W9-DCZ-168

LOVE'S FOOLS:
AUCASSIN, TROILUS, CALISTO AND
THE PARODY OF THE COURTLY LOVER

JUNE HALL MARTIN

LOVE'S FOOLS:
AUCASSIN, TROILUS, CALISTO AND
THE PARODY OF THE COURTLY LOVER

TAMESIS BOOKS LIMITED

LONDON

Colección Támesis
SERIE A - MONOGRAFIAS, XXI

Depósito Legal: M. 1.512 - 1972

Printed in Spain by Talleres Gráficos de EDICIONES CASTILLA, S. A.
Maestro Alonso, 23 - Madrid
for
TAMESIS BOOKS LIMITED
LONDON

To my Mother and Father

Publication of this book was made possible
with the aid of a Faculty Research Grant
from Middle Tennessee State University

CONTENTS

CONTENTS

LIST OF ABBREVIATIONS

AnM	*Annuale Medievale*
ANQ	*American Notes and Queries*
BHS	*Bulletin of Hispanic Studies*
CA	*Cuadernos Americanos*
CAIEF	*Cahiers de l'Association Internationale des Etudes Françaises*
CCM	*Cahiers de Civilisation Médiévale*
CEJ	*California English Journal*
ChauR	*Chaucer Review*
CL	*Comparative Literature*
DA	*Dissertation Abstracts*
ECr	*L'Esprit Créateur*
ELH	*Journal of English Literary History*
ELN	*English Language Notes*
EUPLL	Edinburgh University Publications Language and Literature
ES	*English Studies*
FilR	*Filologia Romanza*
FR	*French Review*
FS	*French Studies*
HSCL	Harvard Studies in Comparative Literature
HSE	Harvard Studies in English
HR	*Hispanic Review*
ISLL	Illinois Studies in Language and Literature
JAF	*Journal of American Folklore*
JEGP	*Journal of English and Germanic Philology*
LP	*Literature and Psychology*
MA	*Le Moyen Age*
MAe	*Medium Aevum*
MH	*Medievalia et Humanistica*
MLN	*Modern Language Notes*
MLQ	*Modern Language Quarterly*
MLR	*Modern Language Review*
MP	*Modern Philology*
MR	*Massachusetts Review*
MS	*Mediaeval Studies*
NQ	*Notes and Queries*
NRFH	*Nueva Revista de Filología Hispánica*
PL	*Patrologia Latina*
PLL	*Papers on Language and Literature*
PMLA	*Publications of the Modern Language Association of America*

PQ	*Philological Quarterly*
RDM	*Revue des Deux Mondes*
RF	*Romanische Forschungen*
RFE	*Revista de Filología Española*
RFH	*Revista de Filología Hispánica*
RL	*Revista de Literatura*
RomN	*Romance Notes*
RP	*Romance Philology*
RR	*Romanic Review*
SATF	Société des Anciens Textes Français
SP	*Studies in Philology*
SUS	*Susquehanna University Studies*
TLS	*Times Literary Supplement*
UColSSLL	University of Colorado Studies Series in Language and Literature
UCPMP	University of California Publications in Modern Philology
UCSSLL	University of California Studies Series in Language and Literature
UNCSCL	University of North Carolina Studies in Comparative Literature
UNCSGLL	University of North Carolina Studies in the Germanic Languages and Literatures
UNCSRLL	University of North Carolina Studies in the Romance Languages and Literatures
YRS	Yale Romanic Studies
ZFSL	*Zeitschrift für Französische sprache und Literatur*
ZRP	*Zeitschrift für romanische Philologie*

PREFACE

This study seeks to investigate the problem of the distorting mirror of parody applied to the traditional lover of courtly literature as he appears in three works: Aucassin et Nicolette, written by an unknown thirteenth-century poet of Picardy; Troilus and Criseyde, by the fourteenth-century English poet Geoffrey Chaucer; and finally, the Celestina, by the fifteenth-century Spaniard Fernando de Rojas. The choice of these three works is to some extent arbitrary in that they are in no way intended to be representative of a literary period or a national literature. Each was selected solely for its literary merit. The study, therefore, is not intended to be an exhaustive exploration of parody or even of the parodic treatment of the courtly lover. Its aim is simply to see how three individual authors, skilled writers all, utilize the conventional hero of courtly romance, to determine whether they treat him as a serious character or whether they choose to mock him through parody. If the author does parody the hero, I will attempt to show what the parodist is attacking within the convention and how the parodic effect is achieved. These are the central issues, though there will inevitably be peripheral questions that must be confronted. Such questions may involve the authors' philosophical positions, general critical problems of a given work, and the extent of the didactic element within the work, to name only a few possibilities.

Few books are achieved by the sole efforts of their authors. This one is no exception. I would like to express my gratitude, to Dr. James M. Smith, who saw me through the final stages of the preliminary version of this study which was my doctoral dissertation at Emory University; to Dr. Dorothy Sherman Severin, for permitting me to examine her book, Memory in «La Celestina», while it was still in typescript; to Mrs. Nancy Heatherly, who, with undaunted cheerfulness, typed and retyped so many pages; and to the editors of Espasa-Calpe, for permitting me to quote so extensively from the Clásicos Castellanos edition of La Celestina, edited by Julio Cejador y Frauca.

I am deeply indebted also to Professor A. D. Deyermond whose many incisive and stimulating comments and suggestions have been invaluable to me in the preparation of this final version.

A special word of gratitude goes to Professor Thomas R. Hart, Jr., who originally suggested the topic of this study to me and whose advice and encouragement have been extremely helpful during all stages of its preparation, but most especially, whose love of medieval literature proved to be contagious.

CHAPTER I

INTRODUCTION

The courtly lover is a familiar figure in medieval literature, an adoring, humble servant to his lady, ready to obey her slightest whim, to grow ill if she looks on him with indifference, or to give himself up to ecstasy if she views him with favor. It would have been remarkable, indeed, had the conventional lover with his behavioral extremes not been singled out as a target for parody. To investigate the problem of parody in terms of the courtly lover, however, one must first confront two essential questions: What is courtly love, and, by extension, the courtly lover? And what is parody?

One may well question the need for a redefinition of courtly love since countless definitions have already been offered by many fine critics such as C. S. Lewis, A. J. Denomy, Tom Peete Cross and William A. Nitze, Gaston Paris, who re-invented the term *amour courtois* in 1883, [1] Moshé Lazar, and Peter Dronke. But it is precisely the multitude and confusion of available definitions that calls for each critic to make clear to his readers

---

[1] Gaston Paris, «Lancelot du Lac II: Le Conte de la charrette», *Romania*, 12 (1883), 532. The expression *cortez'amors* was used by Peire d'Auvergne:

> Mas so non pot remaner
> cortez'amors de bon aire
> don mi lais esser amaire.

from *Die Lieder Peires von Auvergne*, ed. Rudolf Zenker (Erlangen, 1900), XV, 11. 57-59, p. 124. Another reference *(amor cortes)*, a second medieval forerunner of the expression *amour courtois* that seems to have gone virtually unnoticed by critics, occurs in the thirteenth-century Provençal *Roman de Flamenca*:

> E que faría s'us truanz,
> Que-s fenera d'amor cortes
> E non sabra d'amor ques es,
> L'avía messa en follía!

from *Les troubadours: Jaufre, Flamenca, Barlaam* et *Josaphat*, ed. René Lavaud and René Nelli (Paris, 1960), i, 11. 1196-99 of the *Flamenca*, p. 706.

exactly what he means when he uses the term. Surely, despite their disagreements, all of these scholars have some common basis for their definitions, and it is this fundamental definition that I hope to sift out from among the details. In essence, I hope to determine those features which set courtly love apart from other types of romantic or passionate love.

Andreas Capellanus has long been lauded as one of the first writers to attempt a definition of that kind of love we have come to call courtly. But the term «courtly love» was not a common medieval expression. Andreas was merely attempting to set down the qualities of love as it existed in the twelfth century. [2] He was making no effort to distinguish it from any other sort of romantic love. Because it was Paris who reintroduced the term and who, in the same article, first sought to set courtly love apart from romantic love, he provides the logical starting point. He sets up (pp. 518-19) four essential characteristics: (1) It is «illégitime, furtif»; (2) «l'amant est toujours devant la femme dans une position inférieure»; (3) «Pour être digne... il accomplit toutes les prouesses imaginables, et elle de son côté songe toujours à le rendre meilleur, à le faire plus 'valoir'»; and finally (4) «l'amour est un art, une science, une vertu, qui a ses règles tout comme la chevalerie ou la courtoisie».

Father Denomy, by contrast, sees the novelty of courtly love as derived from three elements which overlap with those listed by Gaston Paris, but are not, *in toto*, the same. They are found «first, in the ennobling force of human love; second, in the elevation of the beloved to a place of superiority above the lover; third, in the conception of love as ever unsatiated, ever increasing desire». [3] Of these three he considers the most important that courtly love is «the fount and origin of virtue» (p. 29). He was, a few years later, to alter his views somewhat when he wrote, «the basic, essential characteristic of Courtly Love is the irresistibility of love on the one hand and the ennobling force of love on the other... These are the two characteristics that make Courtly Love be Courtly Love. The other characteristics, conceits, and affections are but trappings of these essential principles... and belong to the general body of love literature». [4]

---

[2] To determine whether or not he was making a serious attempt to describe reality, as some critics think, or whether he was mocking love which pretends to be a spiritual duty, as others believe, is beyond the scope of the present study. Nonetheless, whether he is serious or ironic, his work must have had some relationship to a current concept of love, whether real or fictional. My concern is not with «courtly love» as a sociological phenomenon, but rather as a literary convention.

[3] A. J. Denomy, *The Heresy of Courtly Love* (New York, 1947), p. 20.

[4] A. J. Denomy, «The Two Moralities of Chaucer's *Troilus and Criseyde*», *Chaucer Criticism, II: Troilus and Criseyde and the Minor Poems*, ed. Richard J. Schoeck and

C. S. Lewis has remarked that the «highly specialized sort» of love we call courtly is characterized by «Humility, Courtesy, Adultery, and the Religion of Love». [5]   Already it is apparent that one element is repeated again and again.   It is that characteristic Lewis labels «Humility».   It is stated in various ways: Paris says that the lover is subordinate to the lady; Denomy claims for the lady «a place of superiority».   But the result is the same, a reversal of the traditional roles of man and woman.   Lewis describes it a bit further: «The lover is always abject.   Obedience to his lady's lightest wish, however whimsical, and silent acquiescence in her rebukes, however unjust, are the only virtues he dares to claim.   There is a service of love closely modelled on the service which a feudal vassal owes to his lord» (p. 2).

Cross and Nitze reaffirm the idea that the submission of man to woman is fundamental, that the love service is the hallmark of courtly love.   They describe it as «the deliberate or chosen obedience» [6] of the man to the woman.   They also suggest that «the extra-conjugal nature of the love affair» is significant, but it becomes clear from later chapters that it is really the love service they consider important.   They suggest that an entirely new concept of the lover develops with Chrétien de Troyes, the concept of the *amis antiers*, «the lover who loves even when his passion appears unrequited and who is willing to sacrifice all for Love» (p. 96).

Peter Dronke's idea of *amour courtois* is based largely on a definition of Joseph Bédier who characterizes it as «un culte qui s'addresse à un objet excellent». [7]   It is a cult which increases the worth of the lover and in which «the way towards winning such a love is infinitely arduous, and would be impossible were it not for the lady's grace». [8]   For Dronke, too, the lady is seen as occupying a position superior to that of the lover, of possessing an excellence to which he aspires.   He accepts in courtly love a fundamental «accord of human and divine love» (p. 6), with the lady occupying the position of «mediatrix of divine grace» (p. 96).   The love-service, as he understands it, is a sort of path to spiritual regeneration, «not the survival of the human personality, but on the contrary its complete

---

Jerome Taylor (Notre Dame, 1961), pp. 148-49; reprinted from *Transactions of the Royal Society of Canada*, 44, Ser. III, sec. 2 (June, 1950), 35-46.

   [5]   C. S. Lewis, *The Allegory of Love* (Oxford, 1936; reprinted New York, 1958), p. 2.
   [6]   Tom Peete Cross and William A. Nitze, *Lancelot and Guenevere: A Study on the Origins of Courtly Love* (Chicago, 1930), p. 68.
   [7]   Joseph Bédier, «Les Fêtes de mai et les commencements de la poésie lyrique au Moyen Age», *RDM*, 135 (mai, 1896), 172. Quoted by Peter Dronke in *Medieval Latin and the Rise of European Love Lyric*, i (Oxford, 1965), p. 4.
   [8]   Dronke, p. 7.

surrender, in the love-service, winning through that love-service regeneration— not in one's self but in the beloved» (p. 94). In effect, every courtly
lover, according to Dronke, perceives his lady, at least in part, in essentially
the same way as Dante perceives Beatrice.

Perhaps the most original aspect of Dronke's ideas on courtly love is
the fact that he denies that it was a new feeling in twelfth-century
Provence, as C. S. Lewis, E. R. Curtius, and Reto Bezzola [9] had suggested
earlier that it was. It is, rather, «universally possible, possible in any time
or place and on any level of society» (p. 2). What *is* new in the Western
European love lyric is, he contends, its mode of expression, its use
of language influenced by centuries of mystical and theological tradition
(pp. 57-97).

At almost the same time Dronke was expanding the concept of what
he calls the «courtly experience» and working out the idea that *amour
courtois* is a universally possible feeling, Moshé Lazar was set upon severely
restricting the use of the term. He formalizes instead the more precise
categories of *fin'amors*, the love concept of the troubadours, *amour
courtois conjugal*, the married love described in some of the works of
Chrétien de Troyes, and *amour-passion*, the passionate love prevalent in
the Tristan and Yseut story and the lays of Marie de France.

Lazar would not accept Dronke's idea that the love professed by the
troubadours is compatible with divine love. He follows Denomy in this
respect, generally agreeing that Christianity could never consider the
notion of desire as the source of virtue. [10] And in accepting desire as a
significant factor, he also accepts Denomy's arguments for the incompatibility by insisting that *fin'amors* is «un amour caché, adultère, dominé par
l'appétit de la chair». [11] And thus conceived, it is unquestionably irre-
concilable with Christian love. Nor does he accept the idea that the
language of the troubadours was influenced by mystical or theological
tradition (pp. 84-85). Yet, in spite of such disagreements, Lazar does see
the lover's humility before his lady as an essential aspect of the convention,
and he refers to it again and again throughout his book. In describing
fin'amors, he asserts: «L'amant courtois oscille toujours entre deux pôles:

---

[9] Lewis, *Allegory*, pp. 2-4; E. R. Curtius, *European Literature and the Latin Middle
Ages*, trans. Willard R. Trask (New York, 1953; reprinted New York and Evanston,
1963), p. 586; Reto R. Bezzola, *Les origines et la formation de la littérature courtoise en
occident*, ii (Paris, 1960), p. 242, 249.

[10] *Heresy*, p. 29.

[11] Moshé Lazar, *Amour courtois et «fin'amors» dans la littérature du XIIe siècle*
(Paris, 1964), p. 136.

protestations de respect et d'humilité d'une part, attente du rendez-vous secret d'autre part» (p. 85). And this *humilité* to which he refers seems to be one aspect that, as he would perhaps phrase it, the *amour passion* of the *Tristan* and of Marie de France and the *amour courtois conjugal* of Chrétien have borrowed from *fin'amors*. Tristan seems to accept his role as *serviteur* of his lady, as Lazar points out: «Il n'a d'autre désir que *servir* dans les ordres d'Amour... Tristan s'adresse à la reine comme un troubadour à sa dame» (p. 159). In discussing a work of Marie de France, he comments, «Cette déclaration de soumission absolue [de l'amant à sa dame] par son fond et sa forme, provient directement de la lyrique provençale» (p. 196). And in discussing the conjugal courtly love of Chrétien's work, he remarks that «Même après le mariage, Laudine conserve son caractère et son rôle de Dame autoritaire, et Yvain l'attitude du suppliant et de l'ami obéissant» (p. 248). Such examples could be multiplied, but these few are adequate to point out that while Moshé Lazar is intent upon demonstrating differences in these three types of love, there is at least one consistent element throughout.

It is little wonder, though, in view of the increasing confusion of definitions and refinements concerning courtly love that a number of scholars have become uneasy with the term. The works of both Dronke and Lazar are, I believe, attempts to gain a proper perspective on the problem. But as one vastly expanded the use of the term and the other narrowly limited it, the unfortunate result has been merely to thrust the critics into a still greater state of confusion. It is not surprising to find that one well-known scholar, expressing a view that seems to be becoming increasingly fashionable, was recently led to remark: «As currently employed, 'courtly love' has no useful meaning, and it is not worth saving by redefinition». [12]

The vast number of available definitions of courtly love are merely hinted at here. One could not, in so brief a space, hope to touch on all the notions of courtly love which abound in medieval criticism today. But as Theodore Silverstein has sensibly concluded, the answer is not «simply to abandon term and concept together in a grand and purifying

---

[12] John F. Benton, «Clio and Venus: An Historical View of Medieval Love», in *The Meaning of Courtly Love*, ed. F. X. Newman (Albany, 1968), p. 37. D. W. Robertson, Jr., also argues in favor of abandoning the term which is used to describe something that would better be characterized, he contends, as «idolatrous passion». The term «courtly love» is, he asserts, but an impediment to our understanding of medieval literature. See «The Concept of Courtly Love as an Impediment to the Understanding of Medieval Texts», in Newman, *Meaning*, pp. 3-5.

holocaust». [13] Surely Moshé Lazar is right in seeking to distinguish between the love concepts of the troubadours, those of Chrétien, and those apparently held by the *Tristan* authors and Marie de France. One should certainly further differentiate the special concepts held by the Minnesingers and the *stilnovisti*. And it is unquestionable that our sub-divisions could be still further sub-divided. Jaufre Rudel and Bernart de Ventadorn did not apparently hold precisely the same views of love, nor did Cavalcanti and Dante. But surely there is a common thread that binds them all together. It would be a great loss, I believe, to see that thread broken and forgotten. The most sensible solution to the problem seems to be to accept the term «courtly love», as a broad generic term, which is how it has been largely used for nearly a hundred years anyhow, comprehensive enough to include all of the aforementioned medieval concepts of love, yet allowing adequate opportunity for definitions of each specific type of courtly love. To argue, because the concepts and forms evolved through the course of some four hundred years, that the convention never existed, is absurd. It is like arguing that because Catholics hold different views from Presbyterians, there is no such thing as Christianity. Or because the plays of Beckett are different from those of Racine there is no such thing as the theatre. Surely there are forms that bind the two into a single, evolving tradition, just as Bernart de Ventadorn and Dante are bound within a single tradition, although the individual views of each man and the society in which he lives play a genuinely significant part in determining the final form his love concepts will take.

And it is with the form that we must concern ourselves. How can we, some eight hundred years after the significant blossoming of courtly love in the warm soil of Provence, hope to determine whether or not the love relationships between the troubadours and their ladies were, in fact, consummated or not? It is very likely that some were and that others were not, that some troubadours, who were somewhat more idealistic than others, adored their ladies *de lonh*, while others, whose desires were not gratified, sought new loves with more willing ladies. How can we hope to determine whether the lovers were motivated by sexual desire or by idealistic admiration? Surely we can only hypothesize about the motives and private actions of lover and lady. It was the *language* and the *formal aspects* of the love relationship that became conventional, and not the emotion itself, which is, after all, a highly individual matter. And, as we have

---

[13] Theodore Silverstein, «Guenevere, or the Uses of Courtly Love», in Newman, *Meaning*, p. 87.

clearly seen, one formal aspect of the love relationship that seems to be agreed upon, regardless of the diversity of opinion, is that of the lady's sovereignty over her lover. [14]

Certainly some of the other characteristics mentioned by the various critics—such as adultery and secrecy—are clearly non-essential to courtly love, though they may readily be found in stories which follow courtly love conventions. These belong, instead, to the overall body of romantic literature. In discussing the importance of adultery to romantic love in general, it is helpful to understand it in its medieval sense. Marital sex in the Middle Ages had a distinctive purpose in the Christian tradition—procreation. Sex for itself alone, whether within the bonds of marriage or outside them, was considered adulterous.[15] Consequently, most marriages were for material rather than romantic reasons. Chrétien de Troyes clearly recognized the possibility of courtly love within marriage, as we see from his *Yvain*. But we must remember that Yvain did not marry Laudine for the usual reasons, but for love; consequently, it is not so difficult to believe that courtly love is possible between them. Andreas Capellanus was somewhat less idealistic and left no doubt that what he had in mind was clearly not married love, though it was not necessarily adulterous in the modern sense, for his dialogues, on occasion, involve unmarried and widowed people. His is perhaps the more realistic attitude. It is rare indeed to encounter stories of passionate love within the bonds of marriage. Passionate love tends to be by nature *hors de mariage*, for such love is forbidden by the mores of society. The desirability of love without the bonds of marriage is not a psychological quirk of the Middle Ages. Such yearning for forbidden fruit has played a significant role in literature (and life) since the time of Adam and Eve. [16]

Secrecy follows as a necessary consequence of the generally illicit

---

[14] While I am not concerned specifically with the origins of courtly love, it should certainly be noted that René Nelli in his study *L'Erotique des troubadours* (Toulouse, 1963), accepting, as did Denomy, Arabic and Hispano-Arabic sources, saw «la soumission de l'amant à la dame» (p. 62) as typical of Arabic «Nubb Odhri», which, he contends, is their version of *amour courtois*. It becomes also a fundamental element of «l'érotique des troubadours» (pp. 58-63).

[15] See D. W. Robertson, Jr., *A Preface to Chaucer* (Princeton, 1963), pp. 71-73, 374-76, 428-30.

[16] E. Talbot Donaldson makes essentially the same point when he suggests that the fact that Troilus and Criseyde are not married «enhances the intensity of the erotic experience—a potentiality that has always been known, in all ages, to all poets». («The Myth of Courtly Love», *Ventures*, 5, ii [Fall, 1965], p. 22.) Donaldson is arguing that what we call courtly love is, in fact, nonexistent, a myth, a «phantom cult of sexual immorality in the Middle Ages» (p. 22).

nature of passionate love, and, within the courtly tradition, the desire to protect the lady's honor. Dronke would disagree. In his view the desire for secrecy «springs from the universal notion of love as a mystery not to be profaned by the outside world, not to be shared by any but lover and beloved» (p. 48). Assuming that this may be true in some instances, it by no means excludes the more usual expressed idea that it is the lover's duty to protect his lady's honor, and one means of doing this is by not revealing her identity or meeting with her except in utmost secrecy. In any case, it is obvious that neither secrecy nor love outside of marriage is essential to the courtly love tradition. And their inclusion as basic characteristics of courtly love by some critics is merely another way of saying that it is, by definition, a type of passionate love.

Other frequently-described characteristics of courtly love follow logically from the more fundamental sovereignty of the lady over the lover. The religion of love is taken over from classical mythology. Venus and Cupid retain their traditional roles. [17] But the religion of love in the courtly framework is often carried one step further in that, in more extreme cases, the lady is substituted for the goddess. In essence, it is a Christianization of a pagan religion. The courtly lady is adored as the Christian adores God. The lover is constantly seeking her grace, or her «mercy»; at times he even prostrates himself before her in an attitude of worship. In this sense, it is only a more extreme manifestation of the lady's sovereignty over her lover. On one level she assumes the role of lord in the feudal sense; on a higher level she becomes Lord in the religious sense.

The ennobling power of love, on the other hand, is not a feature derived from classical sources. And it is, for the most part, alien to Western culture before the twelfth century. Denomy believes that it is derived from Arabic philosophy, particularly from the teachings of Averroes and Avicenna. [18] This concept is clearly contrary to Christian teachings, but the Arab philosophers who see earthly love as an aid in approaching the divine provide a necessary link between love—sinful love by Christian standards—and increased virtue as a result of it. Dronke does not agree that the ennobling power of love should be attributed to Arabic philosophers. He contends, rather, quoting H. I. Marrou, that it springs from

---

[17] On the evolution of these traditional roles see M. J. Ruggerio, *The Evolution of the Go-Between in Spanish Literature Through the Sixteenth Century* (UCPMP 78 Berkeley and Los Angeles, 1966), chapter 2, pp. 24-43. See also Erwin Panofsky, *Studies in Iconology* (Oxford, 1939; reprinted New York, 1962), chapter 4, pp. 95-128.
[18] See *Heresy*, pp. 30ff.

«un secteur du coeur, un des aspects éternels de l'homme». [19] Whether it was a spontaneous reaction to love or whether it was influenced by Eastern philosophy, it follows logically from the elevated position of the lady over her lover. Aspiring to the lady's love, he also aspires to be worthy of her, and to be worthy, he must become more noble than he is already. Unfortunately, this feature of the convention tends to be less often observed than many of the others. Lip service is always paid to it. We are told of the lover's increasing nobility, but only on rare occasions are we permitted to observe it. There are perhaps two reasons for this. True ennoblement would follow only from a *sincere* perception of the lady as superior to the lover, which is not, perhaps, always the case, though the lovers unfailingly claim it to be so. And love also produces another effect—the love sickness. If the evidence of ennoblement is not kept in careful equilibrium with the love sickness, if the love sickness is ever permitted to overweight the scales, then the lover's nobility may appear somewhat questionable.

More fundamental than love as the origin of virtue is the concept of love as an art with definite rules that must be obeyed. C. S. Lewis has referred to courtly love, as we have seen, as love of a «highly specialized sort». Gaston Paris has claimed it to be «un art...qui a ses règles». Lazar, too, speaks again and again of the «code courtois» or the «règles de l'amour courtois». [20] The rules were not, like the name, a phenomenon popularized by a late nineteenth-century critic. They are suggested first in the troubadour lyrics. The *cansos* of Bernart de Ventadorn, for example, seem to touch on every significant rule followed by later courtly lovers. But the codification of love did not emerge full blown. The twelfth-century *De Amore* of Andreas Capellanus, suggested perhaps by Ovid's *Ars Amatoria*, provides the earliest set of rules we know about. And the *Lancelot* of Chrétien de Troyes dramatizes the rules Andreas set up. These twelfth-century developments were still further elaborated in the thirteenth-century *Roman de la Rose*. Edwin J. Webber even goes so far as to posit the existence of «an amatory genre» [21] which persisted throughout the Middle Ages. Even as late as the sixteenth century, Count Baldassar Castiglione in the fourth book of his *Libro del Cortegiano* presents us with a rehashing of the four-century-old problem of how one should conduct oneself in the

---

[19]   *Medieval Latin*, p. ix; see also pp. 50-56.
[20]   *Amour courtois*, pp. 176, 181, 186. See especially Appendice II, «La fin'amors codifiée: André le chapelain», pp. 268-78.
[21]   Edwin J. Webber, «The *Celestina* as an *Arte de Amores*», *MP*, 55 (1958), 147.

game of love. According to William George Dodd, «The result of this process of refinement [which he sees ending with Chrétien!] was the form-ulation of certain doctrines, the observance of which became equally obligatory upon courtly lovers and upon later writers who dealt with the subject». [22] Surely the process of refinement continued at the very least through the thirteenth century and the composition of the *Roman de la Rose* in which allegory and courtly conceits tended to fix love in a rigid system. The rules themselves are, for the most part, symptoms that had always been associated with passionate love. But never in such an inflexible way. Love, being an emotional rather than a rational experience, is by nature irrational. And the lover's behavior, unpredictable. Within the courtly love framework, however, such was no longer the case. The lover was expected to fall in love in a certain way, perform certain rituals in praise and service of his lady, react in established patterns to his lady's rebuffs, caprices, and, even, to her granting «mercy». The courtly world was not that of the palace, nor, strictly speaking, that of nature. In lieu of the unbridled natural world, the system adopted as its setting a garden world, [23] which is itself suggestive of the sort of love it shelters. Love is a natural emotion just as trees and flowers are natural growths. But uncontrolled love is just as inappropriate to the courtly love world as is the unpruned bush or the unweeded promenade to a lovely garden. Both courtly love and its garden setting suggest nature tamed—love hedged in by a set of rules and the artificial aspect of a well-sculptured garden.

The rules themselves, while taken one at a time, belong to the general body of romantic love. But as a system, they are the unmistakable hallmark of courtly love. Even the physical description of the lovers became stereotyped. «The lady is regularly represented as perfect in all her attributes... Her hair is blond or golden; her eyes beautiful; her complexion fresh and clear; her mouth rosy and smiling; her flesh white, soft, and

---

[22] William George Dodd, *Courtly Love in Gower and Chaucer* (Cambridge, Mass., 1913; reprinted Gloucester, Mass., 1959), p. 2.

[23] For a discussion of the garden in medieval literature, see D. W. Robertson, Jr., «The Doctrine of Charity in Medieval Literary Gardens: A Topical Approach Through Symbolism and Allegory», *Speculum*, 26 (1951), 24-49. See also Curtius, *European Liter-ature*, pp. 195-200. The walled garden is a singularly appropriate symbol for the world of courtly love. It is, of course, the *locus amoenus*, which has clear sexual symbolism in such works as the *Roman de la Rose* and the *Celestina*. It is also linked to the religious concept of the *hortus conclusus*, one of the traditional names for Mary. The ambiguity inherent in the symbolic garden world reappears in the twentieth century in the form of T. S. Eliot's rose garden motif. For a discussion of the walled garden as it relates to the *Celestina*, see Raymond E. Barbera, «Medieval Iconography in the *Celestina*», *RR*, 61 (1970), 5-13.

smooth; her body slender, well formed, and without blemish... In short, all that makes the perfect woman,.. the poet's love possesses.» [24] The lover is her masculine counterpart, endowed with the same blond hair and gray eyes and the same physical perfection. Chaucer's squire, according to F. N. Robinson, «exhibits the qualities and accomplishments that were regularly expected of a young courtly lover». [25] He was, Chaucer tells us,

> A lovyere and a lusty bacheler,
> With lokkes crulle as they were leyd in presse.
> Of twenty yeer of age he was, I gesse.
> Of his stature he was of evene lengthe,
> Of wonderly delyvere, and of greet strengthe. [26]

And to top it all off, Chaucer does not fail to include the lover's most necessary attribute:

> Curteis he was, lowely, and servysable.
>
> (1. 99)

The lover is, as we have mentioned, usually expected to fall in love in a certain way. He is attracted by his lady's beauty [27] which pierces his eye and strikes his heart, causing him to fall ill. One of the most strenuously observed rules is the resulting love sickness, the symptoms of which are paleness, sleeplessness, groaning, sighing, loss of appetite,

---

[24] Dodd, p. 10. For a full study of the ideal beauty of the courtly lady, see Alice M. Colby, *The Portrait in Twelfth-Century French Literature* (Genève, 1965), pp. 25-72.

[25] «Explanatory Notes», *The Works of Geoffrey Chaucer*, ed. F. N. Robinson, 2nd ed. (Boston, 1957), p. 653.

[26] *Ibid.*, «The General Prologue», *The Canterbury Tales*, 11. 80-84. One instance of Chrétien's use of conventional description occurs in his presentation of Cligés:

> Si chevol sanbloient fin or
> Et sa face rose novele
> Nes ot bien fet et boche bele,
> Et fu de si grant estature
> Con miauz le sot feire Nature;
> ....
> An Cligés ne failli nus biens.

From the edition of Wendelin Foerster (Halle/Salle, 1901), 2776-80, 2791.

[27] There are cases, the most famous being that of Jaufre Rudel, in which the love results from the lover's merely hearing reports of the lady's beauty. Perhaps, in a case of this sort, the imagined beauty may be said to enter through the «mind's eye».

palpitations of the heart, and even death [28] if the lady does not act the part of the physician and cure his ills by granting that «mercy» he so desires. In seeking his lady's favor he performs services for her, whatever she may desire, for he is, as we have seen, wholly subservient to her will. And seeking always to be worthy of her love, he is perforce ennobled by his desire. The lover is expected to be jealous and furtive, guarding his lady's honor above all else. And interestingly enough, he must be restrained in his loving, for, according to Andreas, a man who is overpassionate usually does not love: «Non solet amare, quem nimia voluptatis abundantia vexat.» [29] The lady is loved to the extent that she replaces God in the lover's eyes. His prayers are directed toward Venus, but worship belongs to his lady. And the lover, if he is very fortunate, will, after many trials of endurance, both physical and emotional, after many cold rebuffs and capriciously assigned errands, be granted what he so desires. Taken as a whole the rules are unmistakably those of courtly love.

By way of summary, what, then, are the fundamental distinguishing features of the tradition? First, it reverses the traditional roles of man and woman, setting woman in the position of overlord. This, in itself, was enough to bring courtly love into conflict with Christianity and with the sacrament of marriage. In the Christian world, man is the unquestioned lord of his wife. In the twelfth-century *Jeu d'Adam* Adam seeks to excuse himself for having eaten of the forbidden fruit by claiming that it was Eve who wished it, and, after all, it was Figura who had given him Eve. This may have been an acceptable excuse in the courtly world, but Figura will have none of it:

> Ta moiller creis plus que moi,
> Manjas le fruit senz mon otroi.
> Or te rendrai itel guerdon:
>
> . . . .
>
> Od grant peine, od grant suor
> Vivras tu nuit e jor. [30]

---

[28] For a more detailed description of the love sickness, see Lewis Freeman Mott, *The System of Courtly Love Studied as an Introduction to the Vita Nuova of Dante* (New York, 1924). See also John Livingston Lowes, «The Lovere's Malady of Hereos», *MP*, 11 (1913-14), 491-546.

[29] See Andreas Capellanus, *De Amore libri tres*, ed. E. Trojel (Havniae, 1892; reprinted Munich, 1964), rule XXIX, p. 331.

[30] *Le Jeu d'Adam*, in *Jeux et sapience du moyen âge*, ed. Albert Pauphilet (Paris, 1961), p. 27.

In addition to reversing the roles of man and woman, courtly love was subject to a set of rules. The codification of love is something of a paradox in that it imposes outward restrictions on inward feelings. What was once a possible reaction to love had been made a mandatory reaction. And lovers, by nature unpredictable, had become stereotyped.

Before determining precisely why courtly love was such a ready target for parody, it is first necessary to clarify what is meant by the term parody as it will be used throughout this study. It is by no means easy to find a good definition of parody. Some critics labor over distinctions between parody, burlesque, travesty, caricature, and so forth, while others go on blithely using them interchangeably. M. H. Abrams bemoans such carelessness with the terms, claiming that «to equate the terms in this way is to surrender very useful critical distinctions». [31] He himself prefers to use burlesque as «the generic term for all literary forms in which people, actions, or other literary works are made ridiculous by an incongruous imitation, and to reserve the other terms as names for various species of burlesque». He sees parody as «a form of high burlesque» which derides «a particular literary work or style, by imitating its features and applying them to trivial or grossly discordant materials». Richmond P. Bond would tend to agree with the generic definition of burlesque, though he subdivides a bit more precisely what he considers «low burlesque», which consists of travesty and Hudibrastic, [32] and «high burlesque», of which the components are parody and mock heroic. Of the latter two he considers parody «the most thoroughly literary of the four species of burlesque—it attempts a criticism of an author's traits (especially the objectionable ones) as they appear in his work as a whole or in an immediate poem» (p. 14). David Worcester accepts Bond's distinctions, and follows him in applying parody and travesty to the specific, mock heroic and Hudibrastic to the general. [33] Gilbert Highet, by contrast, sees mock heroic and burlesque as subdivisions of parody. «A mock heroic parodist pretends to be serious», he claims, while the «writer of burlesque is a vulgarian». [34] Karl Beckson and Arthur Ganz make different sorts of distinctions.

---

[31]   M. H. Abrams, *A Glossary of Literary Terms* (New York, 1957), p. 9.
[32]   Richmond P. Bond, *English Burlesque Poetry 1700-1750* (Cambridge, Mass., 1932), p. 14. Bond defines these terms as follows: «The travesty lowers a particular work by applying a jocular, familiar, undignified treatment, and the Hudibrastic poem [term from Butler's *Hudibras*] uses the same procedure on more general matter, the difference being one of particular and general» (pp. 3-4).
[33]   David Worcester, *The Art of Satire* (Cambridge, Mass., 1940), pp. 43ff.
[34]   Gilbert Highet, *The Anatomy of Satire* (Princeton, 1962), p. 103.

«Though burlesque embraces many types of satirical imitation, it is used to distinguish it from parody, a closely related genre.»[35] Parody, they claim, must ridicule a given work, while burlesque ridicules «attitudes, style, or subject matter». Dwight Macdonald defines them a bit differently. Parody, he says, «concentrates on the style and thought of the original».[36] While burlesque, too, is concerned with style, it «differs from parody in that the writer is concerned with the original not in itself but merely as a device for topical humor» (p. 558). He continues: «If burlesque is pouring new wine into old bottles, parody is making a new wine that tastes like the old but has a slightly lethal effect» (p. 559). Robert P. Falk and William Beare in Alex Preminger's *Encyclopedia of Poetry and Poetics* take a somewhat different approach to the problem. Just as Paul Lehmann had in 1922 distinguished between parody that is primarily critical and parody that is primarily for entertainment, [37] they, too, differentiate comic parody «which is close to burlesque» [38] from literary or critical parody which is «the exaggerated imitation of a work of art» belonging to «the genus *satire*».

While all the distinctions make sense if examined individually, taken as a group the effect is somewhat vertiginous. And the general lack of agreement is rather astonishing. Parody is probably the most widely used of the terms, and I think it sensible, therefore, to submit to usage and define parody somewhat more broadly than do Bond and Worcester in particular. It is generally agreed that it is applied to style and may be a form of literary criticism. Most critics, as we have seen, consider that parody must direct itself at a given work or author. None, however, takes into consideration that it may be directed to an entire convention, which is, in the case of courtly love, as stylistically defined as the works of a single author. The characters tend to look the same and behave in similar fashion. The poets tend to use the same images and similar language. All in all, there is clear justification, assuming that parody functions around a stylistic fulcrum, for asserting that a convention can, indeed, be parodied. For this reason, and because mock heroic, probably the next best term, is, relatively speaking, a little-used term, and perhaps

---

[35] Karl Beckson and Arthur Ganz, *A Reader's Guide to Literary Terms* (New York, 1960), p. 20.
[36] Dwight Macdonald, *Parodies* (New York, 1960), p. 559.
[37] Paul Lehmann, *Die Parodie im Mittelalter* (First published in 1922; 2nd ed. Stuttgart, 1963).
[38] Robert P. Falk and William Beare, «Parody», in *Encyclopedia of Poetry and Poetics*, ed. Alex Preminger (Princeton, 1965), p. 600.

a little too narrowly defined, I have chosen to refer to the phenomenon we are examining as parody.

But we are very little closer to understanding precisely what we mean by the term. Perhaps the most fundamental characteristic of parody is that it must bear an essential similarity to the original, whether it be a specific work, a style, a convention, or a stylized character within that convention. Yet it is not simply imitative. Some basic element must be altered so that the resulting incongruity may reveal some weakness in the original. In the case of courtly love, for example, the lofty style, the elegant manners of the courtly world, may be retained, while the characters are made base. Or an ideal character may be placed in a lowly and, hence, incongruous situation. The result is what is, indeed, a form of literary criticism which underscores some weakness or tendency toward absurdity within the convention. It is, therefore, by definition didactic to some extent. Yet it is also humorous. The two elements—didacticism and humor—always coexist in parody, though it is not uncommon for one of these aspects to be so dominant that it may tend to obscure the other. In short, the tone of the parody may vary considerably, from gay mockery to bitter irony.

The techniques of parody range from subtle exaggeration to total inversion. Wolcott Gibbs claims that parody should be «pitched so little above (or below) the key of the original that an intelligent critic, on being read passages from both, might be honestly confused».[39] And Robert Falk agrees that «subtlety is one of the fundamental qualities of superior parody».[40] While this is often the case, such statements radically limit the scope of parody. Parody may be subtle, but it may also depend upon extreme and very unsubtle exaggerations. But in spite of the potential extremes of parody, the parodist himself requires mental balance and good taste. As Carolyn Wells has said, «a parodist may go to the very edge, but he must not fall over».[41]

Attitudes towards parody have often been extreme, ranging from Matthew Arnold's denunciation of it as «a vile art»[42] to Sir Owen Seaman's effusive encomium of «the noble art of parody».[43] I would see it, rather,

---

[39] Quoted in Robert P. Falk's *The Antic Muse: American Writers in Parody* (New York, 1955), p. 10.
[40] *The Antic Muse*, p. 10.
[41] Carolyn Wells, *A Parody Anthology* (New York, 1904), p. xxiii.
[42] Quoted in George Kitchin's *Survey of Burlesque and Parody in English* (London, 1931), p. xxi.
[43] Quoted *ibid.*

as a genre unto itself, stopping short of both vileness and nobility, but sometimes serious and vindictive, brutally attacking what the parodist considers false or bad, and at other times gentle and light, even sympathetic to the very weaknesses it exposes. It is hoped that this study will in some way help to illustrate the range of parody which is, in summary, a form of imitation which exaggerates or distorts certain features of the original work, style, or convention, thereby revealing its weaknesses and rendering it the object of mockery, ridicule, or scorn.

It is not difficult to see why courtly love should be an inevitable target for parody. Parody ordinarily directs itself towards a work, style, or tradition that is well known to its audience and probably even admired by many among them. «To parody a poem of which no one has ever heard is to court a cold reception; to mock a poet whom the world has learned to regard with pity or indifference is like drawing attention to the blemishes in a face that no one has ever admired.»[44] Or as Carolyn Wells has stated it (p. xxx), parody «is a tribute to popularity, and consequently to merit of one sort or another». Certainly courtly love had both its vogue and its merit. Its popularity is confirmed by the fact that it survived for some four centuries and even beyond if such critics as C. S. Lewis and Otis H. Green are correct.[45] Its merit is well evident in the romances of Chrétien de Troyes who presents us with a courtly lover representative of the chivalric ideal. In his works we are witness to the lover's self-sacrifice and humility for his beloved, recounted with grace and sensitivity. He is striving for perfection, to become the gentle knight for whom love and adventure feed upon one another. But the ideal requires a most delicate balance. One of the major dangers of love is sloth, for «love feeds and nurtures inactivity».[46] That tendency towards inactivity was clearly recognized by Chrétien for whom achieving the proper balance of *amour* and *aventure* became one of the major themes. In the *Yvain*, for example, we see a situation in which the knight loves to such an extent that he neglects his knightly duties and adventures and must be prodded to return to them.

---

[44] Christopher Stone, *Parody* (London [1914]), p. 44. A. D. Deyermond makes the same point in «Some Aspects of Parody in the 'Libro de buen amor'», *Libro de buen amor Studies*, ed. G. B. Gybbon-Monypenny (London, 1970), p. 55: «The essential requirement is, of course, that the thing parodied should be familiar to the audience to whom the parody is addressed, for without this familiarity, the audience cannot grasp the comparison which is at the base of all parody.»

[45] Lewis, *Allegory*, pp. 3-4; Otis H. Green, *Spain and the Western Tradition*, i (Madison, Wis., 1963), pp. 92-263. See also his *Courtly Love in Quevedo*, UCoISSLL, 3 (Boulder, 1952).

[46] Cross and Nitze, p. 83.

16

Another potential danger of the ideal was the tendency of the reversal of male-female roles to emasculate the male. And the young knight who is ever obedient to his lady and who is in the throes of the love sickness with its obligatory weeping and sighing must guard his manhood with care.[47] The necessity of the *militia* element is evident. A knight who proves himself to be totally equal to his manly duties in battle can perhaps afford any weakness that may have been inherent in the love sickness, with its obligatory fears, groans, and sighs. Chrétien was not oblivious of the potential for humor in such a situation if it were carried to an extreme.[48] Describing Cligés' fear before Fénice, he comments:

> Deus! ceste crieme don li vient,
> Qu'une pucele sole crient,
> Foible et coarde, sinple et coie?
> A ce me sanble que je voie
> Les chiens foïr devant le lievre
> Et la tortre chacier le bievre,
> L'aignel le lo, le colon l'egle.
> Einsi fuit li vilains sa megle,
> Don li vit et don il s'ahane.
> Einsi fuit li faucons por l'ane
> Et li girfauz por le heiron,
> Et li gros luz por le veiron,
> Et le lion chace li cers,
> Si vont les choses a anvers.
>
> (3845-58)

He then apparently feels compelled to justify Cligés' behavior by explaining at some length that true lovers typically lose their senses, that a lover's

---

[47] It should, of course, be noted that weeping in appropriate situations (i.e., Charlemagne's reaction to the death of Roland and the twelve peers) was considered a sign of a sensitive and noble man. Tears seem to be fully acceptable, however, only in certain types of situations. According to Paul Rousset («Recherches sur l'émotivité à l'époque romane», *CCM*, XI-XIIe siècles, 2 [1959], p. 58), these situations included «une supplication collective..., ou bien une émotion religieuse, le spectacle d'un malheur, d'un deuil». Still more important in contributing to the nobility of weeping is the fact that it is more effective when counterbalanced by a heroic nature. Tears from a coward could scarcely be called noble, even in the Middle Ages when heroes still wept.

[48] See Norman Susskind, «Love and Laughter in the *Romans Courtois*», *FR*, 37 (1963-64), 651-57.

fear of his lady is necessary to love, and that, therefore, Cligés should not be held guilty for his apparently foolish behavior:

> Mes volantez a moi s'aüne,
> Que je die reison aucune,
> Por quoi avient a fins amanz,
> Que sans lor faut et hardemanz
> A dire ce qu'il ont an pans
> Quant il ont eise et leu et tans.
>
> . . . .
>
> Amors sans crieme et sanz peor
> Est feus sanz flame et sanz chalor,
> Jors sanz soloil, bresche sanz miel
> Estez sanz flor, iverz sanz giel,
> Ciaux sanz lune, livres sanz letre.
> Einsi le vuel a neant metre,
> Que la, ou crieme s'an dessoivre,
> Ne fet amors a ramantoivre.
> Qui amer viaut, doter l'estuet,
> Ou se ce non, amer ne puet.
>
> . . . .
>
> Donc, ne faut ne ne mesprant mie
> Cligés, s'il redote s'amie.
>
> (3859-64, 3893-3902, 3905-06)

A similar awareness of the lover's potential foolishness is apparent in the *Chevalier de la charrette*. Lancelot's discovery of Guenevere's comb with some of her hair still caught in its teeth causes him to become so weak that he seems to swoon and nearly falls from his horse. But the damsel who is accompanying him leaps down from her horse to support him. Sensing Lancelot's embarrassment when he has regained his composure, she tells him that she has dismounted to get the comb. Lancelot allows her to keep the comb, but the hair he keeps as a holy relic. The scene recalls Alexander's ecstasy over the golden hair sewed into his shirt by Sordamors and the wry comment of Chrétien:

> Bien fet amors de sage fol
> Quant cil fet joie d'un chevol
> Et si se delite et deduit.
>
> (1643-45)

Perhaps the occasion in which Chrétien comes closest to letting his hero become a comic figure is when Lancelot approaches the ford, a scene to which we shall need to refer again somewhat later in this study. Lost in dreams of Guenevere, he is oblivious of the knight guarding the ford who challenges him three times before finally unhorsing him. Landing in a most uncourtly manner in the cold stream, Lancelot comes to his senses and berates the knight for having attacked without warning. Fortunately, the knight at the ford is gentleman enough to give Lancelot a second chance. But if he were not, Lancelot would have a good deal of trouble regaining his dignity. It is apparent that the behavior of the courtly lover, particularly in situations which involve people other than lover and lady, requires the ordered and somewhat fantastic world of Chrétien's romances.[49] If the courtly hero were removed intact and injected into the world of a realistic novel, he would clearly be at a loss as to how to behave. The perils of the new and unknown world are not dragons to slay, perilous magic fountains to brave, or razor-sharp bridges to cross, but rather confrontations with petty dishonesty and practical affairs. From such a world the gentle courtly lover could scarcely emerge unscathed and would appear, at best, a foolish, pathetic figure lost in a world which would, in turn, seem more scurrilous and opprobrious by virtue of his presence in it, a situation which Cervantes has explored to the full. Huizinga has pointed out how the concepts of chivalry and courtly love conflict with the reality of medieval life:

> In order to forget the painful imperfection of reality the nobles turn to the continual illusion of a high and heroic life. They wear the mask of Lancelot and of Tristram. It is an amazing self-deception. The crying falsehood of it can only be borne by treating it with some amount of raillery. The whole chivalrous culture of the last centuries of the Middle Ages is marked by an unstable equilibrium between sentimentality and mockery.[50]

---

[49] Prior to the works of Chrétien, courtly love literature, and I am thinking especially of the troubadour lyrics, had been written only within the context of the private relationship between lover and lady. One of the added dimensions of Chrétien's works, as well as those of the *Tristan* authors, Béroul especially, is an exploration of the love relationship within a broader context of society. One particularly interesting study of this problem is Stephen G. Nichols, Jr.'s «Ethical Criticism and Medieval Literature, *Le Roman de Tristan*», in *Medieval Secular Literature: Four Essays*, ed. William Matthews (Berkeley and Los Angeles, 1965), pp. 68-89.

[50] J. Huizinga, *The Waning of the Middle Ages*, trans. F. Hopman (London, 1924; reprinted Garden City, N. Y., 1954), p. 80.

3

While the ideal was beautiful, it was unnatural and unreal. The whole idea of a codification of love attests to this fact. And the idea that an emotion such as love can be governed by a set of rules is inherently absurd. C. S. Lewis has remarked that «To leap up on errands, to go through heat or cold, at the bidding of one's lady, or even of any lady, would seem but honourable and natural to a gentleman of the thirteenth...century».[51] Surely for some this was true, but it seems to me dubious that *all* who called themselves gentlemen in the thirteenth century would have agreed with Lewis that such behavior was «honourable and natural». For many, I dare say, it must have seemed rather extreme behavior. And there are indications that, even then, such love was derided by those less romantic «gentlemen». Bernart de Ventadorn, for example, chides those who criticize such love:

> Amors, cil que·us volon delir
> son enoyos e disliau,
> e si·us deschanton, me qu'en cau?
> No·s podon melhs envilanir;
> be conosc a lor parladura
> qu'ilh renhon mal contra natura.
> Cist an perdut vergonha e paor
> partit de Deu tot per sordeg d'amor
> et eu sui fols si mais ab lor conten.[52]

And Jean Renart in his *Lai de l'ombre* makes a similar defensive comment, striking back at those who were crass enough to mock his worthy tales of love:

> Je ne vueil pas rasambler ceus
> Qui sont garçon por tout destruire,
> Quar, puis que j'ai le sens d'estruire
> Aucun bien en dit ou en fet,
> Vilains est qui ses gas on fet,
> Se ma cortoisie s'aoevre
> A fere aucune plesant oevre
> Ou il n'ait ramposne ne lait.

---

[51] *Allegory*, p. 7.
[52] *The Songs of Bernart de Ventadorn*, ed. Stephen G. Nichols, Jr., and John A. Galm (Chapel Hill, 1962), canso 13, ll. 46-54, p. 76.

20

Fols est qui por parole lait
Bien a dire, por qu'il le sache;
Et s'aucuns fel sa langue en sache
Par derriere, tout ce li doit,
Quar nient plus que je puis cest doit
Fere ausi lonc comme cestui,
Ne cuit je que on peüst hui
Fere un felon debonere estre,
Et miex vient de bone eure nestre
Qu'estre de bons, c'est dit pieça.[53]

While Chrétien apparently recognized the humorous potential of courtly love, he was careful never to let his lovers completely slip over into the comic world. But humiliation, he recognized, was a part of the courtly world. Mounting the cart is, for Lancelot, a lover's test, and one which even he, the most perfect of lovers, almost fails. His hesitation before the cart reveals to Guenevere that he is not yet an *amis antiers*, and, to prove his worth, she bids him undergo other trials of humiliation, particularly on the tournament field where she commands him to let his opponent have the upper hand. And this time Lancelot does not hesitate. Behavior that would seem absurd in any other context is saved from ridiculousness by virtue of its serious framework. Later writers were not so careful as Chrétien. They tended to become less concerned with the lover's virtue and his necessary equilibrium between *amour* and *aventure* and more preoccupied with the rules and conceits of the courtly world. The balance was upset as the rules began to be exaggerated out of all proportion to the sentiment. And exaggeration, as Dwight Macdonald has pointed out (p. 560), «is the meat that parody feeds on». The courtly lover with his blond curls, his paroxysms of weeping, and his transports of joy, was an easy target.

---

[53] Jean Renart, *Le Lai de l'ombre*, ed. Joseph Bédier (Paris, 1913), 11. 4-21.

CHAPTER II

AUCASSIN

While almost all medieval literature is the object of far too little study, the thirteenth-century *chantefable, Aucassin et Nicolette,* is even more critically impoverished than most. Until fairly recently, scholars who had given attention to the text had concentrated primarily on certain linguistic difficulties, disputed readings of various lines or, at best, examinations of single motifs. In the past two decades, however, critics have begun to consider the text as a whole, and their investigations have led to a general agreement that *Aucassin et Nicolette* is not the sweet and simple tale it was once thought to be, but that it is intended to be humorous. Most notable among these recent studies are those of Albert Pauphilet (1950), Omer Jodogne (1959), and Robert Harden (1966).[1] Although their investigations differ in many respects, they agree on one fundamental point— that *Aucassin et Nicolette* is, in some sense, a parody. Pauphilet claims that the author of the *chantefable* is parodying current literary themes of war, adventure and romance. Jodogne goes a step further in asserting (p. 65) that the work is both «pastiche et parodie de trois genres littéraires», the *roman idyllique,* from which the work takes its structure, the *chanson de geste* and lyric poetry. Harden agrees that the parody is directed towards the «vapid plots and equally vapid personages of the idyllic novel» (p. 3). But he, too, is unable to account for all situations within the rather narrow structure he suggests, and he is forced to compromise his position somewhat by admitting that the parody laps over into *chanson de geste, desbats,* and even *fabliaux.*

While these studies undoubtedly point in the right direction, that is,

---

[1] Albert Pauphilet, *Le Legs du moyen âge* (Melun, 1950), pp. 239-48; Omer Jodogne, «La Parodie et le pastiche dans *Aucassin et Nicolette*», *CAIEF,* 12 (1959), 53-65. Robert Harden, «*Aucassin et Nicolette* as Parody», *SP,* 63 (1966), 1-9.

toward parody, in the final analysis they leave something to be desired, for they tend to obscure the fundamental unity of the text. |The parody does not seem to lie in the disunity that a pastiche of several genres or themes would suggest. Nor, indeed, does the parody seem to be one of genres at all, except peripherally. There is a more fundamental unifying element, a character who ties together the actions and tones of the different episodes—Aucassin.| Certainly the importance of Aucassin as a humorous figure in the *chantefable* has not gone unnoticed. Pauphilet has remarked that he is «un personnage sympathique, mais un peu pâle, qui prête souvent à sourire, mais sans hostilité de fond» (p. 246). Jodogne has attributed even greater importance to Aucassin's role, concluding that along with the pastiche and parody of the three literary genres previously mentioned there is also «pastiche et parodie de l'amoureux» (p. 65) whom he characterizes as «un insensé, un réfractaire au statut social, un pusillanime» (p. 59). Harden as well has noted the humorous role of Aucassin and asserts that he is «a veritable anti-hero» (p. 6). Rather than considering the parody of the hero as a secondary issue, or, as in the case of Jodogne, of no greater significance than the generic parodies, I would contend that it is precisely and primarily toward Aucassin that the parodist directs himself, his humor, his criticism, and, as Pauphilet has suggested, his sympathy. |He has seized upon the figure of the courtly lover and has made an amusing quasi-critical commentary on the eccentricities of his behavior and his lack of practical function in the real world.[2]| Virtually all the humor in the *chantefable* is centered, not around the situation nor the individual episodes *per se*, but around the behavior of the protagonist within each episode. Even the land of Torelore which is constructed around an inherently ludicrous situation is rendered more humorous by the thrashing about of Aucassin, who exhibits there a bravura he has not shown in the outside world.[3] Aucassin, and this episode merely tends to confirm it, is fundamentally a misfit. He shares with Don Quixote an existence in a world that is not especially prepared for him. The world of Aucassin should be one of dwarfs, magic rings, and strange, heroic adventures, for it is in this sort of world that he could properly function as a courtly lover. Placed in such a world as that of Beaucaire, which is by no means the «random, everyday, real world»[4] of Don Quixote but which

---

[2] See Erich Auerbach, «The Knight Sets Forth», *Mimesis*, trans. Willard Trask (Princeton, 1953; reprinted Garden City, N. Y., 1957), pp. 120-21.

[3] For a delightful discussion of the Torelore episode see Sister M. Faith McKean, «Torelore and Courtoisie», *RomN*, 3, ii (Spring, 1962), 64-68.

[4] Auerbach, p. 120.

does concern itself with practical considerations, Aucassin is remarkably inept at almost everything. He is as awkward as the young Perceval entering for the first time into the world of chivalry, and the only lover's «duties» he can properly perform are those of mourning, sighing, and weeping, which he does abundantly, precisely the behavior most likely to be picked up and put into perspective by the mocking pen of the parodist.

From the very beginning Aucassin is described in conventional courtly-love terms. The first *laisse* announces that the tale is about Nicolette and Aucassin, emphasizing the role of Aucassin:

> Qui vauroit bon vers oïr
> . . . .
> des grans paines qu'il soufri
> et des proueces qu'il fist
> por s'amie o le cler vis.[5]

These last three lines sum up the essential actions of the traditional courtly lover who, as we see in a more or less ideal state in the romances of Chrétien, suffered «grans paines» and performed «des sproueces... por s'amie». That the parodist felt compelled to mention Aucassin's «proueces», which can only be read ironically, merely confirms the hypothesis that we are indeed dealing with a «courtly lover» called Aucassin. His physical description in the second division of the work is also traditional: «Biax estoit et gens et grans et bien tailliés de ganbes et de piés et de cors et de bras; il avoit les caviax blons et menus recercelés et les ex vairs et rians et le face clere et traitice et le nes haut et bien assis» (II, 10-14). Blond curls, grey eyes, and a well-made nose are almost as necessary to the courtly lover as his horse and sword.

The beginning of the tale finds Aucassin already in such an unbalanced state of development between *paines* and *proueces* that he is almost immediately recognizable as a parody or a bad copy of the conventional courtly lover. «... si estoit soupris d'Amor, qui tout vaint, qu'il ne voloit estre cevalers, ne les armes prendres, n'aler au tornoi, ne fare point de quanque il deust» (II, 15-18). He is not without literary precedent, however, for even within the works of Chrétien, as we have seen, this sort of conflict between love and prowess plays a significant role. Aucassin is in essentially the same position as Erec and Yvain shortly after their

---

[5] *Aucassin et Nicolette*, ed. Mario Roques, 2e ed. (Paris, 1963), I, 1-7. All subsequent references are to this edition and will be given within the text.

respective marriages. Such apparent recreancy is one of the pitfalls of love, one into which better men than Aucassin have fallen. But if the parody did not go beyond this point Aucassin would remain a mere caricature of a courtly lover. The success of the parody is derived not just from Aucassin himself, but from an essential conflict between our courtly lover and the other characters who inhabit Beaucaire, none of whom appears to know the rules of the courtly world. In Beaucaire, for example, one cannot even trust a father to keep his word. Aucassin makes a bargain with his father Count Garin, agreeing to don his armor and defend his land against an invading army in exchange for a kiss and a few words from Nicolette. But when Aucassin has fulfilled his promise and captured the enemy leader, Garin pretends to have forgotten his pledge. How different this is from the world of Chrétien's heroes where a captured knight gives his word to return to Arthur's court and recount the story of his own defeat and fulfills his promise!

Aucassin often finds himself in situations which parallel episodes in Chrétien's romances. He behaves in many instances very much as Lancelot or Yvain before him has behaved, but the same set of rules is not followed by the other characters. For example, as Aucassin rides into battle, his mind is so preoccupied with thoughts of Nicolette that he drops his reins, totally oblivious of the fact that his horse has borne him into the thick of battle. The enemy captures him without warning. Lancelot, in search of Guenevere, finds himself in a similar situation which has been referred to in the introduction to the present study. He rides toward a forbidden ford, lost in thought:

> et ses pansers est de tel guise
> que lui meïsmes en oblie,
> ne set s'il est, ou s'il n'est mie,
> ne ne li manbre de son non,
> ne set s'il est armez ou non,
> ne set ou va, ne set don vient;
> de rien nule ne li sovient
> fors d'une seule, et por celi
> a mis les autres en obli;
> a cele seule panse tant
> qu'il n'ot, ne voit, ne rien n'antant.[6]

---

[6] Chrétien de Troyes, *Le Chevalier de la charrette*, ed. Mario Roques (Paris, 1958), 11. 714-24.

Struck down by the knight who guards the ford, Lancelot asks to be allowed to rearm and joust fairly with the knight who agrees willingly.

Having been taken prisoner by the forces of Bougar de Valence, Aucassin remembers suddenly that if his head is cut off he can no longer converse with Nicolette. He realizes then that they have neglected to take away his sword; and singlehanded he captures Bougar and takes him back to his father. But when he learns of his father's perfidy, he releases Bougar, demanding from him only a promise that he will do some evil toward Count Garin every day for the rest of his life. Bougar thinks he is joking: «Sire, por Diu, fait il, ne me gabés mie; mais metés moi a raençon: vos ne me sarés je demander or ni argent, cevaus ne palefrois, ne vair ne gris, ciens ne oisiax, que je ne vos doinse» (X, 66-69). Bougar is a practical man; he cannot understand Aucassin's request for a mere promise when he could have any ransom he asked. But Aucassin insists on the promise and Bougar agrees, although there is no evidence within the text that he fulfilled the agreement. Jodogne interprets the fact that we hear from Bougar no more as conclusive evidence that he has lied to Aucassin just as his father the Count had lied. «Ces deux personnages ne sont pas déloyaux; ils ont menti comme on ment à un malade, ou mieux à un fou qu'on voudrait interner. Ils sont très sages, en somme; ils ne veulent pas 'baer a folie'» (p. 60). For Jodogne Aucassin is «un fou au pays des sages», but such a conclusion seems to me a gross oversimplification. What we have here is a conflict of social systems. While it is true that Aucassin usually comes out looking a little foolish, the reader tends to smile *sympathetically*, for however often he is the butt of the joke, he is usually right. And he has little understanding of the materialistic world of Beaucaire.

Material values are brought into play also when Aucassin meets the various rustics in the woods. Jodogne has attributed their appearance in the *chantefable* to an intended parody of the *pastourelle*, but the rustic is by no means an unfamiliar figure in the romances of Chrétien. The giant herdsman in the *Yvain*, for example, is almost copied in the *Aucassin*.[7] Both are described as large and black; both are depicted as leaning upon a club. Even identical terms are used in the descriptions. For example,

---

[7]   U. T. Holmes, Jr., in his preface to *Aucassin and Nicolette*, translated by Edward Francis Moyer and Carey DeWitt Eldridge (Chapel Hill, 1937), p. vii, first called attention to the similarity between these two rustics. Both of them undoubtedly owe much to the wild man lore of the Middle Ages. For a thorough discussion, see Richard Bernheimer, *Wild Men in the Middle Ages: A Study in Art, Sentiment and Demonology* (Cambridge, Mass., 1952). See also Alice M. Colby, *The Portrait*, pp. 72-88 for a discussion of what she calls «ideal ugliness».

«leiz et hideus» in the *Yvain* becomes in the thirteenth-century Picardian dialect of the *Aucassin* «lais et hidex». Instead of being adorned with «danz de sengler aguz et rous», the rustic of the *Aucassin* has «uns grans dens gaunes et lais». Yvain's rustic is described as «apoiez fu sor sa maçue», while Aucassin's is «apoiiés sor une grande maçue». And both are clad in skins of cattle. The similarities of the descriptions, while Chrétien's is considerably more detailed, are rather remarkable.

Just as the descriptions of the rustics are strikingly similar, so, too, in some respects, are the actions of Calogrenant, the hero of this episode of the *Yvain*, and Aucassin. The notable exception is the vastly different greetings proffered by our two protagonists. Calogrenant, who would not be too surprised to meet such a monster in the woods, is primarily concerned with the moral position of the giant rustic. He exclaims:

> ... Va, car me di
> se tu es boene chose ou non.[8]

Calogrenant's question shows a certain sophistication, a certain awareness of several possibilities, particularly when it is compared to Aucassin's innocent «Biax frere, Dix t'i aït!» (XXIV, 25). Aucassin's greeting to the rustic is no less courtly than is his greeting to Nicolette. He has a rather undefined sense of propriety and behaves somewhat like a novice who tries very hard not to make mistakes yet errs through his over-caution.

Calogrenant inquires of the cowherd what he is doing in the woods, and the rustic answers immediately,

> ... Ge m'i estois,
> et gart les bestes de cest bois.
> (331-32)

Aucassin asks the same question: «que fais tu ilec?» (XXIV,26), but the rustic is not so accommodating. He asks suspiciously, «A vos que monte?» (XXIV, 28). The rustic of the *Yvain* is a herdsman who guards the wild cattle of the woods and who controls them utterly. They tremble, he says, to see him punish one among them by wrenching its horns, and they stand still, seeming to beg for mercy. The story of the rustic Aucassin encounters is less fanciful. He has been hired to drive a plough with a yoke of four oxen, but he has lost one and is out seeking it. The herdsman of the

---

[8] Chrétien de Troyes, *Le Chevalier au lion (Yvain)*, ed. Mario Roques (Paris, 1960), 11. 326-27. All subsequent references are to this edition and will be given within the text.

Yvain is the sort of creature one would expect to find in a courtly romance. He is superhuman, monstrously ugly, and placed within the story only for the hero's benefit, for he serves to direct Calogrenant to the marvelous fountain. The only vestige of the original herdsman left in the «demythologized» rustic of *Aucassin et Nicolette* is his ugliness. He seems incompetent since he cannot even keep up with his domesticated ox. And the melodramatic story he tells of not having eaten for three days, of the prison that awaits him if he cannot pay for the ox, of his poor old mother whose very mattress has been taken from under her and who must lie on straw, is just a bit too familiar for us to accept it entirely at face value. In any case, whether the story is true or not, the rustic succeeds in relieving Aucassin of twenty sous.

The herdsmen ask in turn the purpose of the knights' presence in the woods. Calogrenant answers truthfully that he seeks adventure whereby to test his prowess and courage, but Aucassin replies with a lie (or perhaps the truth garbed in symbolic language) as though the naked truth were insufficient for such a world. «Je vig hui matin cacier en ceste forest, s'avoie un blanc levrer, le plus bel del siecle, si l'ai perdu: por ce pleur jou» (XXIV, 39-41). The peasant snorts, «Os!... por le cuer que cil Sires eut en sen ventre! que vos plorastes por un cien puant?» (XXIV, 43-44). Once the twenty sous has changed hands the encounter is ended; the rustic has served no useful purpose to Aucassin. Earlier in the story, however, Aucassin does receive directions from some younger herdsmen to whom Nicolette has paid five sous to deliver a message to him. Instead of delivering the message as soon as they see Aucassin, they tease him with a song:

> ... Bel conpaignet,
> Dix aït Aucasinet,
> voire a foi! le bel vellet;
> et le mescine au corset
> qui avoit le poil blondet,
> cler le vis et l'oeul vairet,
> ki nos dona denerés
> dont acatrons gastelés,
> gaïnes et coutelés
> flaüsteles et cornés,
> maçüeles et pipés!
> Dix le garisse!
>
> (XXI, 5-16)

Aucassin, hearing their words, rides joyfully forward and asks them to repeat their song, but they coyly refuse until Aucassin offers them ten sous, whereupon one of the boys tells the tale in prose. It is significant that in both encounters some reference is made early in the conversation to Aucassin's wealth. On this occasion, one of the young herdsmen remarks, «... il n'a si rice home en cest païs sans le cors le Conte Garin» (XXII, 16-17), a statement which is echoed by the hideous rustic, «... se j'estoie ausi rices hom que vos estes, tos li mons ne me feroit mie plorer» (XXIV, 32-33). In each case Aucassin asks immediately if they know who he is, and the answer is a rapid «Oïl, nos savions bien que vos estes Aucassins nos damoisiax» (XXII, 11-12) or «Oie, je sai bien que vos estes Aucassins, li fix le conte» (XXIV, 35). Aucassin's reputation is apparently widespread, and he seems to be considered quite gullible.

A world like Beaucaire in which men are not always honorable and do not live by the rules of chivalry, where even herdsmen take advantage of a simple heart, is a difficult world for the courtly lover to operate in. But perhaps even these obstacles would not be insurmountable for Aucassin if only Nicolette behaved like a courtly lady. Physically she is perfect for the role:

> Ele avoit les caviaus blons et menus recercelés, et les ex vairs et rians, et le face traitice, et le nes haut et bien assis, et lé levretes vremelletes plus que n'est cerisse ne rose el tans d'esté, et les dens blancs et menus; et avoit les mameletes dures qui li sous-levoient sa vesteure ausi con ce fuissent deus nois gauges; et estoit graille par mi les flans qu'en vox dex mains le peusciés enclorre; et les flors des margerites... estoient droites noires avers ses piés et ses ganbes, tant par estoit blance la mescinete.

> (XII, 19-28)

This portrait of Nicolette, as Barbara Sargent points out, «could hardly be more conventional: an enumeration from head to foot of the qualities essential to feminine beauty».[9] And one can scarcely fail to notice the physical characteristics she shares with Aucassin—«caviaus blons et menus recercelés... ex vairs et rians... face traitice... nes haut et bien assis». But in spite of her physical qualifications for her role as Aucassin's «douce amie»,

---

[9] Barbara Sargent, «Parody in *Aucassin et Nicolette*: Some Further Considerations», *FR*, 43 (1969-70), 597-605. See also Edmond Faral, *Les Arts poétiques du XIIe et du XIIIe siècle* (Paris, 1924), pp. 75-81, 214-15.

she seems to know little more about a proper sort of courtly romance than does Aucassin's father, and she repeatedly shows Aucassin up in comic perspective by acting as a contrast to him. Throughout the work, the author plays with the inherent reversal of male-female roles in the courtly love relationship. For example, when they are both imprisoned, it is Nicolette, not Aucassin, who escapes. It is *she* who comes to *his* tower where they engage in a love debate before dawn. In his article «The *Aube* in *Aucassin et Nicolette*», William S. Woods contends that the separation of Aucassin and Nicolette in sections XII-XVI of the *chantefable* parodies the themes of the usual *aube* pattern. Here again, the parody is aimed not at the genre, but at the male protagonist. Woods notes, significantly, that the «usual roles are reversed here and it is the woman who is leaving the man».[10] The psychological roles are also reversed. «The man is passive, helpless, tearful, devoid of practical solution to the problem and full of idle threats. It is the woman, on the other hand, who is practical, sensible, active, stoical, and she doesn't shed a tear» (pp. 213-14). Warned by the watchman, Nicolette slips into the forest where she builds a bower for Aucassin and hides to wait for him. When Aucassin is finally released from his tower and goes off in search of Nicolette, he stumbles across the *loge* she has made. The discovery in the forest of evidence of the lady's presence recalls Lancelot's finding Guenevere's comb with some of the Queen's golden hairs still caught in its teeth. Lancelot, pale from love and grief, becomes suddenly weak and nearly falls from his horse. Aucassin, dreaming of Nicolette, *does* fall, hits a rock, and dislocates his shoulder. Traditional courtly-love imagery pictures the beloved as a physician, curing the love-malady by returning the love. In this scene by the bower, Nicolette becomes the literal physician of Aucassin, working his shoulder back into place and binding it up with a piece of cloth torn from her petticoat. «... et il fu tox garis» (XXVI, 14). The humor of the scene is derived, not from the transformation of a love image into literal reality *per se*, but rather from Aucassin's comical ineptness which forces the lady to become literally what she is intended to be only symbolically.

The scene echoes even more strongly, perhaps, the *loge* scene of the Tristan and Yseut story, thereby emphasizing once more the exaggerated

---

[10] William S. Woods, «The *Aube* in *Aucassin et Nicolette*», in *Mediaeval Studies in Honor of Urban Tigner Holmes, Jr.*, UNCSRLL, 56 (Chapel Hill, 1965), p. 213.

reversal of male-female roles. For it is Tristan who builds the *loge* for Yseut:

> Sa loge fait; au branc qu'il tient
> Les rains tranche, fait la fullie;
> Yseut l'a bien espes jonchie.[11]

This building of the *loge* is by no means the only echo from the Tristan and Yseut legend.   The fact that the bower is built at a point where seven roads converge, a place where Aucassin was sure to pass by, the fact that Nicolette hides, leaving the bower as a sort of lover's test, recalls Marie de France's *Lai du chevrefeuille* in which Tristan leaves a sign, a branch of hazel enlaced with honeysuckle, as a sort of test for Yseut, and withdraws to wait for her in the forest.   Wayne Conner has pointed out that just as the honeysuckle was Tristan's identifying flower, so are the lilies entwined in Nicolette's bower her special sign, one which Aucassin, who calls her «flor de lis», recognizes immediately.[12]   Nicolette's return to Beaucaire disguised as a *jongleur* is an unmistakable echo, as Jodogne has pointed out,[13] of a similar disguise of Tristan returning from exile to see Yseut. In each instance it is significant that Nicolette assumes the role of Tristan, not that of Yseut.   She is not the typical swooning courtly lady of twelfth-century romances.   Rather, she is a clever, active young woman who is, at one point, even described in virile terms as «Nicole li preus, li sage» (XXXVII, 1).   Nicolette is practical; Aucassin is a dreamer.   She is active; he is passive.   It is not difficult to see how such a reversal suggests the extreme courtly love situation which makes a virtual *seigneur* of the lady and tends to emasculate the man who must always bow in obeisance to her will.   Carried to its logical conclusions such a situation could well result in the total inversion of roles that exists in Torelore.

Gaston Paris has claimed that the Torelore episode is boring and absurd.[14] But, as Pauphilet has said, «on a commis, jadis et naguère, le contre-sens de ne pas reconnaître dans toute l'oeuvre la veine parodique de l'épisode de Torelore et de supprimer cet épisode comme une dissonante

---

[11]   Béroul, *Le Roman de Tristan*, ed. Ernest Muret (Paris, 1903), 11. 1290-92.

[12]   Wayne Conner, «The *Loge* in *Aucassin et Nicolette*», *RR*, 46 (1955), 85.

[13]   Jodogne has noted that this motif appears in the *Folie Tristan* of Oxford as well as that of Berne, 61.

[14]   Gaston Paris, Review of *Aucassin et Nicolette*, trans. A. Bida and *Aucassin und Nicolette*, ed. Hermann Suchier, *Romania*, 8 (1897), 291.

interpolation».[15]   Those who have judged the visit to Torelore a poorly
integrated episode, in some cases the same critics who have called Chrétien's
romances badly constructed, have apparently not attempted to see the
episode in terms of the entire work.   First of all, it provides a traditional,
almost essential, motif from the courtly romance—that of the visit to an
otherworldly kingdom.   Lancelot's visit to the Kingdom of Gorre,
Yvain's adventures in the land of the marvelous fountain, even Erec's
search in the strange garden for the «Joie de la cour» serve to affirm the
knight's prowess.   His deeds in the otherworld are often a sort of culmination of his deeds of everyday.   But Torelore is an upside-down world,
where the king lies in childbed while the queen leads the army against
the enemy, a more extreme situation of inversion, but one that is certainly
not unrelated to the reversed roles of Aucassin and Nicolette.   The Torelore
incident also recalls the visit to the magic castle which transforms all
qualities into their opposites in the *Lanzelet* of Ulrich von Zatzikhoven,
written sometime after 1194 and supposedly based on a French original
by one Hugh de Morville.   During his captivity at the magic castle of
Schâtel le Mort, the hero, the best of knights in the outside world, is
transformed into a cowardly wretch.[16]   Torelore is apparently the same
sort of world and provides for the reader a sort of parody within a
parody.   Within this world *à rebours*, Aucassin and Nicolette seem to
exchange roles.   He who is described as «li biax, li blons,/ li gentix, li
amorous» (XXVII, 1-2) only moments before setting foot on the shore
of Torelore becomes within that land «li prex, li ber» (XXXI, 11).   And
she who, upon leaving Torelore and arriving in Carthage is immediately
described as «Nicole li preus, li sage» (XXXVII, 1-2) was in Torelore
«a gentle, retiring lady from the moment of their arrival».[17]   Sister M. Faith
McKean has claimed, and quite rightly so, that the Torelore episode
«is deliberately cut off from the fictional real world not because it is an
interruption but because it is the key passage, a necessary interlude
highlighting the prime target of the poet's irony» (p. 68).   Explaining her

---

[15]   *Le Legs*, p. 248.
[16]   See Ulrich von Zatzikhoven, *Lanzelet*, ed. K. A. Hahn (Frankfurt, 1845; reprinted
Berlin, 1965), 11. 3536-3825. English prose translation by Kenneth G. T. Webster,
revised by R. S. Loomis (New York, 1951), pp. 73-77. A land that automatically transforms qualities into their opposites would also account for an inconsistency of description
pointed out by Barbara Sargent (p. 603) and earlier by Kaspar Rogger, «Etude déscriptive
de la chantefable 'Aucassin et Nicolette'», *ZRP*, 67 (1951), 421. Nicolette is described
while in Beaucaire as extremely slender, yet in Torelore she describes herself as «grasse
et mole» (XXXIII, 5).
[17]   McKean, 67.

reasons for considering the Torelore episode a key passage, she comments: «Catching the fundamental reversal implicit in courtly love, he [the author] created the perfect parody by creating the perfect courtly lover, and climaxed his work in the much maligned Torelore episode by making the reversal of roles so obvious that even the courtly lover had to recognize its foolishness» (p. 64). Aucassin does, indeed, recognize the foolishness of Torelore. He is even offended by the king's lying in childbed, while the queen fights with the army, but there is no indication whatsoever that he understands the implications of the episode as they relate to himself. Nor does he carry away from Torelore any of his indignation. Whatever situation he is in, Aucassin is still fundamentally a misfit. His new virility and energy are just as much out of place in Torelore as were his weeping and inertia in Beaucaire. Torelore provides a sort of culmination for the everyday deeds of Aucassin as an otherworld adventure should, for his thrashing about in this gentle land brings him to the maximum point of foolishness. He nearly beats to death the poor king who has just given birth to a son; he cheerfully enters into battle killing the enemy who have only eggs, cheeses, apples, and mushrooms with which to defend themselves. In short, the episode shows Aucassin to be hopelessly out of step with the rest of the world; and moreover, it reveals to the reader, if not to Aucassin, the potential humor inherent in the fundamental reversal of roles in the courtly love relationship when carried to its logical extremes.

Harden concurs with the notion that there is a reversal of roles in the *Aucassin*. Indeed, he sees inversion as the essential technique of the author:

> Inversion, especially in character, has always been an effective device for parody, one in which the great are made small and the small great, in which the solemn are made absurd and the absurd solemn, in which the ideal are made ridiculous and the ridiculous ideal. ...It is, we believe, the very method and intention of the author of *Aucassin et Nicolette* as he mocks the vapid plots and equally vapid personages of the idyllic novel (p. 3).

Despite the fact that Harden's study is one of the best that has been done on *Aucassin et Nicolette*, I believe that he has, to some extent, oversimplified the question of parody by seeing inversion as «the very method and intention of the author». Clearly inversion plays a key role in the author's technique, but one is hard put to find it extensively used in situations outside of the Aucassin-Nicolette relationship. And within this love relationship it is perhaps not so much that the author reverses their roles, but rather that he exaggerates a reversal already implicit.) One may point out the Torelore episode as an exception, but I have attempted to suggest its essential relationship with the roles of the lovers. Harden points out several details that bear clear markings of this inversion technique. / The names are a good example. Aucassin is a French hero with an Arabic name; Nicolette, a North African heroine with a French name.[18] Aucassin muses about life after death, finding pleasure in Hell rather than in Heaven. But even these details are in some way related to the lovers or the love relationship, the latter suggesting in a comparatively mild way the essential conflict between courtly love and Christianity. To see the technique of parody as limited to inversion alone, however, is to miss the fun of a hero who, when he behaves according to the code, as Aucassin attempts to do, meets continually with situations which are not quite what one expects them to be, although they may bear all the hallmarks of tradition. They are not necessarily inverted in any way. In fact, I believe that inversion, rather than being *the* technique of the parodist-author of *Aucassin et Nicolette*, falls under the more comprehensive category of incongruity, which is an essentially comic device. It may be incongruity between the character and the situation, between the words and their meaning, between style and content, between lover and lady. And to this technique one must add, for any good parody, a greater or lesser degree of exaggeration. In the *Aucassin* exaggeration is strong, so strong, in fact, that it leads logically to the inversion that is already hinted at within the convention itself.

Grace Frank has stated that «If parody alone were the author's motive then his sense of reality and his delight in his own playfulness got the better of him. And mere parody of forgotten chivalric romances would hardly charm us today, as this unpretentious trifle continues to do».[19] I am not quite sure what Mrs. Frank means by the author's «sense of reality»; certainly there is nothing markedly «realistic» about the *Aucassin*. Nor are the chivalric romances quite so forgotten as she suggests. The courtly love triangle of Arthur, Guenevere, and Lancelot has even succeeded as a Broadway musical, albeit in a rather spurious form. But most difficult of all to understand is why the author's «delight in his own playfulness» carries him so far beyond parody. Such delight and playfulness are part and parcel of the makeup of the parodist. It is unlikely, in view

---

[18] Harden, 8. Jodogne has also pointed this out in his earlier article, 56.
[19] Grace Frank, *Medieval French Drama* (Oxford, 1954), pp. 238-39.

of her statement about «mere parody», that Mrs. Frank is using the term as I have used it here. She seems to consider parody as a debased art form. Surely it is no more so than satire when used in connection with the writings of Swift. Nor is it simply a mockery. While there is always a barb in parody, there may also be affection for the thing parodied. Robert P. Falk, in fact, claims that successful parody «holds in equilibrium two opposing attitudes towards its subject—satire and sympathy».[20] If this is so, then one may well claim that *Aucassin et Nicolette* is successful as parody. The juxtaposition of the exaggerated courtly lover with a world of practical considerations, suspicious rustics, and unreliable fathers, renders not only Aucassin, but also the people of Beaucaire, somewhat ridiculous. But the mockery is light, the criticism gentle. It is quite possible that, in parody, the didactic instinct of the author is in inverse proportion to his sense of humor. If so, one may conclude that, while *Aucassin* is, to some extent, didactic in that it inevitably points up the weaknesses of the courtly lover in conflict with a less romantically inclined society, its essential quality is humor. We laugh at Aucassin; we enjoy him. And while we have no desire to emulate him, we also have no desire to see him changed.

---

[20] *The Antic Muse*, p. 10.

CHAPTER III

TROILUS

Much has been written about the tribulations of Troilus, the deserted lover of the sprightly Criseyde. By some critics he has been considered noble, sincere, and totally conventional, a tragic young lover cruelly betrayed by an unworthy woman. For others, he is the butt of a Chaucerian joke. The more sensitive and more recent readings of the *Troilus* tend to focus on an interpretation that lies somewhere between the two, to reveal a character who is neither wholly comic nor wholly tragic, but, in essence, <u>tragicomic</u>. Neither element is treated in the extreme. Both are delicate portrayals, more aptly described, perhaps, as gentle parody of a single figure seen from two different points of view. Charles Muscatine describes Chaucer's complexity of viewpoint in the *Troilus* in terms of three levels of perspective:

> He sees, as Jean [de Meung] does, the elements of presumption, of naïveté and of <u>impracticality in courtly idealism</u>, and he admires the wholesome sanity of ordinary life. But, unlike Jean, he <u>also prizes courtly idealism</u> for its <u>very real virtues</u>, for its recognition of nobility, of beauty, and <u>of spirit</u>, and he detects in the incessantly practical pursuits of common life the shadow of futility cast over any human activity in which these higher concerns are neglected. [1]

In short, Troilus and Pandarus, and even Troilus and Criseyde, for in practicality she surpasses even Nicolette, serve as foils for one another, each revealing the other's strengths and weaknesses. But the complexity

---

[1] Charles Muscatine, *Chaucer and the French Tradition: A Study in Style and Meaning* (Berkeley and Los Angeles, 1957; reprinted, 1964), p. 131.

of viewpoint does not end here, and the structure of the poem will bear out Muscatine's assertion that:

> Beyond this lies another level of perspective. Chaucer is a spiritual pupil of Boethius. He sees in turn the whole sphere of human experience against eternity. He sees the imperfection inherent in any mode of life—be it practical or idealistic—wherein the end itself is *earthly* joy, and hence wherein the prize may at any moment be washed away by the same tides that brought it in (p. 132).

It is only logical that Chaucer should, in his maturity, arrive at such a philosophical position, and it has strongly colored his depiction of Troilus. How different he might have been had the poem been written earlier, say, at about the same time as the *Book of the Duchess!* It is also logical to find in Chaucer's characterizations of both Pandarus and Troilus not ultimate condemnation, but sympathy, at the same time that he definitively rejects both positions. And while one would be in error to attempt to see in the characters of the poem any deliberate attempt at self-portrayal, one cannot help but notice how clearly the male protagonists delineate the general tendencies of the young and the older Chaucer. There are good reasons for believing that as a young man, before he reached the age of about thirty, Chaucer was heavily influenced by the French courtly tradition, by Guillaume de Lorris, Machaut, Froissart and Deschamps. The works of the earlier period are imbued with a rather light but sentimental view of love. From this period, according to the literary chronology of F. N. Robinson,[2] we have the *ABC*, the *Book of the Duchess*, a translation of the *Roman de la Rose*, and some early complaints and lyrics composed on French models.   Aside from the shorter works, the *Book of the Duchess*, a springtime love vision told in allegorical terms, clearly bears the mark of French romantic influence, and particularly, as Robinson points out (p. 266), of Froissart's *Paradys d'Amours*. It is, of course, uncertain whether the extant Middle English translation of the *Roman de la Rose* is correctly attributed to Chaucer; nevertheless, we have no reason to doubt that he did, in fact, make such a translation as he claimed to have done in the *Prologue* to the *Legend of Good Women*, and that it belongs to this period of his work.

A number of critics have pointed out a shift in Chaucer's attitude as a result of influences operating on him after his first trip to Italy in December

---

[2] «Introduction», *The Works of Geoffrey Chaucer*, pp. vii-xxx.

1372 to May 1373, when he must have encountered the works of Boccaccio and Petrarch. Exposure to Boccaccio, in particular, seems to have awakened in the maturing Chaucer a keen sense of irony, particularly toward the romanticism to which he had been drawn in the courtly tradition. Possibly this sense of irony had been aroused as early as 1366 during a visit to Spain, where he may have been introduced to the *Libro de buen amor*.[3] Before 1380 Chaucer had been again to Italy, which served apparently only to strengthen his new direction, more ironic, yet more serious. It is during the period between 1380 and 1386 that he is believed to have composed both *Palamon*, later incorporated into the *Canterbury Tales* as the tale told by the knight, a character who does not directly concern us here, but towards whom, it might be pointed out, Chaucer expresses a sincere admiration coupled with a gentle mockery, as though it were directed at the quaint ways of a good friend, and *Troilus*, a tale which expresses the same sort of discrepancy between the sincerity and naïveté of both the narrator and the protagonist and the irony of the author who views the entire situation from another level of understanding.[4] From this same period we have also the *Legend of Good Women*, the *Parliament of Fowls*, and, more significant, Chaucer's translation of Boethius. The fact that the *Troilus* and *Boece* were composed at about the same time, coupled with the fact that Chaucer mentions them both in the same breath in his *Adam Scriveyn* («Adam Scriveyn, if ever it thee bifalle/ Boece or Troylus for to wryten newe...»),[5] tends to substantiate the hypothesis that Boethian ideas were uppermost in Chaucer's mind at the time he wrote the *Troilus* and that, indeed, he felt a necessary connection between the two works. This developing dual tendency towards irony and serious philosophical considerations was strengthened even further

---

[3] See T. J. Gárbaty, «The *Pamphilus* Tradition in Ruiz and Chaucer», *PQ*, 46 (1967), 457-70. Gárbaty points out the parallel between Juan Ruiz's opposition of *buen amor* and *loco amor* and the similar dichotomy in the epilogue of *Troilus and Criseyde*. While such dichotomies exist in many medieval works, he argues convincingly for the influence of the *Libro de buen amor* on the *Troilus* by showing a number of parallels between the two that are not derived from the *Pamphilus*.

[4] Robert M. Jordan suggests a very sensible «four-level hierarchy of perception» (p. 109) based on the Boethian principles of Divine Intelligence, Reason, Imagination, and the Senses. He relates these four levels in the *Troilus* to the perceptions of the poet, the narrator, Pandarus, and Troilus; *Chaucer and the Shape of Creation* (Cambridge, Mass., 1967), pp. 95-110. Jordan's view of four levels of perception by no means excludes that of Muscatine. Rather, it seems to expand Muscatine's third level by distinguishing between the viewpoint of the narrator and that of the poet. For this discussion, Muscatine's three levels are adequate and avoid unnecessary complexity, since I am not concerned with the narrator as such; nonetheless, the distinction is an important one.

[5] *The Works of Geoffrey Chaucer*, ed. Robinson, p. 534.

in his later works, and, as a result at least in part of this mature perspective, the *Canterbury Tales* remains today one of the most sophisticated works of English literature.

This is not to say that when Chaucer discovered realism and irony, Chaucer the romantic ceased to exist. On the contrary, he simply grew up. The two tendencies remain very much a part of the mature Chaucer, keeping one another in check. They are personified in the characters of Troilus the extreme romantic and Pandarus the extreme realist, neither of whom is, by himself, wholly effectual. Perhaps aware of both tendencies within himself, Chaucer notes their dangers within the work, superseding them by a third, more philosophical attitude, that which recognizes them as earthly and, therefore, limited positions.

In discussing the *Troilus* the critic cannot ignore any of the three levels of perspective. They are particularly important in understanding the characterization of Troilus himself. He is on one level the time-honored young lover, wholly romantic, given over to the arts of love. But his functions within the text are severely limited, somewhat like Aucassin's, by the context in which he operates, a context which could have been conceived and executed only by the more mature Chaucer who is capable of accentuating Troilus' inherent absurdity by juxtaposing him with a jaded lover-turned-realist, Pandarus. And both are ultimately seen from a loftier angle, their follies softened somewhat by the compassion of a clearer vision. Both had placed their hopes wholly on this world, which, in its essential mutability, could not endure. In short, what we have in the *Troilus* is Chaucer's fully developed conception of the lover.

Agnes K. Getty has noticed what she terms «Chaucer's changing conception of the humble lover».[6] She points out, much as has been done here, that in Fragment A of the *Romaunt of the Rose* (that part most widely accepted as the authentic work of Chaucer), the *Complaint unto Pity*, the *Complaint of Mars*, the *Complaint to his Lady*, the *Book of the Duchess*, and the *House of Fame*, all from the earlier period, the lover is treated conventionally. But the *Parliament of Fowls*, she believes, «marks a departure from Chaucer's usual passive acceptance of the formal code» (p. 205). She sees Pandarus and Criseyde as *hors de code*, but Troilus as completely conventional. And she concludes that «except for a temporary renewal of allegiance to formal love standards in the *Legend of Good Women*, Chaucer's rebellion against the conventional concept of the humble

---

[6] Agnes K. Getty, «Chaucer's Changing Conception of the Humble Lover», *PMLA*, 44 (1929), 202-16.

lover developed and increased in intensity after the writing of the *House of Fame*» (p. 216). Miss Getty is on the right track, but she is, I believe, mistaken in seeing the later works as real departures from Chaucer's earlier views. Rather they are simply developments of them. Chaucer never gives up his courtly lover. He even reappears as Absolom in the *Miller's Tale*, where, as E. T. Donaldson has pointed out, Chaucer uses in ironic and comic contexts «clichés borrowed from the vernacular versions of the code of courtly love».[7] The mature Chaucer who wrote both the *Miller's Tale* and the *Knight's Tale* and used, as Donaldson also reminds us, one to «quite» the other, could hardly have looked upon courtly love seriously in either. The very fact that he saw in it a fit subject for parody suggests that the reader should be wary of taking Palamon (or Troilus, who was conceived during the same period) too seriously. Here the courtly lover is clearly revealed from a new point of view. Troilus, likewise, is not just the offspring of one period, and Pandarus and Criseyde, of another, as Miss Getty seems to suggest. They are all born of a new philosophical position, of a depth lacking in the earlier works. Pandarus is not a comic figure and Troilus a tragic one. Rather they are all together playing out a sort of *comédie humaine*, enduring with absurd seriousness the trials of this world, both comically and tragically unaware of the greater perspective.

Part of the problem of interpreting the character of Troilus is derived from the fact that within the text the reader is not permitted to see all three levels of perspective from the beginning. Chaucer's method is, rather, to permit them to unfold, and it is only at the end or in rereading that we are given the triptych view and are permitted to see the three levels functioning simultaneously. The parody-pathos situations are, in a sense, interdependent in that both are strictly worldly views of the story, and, as such, they *do* develop side by side to a certain extent. Books I and II, however, lean most sharply in the direction of comedy. Book III is the culmination of the romance, in which Troilus' ride on the Wheel of Fortune[8] reaches its highest point, the possession of Criseyde. It must of necessity begin its downward swing in the opening lines of Book IV:

> But al to litel, weylaway the whyle,
> Lasteth swich joie, ythonked be Fortune,

---

[7] E. Talbot Donaldson, «Idiom of Popular Poetry in the *Miller's Tale*», *English Institute Essays, 1950*, ed. Alan S. Downer (New York, 1951), pp. 121-22.

[8] For a full discussion of the Wheel of Fortune, see Howard R. Patch, *The Goddess Fortuna in Medieval Literature* (Cambridge, Mass., 1927; reprinted New York, 1967), pp. 147-77.

That semeth trewest when she wol bygyle,
And kan to fooles so hire song entune,
That she hem hent and blent, traitour comunne!
And whan a wight is from hire whiel ythrowe,
Than laugheth she, and maketh hym the mowe.[9]

Books IV and V develop more strongly the pathos of the situation, the all-but-tragic in strictly human and medieval terms, the loss of Criseyde and the downfall and death of Troilus. At the end of Book V, however, in nine swift stanzas, Chaucer effectively erases the «litel...tragedye» he has erected, revealing it to be, in truth, but a pathetic situation created by the limited vision of man.

Our first view of Troilus prepares the comic development that will follow. He is, in the first «scene» of his story, found striding up and down in the temple, followed by «His yonge knyghtes» (I, 184), the local playboy looking over the ladies of the town, mocking any of the knights and squires of his company who might be caught by the snares of love. Unwittingly he foresees himself as he will be when stung by love's arrow:

He wolde smyle and holden it folye,
And seye hym thus, «God woot, she slepeth softe
For love of the, whan thow turnest ful ofte!

«I have herd told, pardieux, of youre lyvynge,
Ye loveres, and youre lewed observaunces,
And which a labour folk han in wynnynge
Of love, and in the kepyng which doutaunces;
And whan youre prey is lost, woo and penaunces.
O veray fooles, nyce and blynde be ye!
Ther nys nat oon kan war by other be.»

And with that word he gan caste up the browe,
Ascaunces, «Loo! is this naught wisely spoken?»
                                        (I, 194-205)

---

[9] *Troilus and Criseyde,* IV, 1-7. Quoted from *The Works of Geoffrey Chaucer*, Robinson edition. All subsequent references to the *Troilus* are from this edition, and book and line references will be given within the text.

But Troilus is the strutting and dapper young man-about-town, a little too sure of himself, and he is about to fall flat on his face. In the very next line «The God of Love gan loken rowe» (I, 206), takes aim with his bow and fires, thereby reducing Troilus to the object of his own mockery. In «an elaborate simile», as Robert Jordan has commented, «epic in form and in verbal style but barnyard in content»,[10] love's power over Troilus is described. He is «proud Bayard» (I, 218), who is a bit headstrong until he feels the lash of the whip which reminds him that he is «but an hors» (I, 223). The limited vision of man is already drawn in as a theme, one which, as yet, the reader is not encouraged to take too seriously:

> O blynde world, O blynde entencioun!
> How often falleth al the effect contraire
> Of surquidrie and foul presumpcioun;
> For kaught is proud, and kaught is debonaire.
> This Troilus is clomben on the staire,
> And litel weneth that he moot descenden;
> But alday faileth thing that fooles wenden.
>
> (I, 211-17)

These lines apply clearly to the situation at hand, Troilus' fall from pride into the humility of love. It is only in retrospect that they may be seen to foreshadow his later behavior viewed from the third level of perspective, when he is again «clomben on the staire,/ And litel weneth that he moot descenden». With a single blow from Cupid's arrow, Troilus is toppled from his position as a leader of men, like Bayard «First in the trays, ful fat and newe shorn» (I, 222), to one «moost subgit unto love» (I, 231). From this point to his death, Troilus is incapacitated by love. The adolescent mocker has been miraculously transformed into the equally adolescent romantic, whose first utterance as a lover is a song, a conventional song full of the paradox of love, the suffering and humility he has made such fun of earlier. He has become an all too typical young lover, who suddenly discovers all the profound «truths» in the love ballads he has previously considered trite and sentimental. The reader is left with Troilus' own laughter still ringing in his ears and the inevitably amusing realization that the young man has, because of his unsympathetic mockery of other lovers, deserved exactly what he is getting.

---

10 *Chaucer*, p. 74.

It is a bit surprising, considering this clearly comic initiation, that some critics have insisted on an interpretation of Troilus as a totally serious character, and even as «a valiant and thoroughly practical knight»[11] who is for Chaucer the ideal courtly lover. And yet such notions have been, until fairly recently, something of a critical commonplace. For W. G. Dodd, Troilus is a young man, not in the least amusing, completely determined by the courtly conventions, and it is by these conventions, he asserts, «rather than by present day ideas» (p. 143), that we must judge Troilus. Thomas A. Kirby, writing almost thirty years later, is still essentially in agreement with Dodd that Troilus is «Chaucer's conception of... the ideal lover»,[12] whose conduct the author fully approved. He adds, in an apparent attempt to account for the extravagances of Troilus' behavior, that «the reader unmindful of courtly love conventions may easily be annoyed at his conduct» (p. 246). Even C. S. Lewis holds the view that Chaucer's Troilus is, to a large extent, predetermined by convention. «He can be, to some extent, assumed: he is in one sense unimportant, because he is, in another, all important. As an embodiment of the medieval ideal of lover and warrior, he stands second only to Malory's Lancelot: far, I think, above the Launcelot of Chrétien. We never doubt his valour, his constancy, or the 'daily beauty' of his life.»[13] Still more recently, Siegfried Wenzel contends that «Chaucer presents him primarily as an idealized hero in whom *courtoisie* reaches perfection».[14] Because of the notion that Troilus is wholly conventional, and therefore essentially uninteresting, «the least satisfying of the major characters of the poem, somewhat flat and characterless»,[15] he has been largely ignored by many critics, who have been far more interested in the «realistic» Criseyde and Pandarus. I agree wholeheartedly with Kirby that a sound critical opinion of Troilus must be founded on a knowledge of medieval standards of love, and I could not disagree more with D. W. Robertson, Jr., that «the 'courtly love' interpretation [of the *Troilus*] takes all the humor out of the poem».[16]

---

[11]   W. G. Dodd, *Courtly Love in Chaucer and Gower* (Boston, 1913; reprinted Gloucester, Mass., 1959), p. 142. Percy Van Dyke Shelly concurs with Dodd's view of Troilus as an essentially practical character. See *The Living Chaucer* (Philadelphia, 1940; reissued New York, 1968), p. 136.

[12]   Thomas A. Kirby, *Chaucer's Troilus: A Study in Courtly Love* (Baton Rouge, La., reprinted Gloucester, Mass., 1958), p. 282.

[13]   *Allegory*, p. 195.

[14]   Siegfried Wenzel, «Chaucer's Troilus of Book IV», *PLMA*, 79 (1964), 547.

[15]   G. T. Shepherd, «Troilus and Criseyde», in *Chaucer and Chaucerians: Critical Studies in Middle English Literature*, ed. D. S. Brewer (University, Ala., 1966), p. 79.

[16]   «The Concept of Courtly Love», p. 17.

I believe it can be demonstrated that by using these standards as a yardstick, we will find that Troilus measures up as an effective parody, treated sympathetically but humorously, rather than as a completely serious treatment of the courtly lover. While the reader who is not familiar with the courtly love conventions may be, as Kirby points out, «easily annoyed» by Troilus' behavior, the reader who *is* familiar with them may well be amused by it.

A scene frequently cited to illustrate the conventional behavior of Troilus depicts him groaning alone in his bedroom shortly after he is first struck down by the arrow of Love. The «painful» scene continues for some twenty-seven stanzas before the laments are broken up by the entrance of Pandarus, but the essential situation is summed up in the following lines:

> But thanne felte this Troilus swich wo,
> That he was we neigh wood; for ay his drede
> Was this, that she som wight hadde loved so,
> That nevere of hym she wolde han taken hede.
> For which hym thoughte he felte his herte blede;
> Ne of his wo ne dorste he nat bygynne
> To tellen hir for al this world to wynne.
>
> (I, 498-504)

This is not to say that he never left his room in all the twenty-seven stanzas, for the time span covered seems to be several weeks. At least two stanzas are given over to the war, the central political issue dominating Troy. And Troilus, as the second prince of Troy, was bound to participate. But he has lost any patriotic reason he might have had for fighting and fights only that Criseyde might hear good reports of him:

> But for non hate he to the Grekes hadde,
> Ne also for the rescous of the town,
> Ne made hym thus in armes for to madde,
> But only, lo, for this conclusioun:
> To liken hire the bet for his renoun.
>
> (I, 477-81)

Troilus is at least one step more dignified than Aucassin in his reasons for fighting. Aucassin, we may recall, also fights for love, not so that Nicolette might hear of his valor, but rather because he has made a deal

45

with his father that he might have a few words with Nicolette and a kiss if he goes to war against the enemy. And we must not forget the precept that love breeds valor. Auerbach has stated it as follows:

> Love in the courtly romances is already not infrequently the immediate occasion for deeds of valor. There is nothing surprising in this if we consider the complete absence of practical motivation through a political and historical context. Love, being an essential and obligatory ingredient of knightly perfection, functions as a substitute for other possibilities of motivation which are... lacking.[17]

But we must not forget either that, contrary to the romances of Chrétien, the authors of *Aucassin* and *Troilus* have placed their lovers in both a political and a historical context, though in the *Aucassin* a fictional one. Indeed, it is their contexts which so often reveal their absurdity. The courtly lover is essentially at odds with the real world and is at pains to operate as a serious figure within it. Neither Aucassin nor Troilus is a coward; they simply place love above any other value. For Aucassin, who functions outside any real philosophical framework (and in a fictional world which admits fantastic and burlesque elements much more readily than does Chaucer's), this system of values has no unpleasant consequences of any significance. But for Troilus, whose homeland, as the reader knows from the beginning, is doomed, whose brother, valiantly fighting to defend his people, is to be cruelly killed and dishonored by Achilles, and whose context is, at the same time, historical, political, *and* philosophical, the result is a ludicrous superficiality. Nor is his valor depicted as even a major part of his activity, if, indeed, one may use the word «activity» at all in connection with Troilus. His chief characteristic as a courtly lover is the constant love sickness which he undergoes. And it is in the midst of his suffering that Pandarus enters the story:

> Bywayling in his chambre thus allone,
> A friend of his, that called was Pandare,
> Com oones in unwar, and herde hym groone,
> And say his frend in swich destresse and care.

> (I, 546-49)

---

[17] *Mimesis*, p. 123.

Briefly, the result of this encounter is that Pandarus learns the cause of Troilus' sorrows and sets out to do something about it.

It is quite true that Troilus' behavior in this scene is conventional, though twenty-seven stanzas of «conventional» weeping and moaning do seem a trifle exaggerated, and it has, as we have already seen, been rendered somewhat ludicrous by its serious context. If it is true, as C. S. Lewis asserts, that Troilus «can be, to some extent, assumed», then Chaucer must have had some reason for dwelling on Troilus' miseries other than to illustrate the conventional behavior of courtly lovers, which was already quite well known. The lover's suffering, because it is tacitly accepted as part of his normal behavior, may be dealt with quite briefly. Chaucer's insistence on Troilus' prolonged suffering is, perhaps, for purposes of exaggeration. Certainly that is the effect it achieves. The young Troilus' over-conventional behavior reminds one somewhat of Aucassin's «biax frere» addressed to the hideous herdsman.

Pandarus interrupts Troilus in the midst of his extended suffering, finds out its cause, and determines to take steps to remedy it. It has been frequently pointed out that he is the familiar go-between of courtly romance. Intermediaries, like Lunete in the *Yvain*, were indeed conventional characters, but, unlike Pandarus, they act as aids to the lover only when his own actions have proven futile. Ami in the *Roman de la Rose* comes to the aid of the lover only when his approach to the rose on his own has been rebuffed. Even Celestina, who herself departs from the conventional ideal in many other ways, does not enter the affair until Calisto's suit has failed. And then she functions in such a way as to let Calisto think, quite falsely, that he is directing his own circumstances. Pandarus, on the contrary, takes over completely. There is never any question of Troilus' directing matters. He has not, apparently, the vaguest idea what to do. The only aspect of the convention that comes naturally to Troilus is the weeping and the wailing, and as a one-sided lover he is inherently foolish. It is true that, by modern standards and, most likely, by normal behavioral standards in the Middle Ages, «Medieval lovers... were an extraordinarily lachrymose lot».[18] And it is precisely this sort of behavioral extreme that makes the convention most ripe for parody. Chaucer has taken every advantage of it in making Troilus appear ludicrous. In his «lachrymose» state he is totally passive. As Nevill Coghill has pointed

---

[18] Dodd, p. 123. Concerning weeping as conventional behavior, see chapter I, note 47, of the present study.

out, the «artifices practised... are all Pandar's».[19] Pandarus suggests that he write a letter to Criseyde; he writes. Pandarus suggests that he ride by Criseyde's house at a given hour; he appears without fail. Pandarus suggests that he feign sickness; Troilus becomes sick «in ernest» (II, 1529). Even so early in the story, Pandarus has become a foil for Troilus. He is a clever, practical fellow whose «conventional» role has been exaggerated to such an extent that he overshadows the hyper-emotional lover.

One scene in which Troilus' passivity seems particularly inappropriate and indefensible takes place in parliament as the Trojans are deciding whether or not to accept the proffered exchange of Antenor for Criseyde. Troilus might have stood up for Criseyde, but, argues Dodd, «what good would it have done? What good did Hector's opposition to the proposed exchange do? Yet Hector was more influential in Troy than was Troilus; and he was not actuated by any motives of personal interest» (p. 147). Karl Young, too, argues on Troilus' behalf. For him Troilus in the parliament scene is «a model of fortitude, concealing his extreme distress, and in the midst of the turbulence planning a courageous course of action».[20] I can see no «courageous course of action» planned by Troilus in this scene. He decides simply to leave matters to Criseyde, for like a «good» courtly lover, he dares to do nothing «Withouten assent of hir» (IV, 165). When the situation concerns his lady's safety, however, and when immediate action is so urgently needed, it seems somewhat absurd to wait for her approval. Lancelot did not delay in his attempt to rescue Guenevere from Meleagant. He rode his horses until they were dead of exhaustion and then went on foot until the dwarf and his cart appeared. But Troilus is apparently less determined. He ponders a few possibilities, but finds no quick solution—or none that he is sure will work—and hence, he does nothing. Troilus' refusal to intervene is based on the assumption that if he speaks up, men will know of his love for Criseyde, and her reputation will be endangered. Yet why should this be the case? Part of the courtly lover's excellence lies in his restraint, his *mezura*, his being able to control his emotions before others, as Tristan is able to do in the presence of King Mark, or as Lancelot does before the court of Arthur. Restraining his emotions should not, in any way, curtail his political activity. The most

[19] Nevill K. Coghill, «Love and 'Foul Delight': Some Contrasted Attitudes», in *Patterns in Love and Courtesy: Essays in Memory of C. S. Lewis*, ed. John Lawler (London, 1966), p. 143.
[20] Karl Young, «Chaucer's *Troilus and Criseyde* as Romance», *PMLA*, 53 (1938), 50.

important men would have been expected to speak up on such a significant parliamentary issue, yet Troilus, as second son of King Priam, remains silent, waiting meekly to hear what the other lords will say. Only Hector, who is continually described as the best and bravest knight in the kingdom, speaks up in Criseyde's defense. His speech is logical and impersonal and does not suggest to anyone that Hector is Criseyde's lover, which, of course, he is not. His reasons should have occurred to any worthy knight dedicated, in the medieval rather than the classical manner (for the system is essentially medieval despite the classical framework), to the protection of womanhood:

> «Syres, she nys no prisonere», he seyde;
> «I not on yow who that this charge leyde,
> But, on my part, ye may eftsone hem telle,
> We usen here no wommen for to selle.»
>
> (IV, 179-82)

Hector's speech, though brief and to the point, is designed to make the men feel ashamed of their cowardice and selfishness, but it fails for lack of support. Regardless of the failure, Hector is clearly to be admired for his stand. Troilus might at least have spoken in support of his brother without revealing his personal interest. It is, in fact, his duty, not just to Criseyde and to his knighthood, but to the honor of his kingdom as well. But the decision is made to exchange Antenor who, as Chaucer points out, «was after traitour to the town/Of Troye» (IV, 204-05), for Criseyde, «Altheigh that Ector 'nay' ful ofte preyde» (IV, 214). Troilus' silence is far more conspicuous than his speech would have been. Chaucer then tells us that Troilus, who had remained so silent, ironically, «withouten wordes mo,/ Unto his chambre spedde hym faste allone» (IV, 219-20), where he gives in to his emotions in a rather violent way, suggesting less the wan figure of the sorrowing lover than the misunderstood adolescent in the throes of a temper tantrum.

> Right as the wylde bole bygynneth sprynge,
> Now her, now ther, idarted to the herte,
> And of his deth roreth in compleynynge,
> Right so gan he aboute the chaumbre sterte,
> Smytyng his brest ay with his fistes smerte;
> His hed to the wal, his body to the grounde
> Ful ofte he swapte, hymselven to confounde.
>
> (IV, 239-45)

And, of course, all this rage is accompanied by the ever present «heighe sobbes of his sorwes smerte» (IV, 248). He calls for death as he will over thirty more times before the end of the book, yet, when death comes, it comes inconspicuously, as Troilus is dispatched in a single line:

Despitously hym slough the fierse Achille.
(V, 1806)

A second time Pandarus interrupts Troilus' misery to try to put a little spirit into his protégé. Chaucer has here, as he does in many instances, deliberately placed the two in a situation which will show them both in the harsh light of what they really are—one ineffectual in the game of love because of his absurd japing and his uncourtly, realistic way of looking at things; the other, equally ineffectual because of his total submission to the love sickness, extreme even by courtly standards, which renders him virtually inert. A fine pair they make! As for Troilus' decision to do nothing because he does not wish to endanger Criseyde's or his own reputation and because he would be defying parliamentary decision, one immediately thinks of other courtly lovers for whom love gained the upper hand and who were willing to risk their reputations and their lives in defense of their ladies. Lancelot, for example, defies a «court decision», Arthur's rash boon which permitted the abduction of Guenevere, to go into the otherworld of Gorre in search of his lady. His only precaution is that he remains nameless throughout much of the adventure. Tristan, too, can hardly be seen as submitting to the wishes of King Mark in his actions concerning Yseut. Even Aucassin, parody though he be, sets out in an abortive search for Nicolette against the wishes of his father the Count.

Such comparisons of Troilus' behavior with that of other traditional courtly lovers can be very fruitful in pointing up Chaucer's use of convention. We have already noted the exaggerations of Book I, more clearly drawn because of the contrast between Troilus the cynic and Troilus the senti-mentalist. Here the lover has been struck by the arrow of Cupid and has, typically, been brought low by the resulting love sickness. The God of Love describes the symptoms to the Lover of the *Roman de la Rose:*

Sovent, quant il te sovendra
De tes amors, te convendra
Partir des genz par estovoir,
Qu'il ne puissent apercevoir
Le mal don tu es angoisseus.

50

> A une part iras toz seus:
> Lors te vendront sospir e plaintes,
> Friçons e autres dolors maintes;
> En plusors sens seras destroiz,
> Une eure chauz e autre froiz,
> Vermauz une eure, une autre pales:
> Onques fievres n'eüs si males,
> Ne cotidianes ne quartes.[21]

For some three hundred lines he coaches the Lover in the duties he must perform and the pain he will endure. But we seldom see the Lover of the *Roman* actually in the throes of the love sickness. His role lies in action, his innocent approach to the rose who at first welcomes him before he is driven away by Danger, and in thoughtfulness, his debate with Raison, then again in action, as he seeks a second time the affections of the rose, though this time his goal is a bit more modest, a kiss rather than the plucking of the rose. Whatever inactivity there may be in the traditional lover is clearly exaggerated in Troilus, and he becomes ridiculous, much as Chrétien's Lancelot is rendered ridiculous through his preoccupation with love which makes him incapable of coping with the practical problem of the knight guarding the ford.

Perhaps the single scene in the *Troilus* which most clearly points up the protagonist's tendency towards parodying the perfect knight rather than being one is the unforgettable bedroom scene, unmatched in English literature for boudoir comedy until, perhaps, the advent of Fielding. It is not unusual for the lover to be awed, raptured, and in utter reverence at the prospect of finally being granted the lady's «mercy». One is reminded of the troubadour lyrics which mention the lover's religious postures before his lady and of Lancelot's genuflection before Guenevere's bed. But nothing has matched Troilus' fainting away at the crucial moment and having to be bodily tossed into bed by the more pragmatic Pandarus who, at the moment, can think of no more effective way of getting him there. Troilus' incapacity has reached its culmination in this scene. Yet critics remain who would seek to justify and even ennoble Troilus' absurd behavior. Robert apRoberts, for example, contends that his «weakness under the onset of love is meritorious—it is in the best Courtly tradition. It impresses upon the reader not only the power of love which can reduce a strong man

---

[21] Guillaume de Lorris and Jean de Meun, *Le Roman de la Rose*, ed. Ernest Langlois, SATF edition (Paris, 1914-24), II, 2269-81.

51

5

to a state of utter weakness but also the completeness of his surrender to love and the overwhelming sincerity of his passion». [22] Certainly a degree of submissiveness is a part of the convention; but I cannot think of a single prior instance in which the hero has been so utterly incapacitated by love at such a crucial moment. The thought of consummating his love with Guenevere, for example, seems to give Lancelot superhuman strength, for despite his wounds, he is capable of bending back the bars that separate them and leaping from the window to the Queen's bed.[23] As Howard R. Patch has pointed out, «All the rules of Courtly Love in a thousand handbooks do not explain the hero's lassitude before his first union with the lady».[24] Helen Storm Corsa takes essentially the same view of the situation:

> The comedy of this scene...that makes of the hero a figure not only quite unheroic, but even somewhat ridiculous, is undeniably intended by Chaucer. Boccaccio's Troilo had not swooned, nor had his coming into the bed of Criseyde needed any help from anyone. Nor is his faint a part of the «courtly love tradition.» [25]

If Chaucer had intended us to admire Troilus' swoon before the awesome splendor of Criseyde's bed, he would surely have kept Pandarus out of the room. The startling contrast between Troilus' inertia and Pandarus' bustling about in the bedroom renders the scene all the more humorous. Pandarus clearly cuts a most uncourtly figure, one who has no place at all in the bedroom scene. To a certain extent, he foreshadows the presence of Celestina and Lucrecia in similar key seduction scenes in the *Tragico-media de Calisto y Melibea*. Neither Celestina nor Lucrecia actually remains present throughout the entire love scene, but in each case they remain long enough to leave the reader gasping at the indiscretion. There is no indication in the text that Pandarus left the room at all, though he surely does not seem to be there the next morning. We should very likely presume that Pandarus remained long enough to put Troilus into

---

[22] Robert P. apRoberts, «The Central Episode in Chaucer's *Troilus*», *PMLA*, 77 (1962), 384.

[23] It should be pointed out that despite the fantasy-world context of Lancelot and despite his relative balance of love and adventure, some critics have contended that even he is a caricature of the perfect knight. See, for example, R. S. Loomis, *The Development of Arthurian Romance* (London, 1963; reprinted New York, 1964), pp. 51-52. Yet how much greater is the imbalance of Chaucer's Troilus.

[24] Howard R. Patch, *On Rereading Chaucer* (Cambridge, Mass., 1939), p. 21.

[25] Helen Storm Corsa, *Chaucer, Poet of Mirth and Morality* (Notre Dame, 1964), pp. 60-61.

bed, caution him («Swouneth nought now» III, 1190), and make sure that the situation was under control before quietly slipping out of the room. Still, it is a curious omission on Chaucer's part since he has made us so aware of Pandarus' presence up to this point. And it is a presence that has made us ever conscious of the humor of the situation. In his own way, Pandarus is as comical as Troilus. His impatience to «get on with it» is sharpened by Troilus' abject kneeling, his swooning immobility, like that of a man frozen with fear. Troilus is so completely undone that it is Criseyde who must finally make the first move to actuate the seduction. She helps Pandarus to rub Troilus' wrists and palms and to wet his temples. Not unlike Nicolette she has been forced to become the literal physician of her lover as a result of his amusing and rather foolish behavior. Upon his reviving she chides him, «Is this a mannes game?/ What, Troilus, wol ye do thus for shame?» (III, 1126-27). And it is she who reaches out for him. One is hard put to discover here, or elsewhere for that matter, the heroic Troilus described by G. T. Shepherd, still echoing the earlier pronouncements by Dodd, a Troilus who is

> strong, resolute in action and successful in war...both masterful and humble in the consummation of his love...the ideal young male character, quick, proud, active, passionate, easily cast down, resolute when his course is clear, delighted by success, impatient of delay—psycho-biologically, the perfect specimen. [26]

While he may be biologically «the perfect specimen», I think there is some question as to whether he is equally fit psychologically.

If Criseyde has had to assume the masculine role, at least temporarily in the seduction scene, she reassumes it the following morning, according to R. E. Kaske. Like Nicolette departing from Aucassin, Criseyde in the *aube* scene plays the masculine role. «Chaucer seems to have bestowed on Troilus several speeches usually assigned to the lady in an aube, and on Criseyde certain speeches usually assigned to the lover, thus enriching a theme sometimes detected in other parts of the poem: the reversal of the roles of man and woman as they are popularly or romantically conceived.»[27] While inversion plays less of a key role for Chaucer than it does for the author of the *Aucassin*, it is implicit in any courtly romance in which the lover is passive and the lady, active. And we should never lose sight of

---

[26] «Troilus and Criseyde», pp. 78-79.
[27] R. E. Kaske, «The *Aube* in Chaucer's *Troilus*», in *Chaucer Criticism*, II, ed. Richard J. Schoeck and Jerome Taylor (Notre Dame, 1961), pp. 170-71.

the fact that a reversal of male-female roles is implicit in the courtly love relationship itself.

We have seen a sharp contrast drawn between Pandarus' activity and Troilus' inactivity in the bedroom scene. A similar contrast is evident in terms of their reactions to a reversal in love. We have already noted that the slightest upheaval sends Troilus, typically, straight to bed where he weeps and moans and cannot be budged until Pandarus is off and doing something to set things aright. But Pandarus himself is not without problems. He, too, has known «his part of loves shotes keene» (II, 58). But how differently he reacts to them! The reader learns of one instance in particular, on the third of May: [28]

> So shop it that hym fil that day a teene
> In love, for which in wo to bedde he went,
> And made, er it was a day, ful many a wente.
>
> (II, 61-63)

His initial reaction is not unlike that of Troilus. He tosses all night in his bed, but when morning comes, he remembers his promise to his young friend and knows that the astrological signs for the day are good, so, despite his own sorrow, he rises, and before the sun is high, he is about his work on Troilus' behalf. It is ironic, almost comical, to see Pandarus, who admits that in the dance of love he hops always behind seeking to further the romance of someone else.

One might argue that Pandarus has no place in this discussion, that what I have set out to do is to measure the behavior of Troilus by the yardstick of courtly love conventions. But we must always bear in mind that these conventions tend to take on a particular quality of inherent foolishness when placed against a background of practicality or of a realistic world which does not honor the courtly code. Pandarus plays essentially the same role as the father of Aucassin, who is somewhat less than sympathetic toward the unpragmatic attitude of his son. Pandarus represents, to a certain extent, the same attitude as the inhabitants of the «real» world in which Don Quixote functions. The impractical ideal-driven knight is revealed as something of a fool by the standards that operate in the quotidian world of practical affairs. But the contrast works also in reverse. The world is revealed as harsh and cold, having lost sight of

---

[28] See John P. McCall, «Chaucer's May 3», *MLN*, 76 (1961), 201-05. See also D. W. Robertson, Jr., «Chaucerian Tragedy», in *Chaucer Criticism*, II, ed. Schoeck and Taylor, p. 101.

beauty and truth. Chaucer seems to be aiming at a similar goal as he points up the limitations and absurdities of both Troilus and Pandarus. Though neither has the whole answer, neither is to be wholly condemned.

Leaving aside the contrast of Pandarus for the moment, we may ask whether or not there are other ways in which Troilus falls short of (or overshoots) the mark on his own. Outwardly his behavior seems to fulfill most of the conventional requirements. The narrator is at pains to *mention* virtually every element of the convention. That the relationship is «adulterous» by medieval standards, which is to say carnal and concupiscent,[29] goes without saying. And those stanzas that separate the striking of Cupid's arrow and the *Canticus Troili* are packed with references to the predominant characteristics of the convention. The narrator tells us of Troilus' desire to participate in the traditional love service:

> It was to hym a right good aventure
> To love which oon, and if he dede his cure
> To serven hir, yet myghte he falle in grace,
> Or ellis for oon of hire servantes pace.
>
> (I, 368-71)

This is, however, merely a verbal token, for in reality, Troilus' «love service» involves a good deal more love than service. He fails Criseyde at the one moment she needs him most, when she is virtually on trial in the parliament. And once the decision is made, Troilus backs away from taking steps to remedy it. His plight is rather pathetic. He has thought of several solutions, but has rejected them all because they seemed imperfect. He has thoughts for Criseyde's honor, but none for the pain she might feel at their parting. The following scene, however, presents us with a grief-stricken Criseyde, who, when Pandarus arrives, pours out her sorrow to him somewhat bitterly, heaping blame upon him for helping to bring her to this end. But when Pandarus tells her that he comes with a message from Troilus, she turns to him, not daring to hope:

> «Allas!» quod she, «what wordes may ye brynge?
> What wol my deere herte seyn to me,
> Which that I drede nevere mo to see?
> Wol he han pleynte or teris, or I wende?
> I have ynough, if he therafter sende!»
>
> (IV, 857-61)

---

[29] See Chapter I, p. 7.

Pandarus offers no solution from the lips of Troilus, but a proposal that
Troilus should come «With yow to ben al nyght, for to devyse/ Remedie
in this, if ther were any wyse» (IV, 888-89).   When Troilus arrives, Criseyde
swoons in his arms with a helpless plea for succor:

> «O Jove, I deye, and mercy I beseche!
> Help, Troilus!»
>
> (IV, 1149-50)

Thinking her dead, Troilus draws his sword to kill himself so that «Shal
nevere lovere seyn that Troilus / Dar nat, for fere, with his lady dye»
(IV, 1200-01).   We seem on the verge of witnessing the Piramus-Thisbe
death motif, but, as usual, Troilus has delayed so long in acting—taking
time out first to wring his hands, beat his breast, cry out, cover Criseyde's
face with kisses, and make his last farewells—that Criseyde is given ample
time to revive.   Finding Troilus without the will or ability to respond to
her cry for help, she takes him to her bed and chides him gently for his
complaints and his failure to take action:

> «Lo, herte myn, wel woot ye this», quod she,
> «That if a wight alwey his wo compleyne,
> And seketh nought how holpen for to be,
> It nys but folie and encrees of peyne;
> And syn that here assembled be we tweyne
> To fynde boote of wo that we ben inne,
> It were al tyme soone to bygynne.»
>
> (IV, 1254-60)

They have both been grieving over their plight, but it is Criseyde who has
an idea and who takes the initiative.   Troilus offers no assistance.   She
will go to the Greeks, but within ten days she will return to Troy.   We are
reminded of Nicolette who despairs of Aucassin's rescuing her from prison
and escapes of her own accord.   For Troilus the love service consists
more of standing and waiting than anything else.   The interdependence
and balance described by Cross and Nitze [30] are missing.   Service implies
action.   For Troilus it is limited to lip service.

---

[30]   See *ibid.*, p. 16.

The religion of love is pointed out by the narrator as he recounts a prayer of Troilus to the God of love immediately following his love lyric:

> And to the God of Love thus seyde he
> With pitous vois, «O lord, now youres is
> My spirit, which that oughte youres be.
> Yow thanke I, lord, that han me brought to this.
> But wheither goddesse or womman, iwis,
> She be, I not, which that ye do me serve;
> But as hire man I wol ay lyve and sterve.
>
> «Ye stonden in hir eighen myghtily,
> As in a place unto youre vertu digne;
> Wherfore, lord, if my service or I
> May liken yow, so beth to me benigne;
> For myn estat roial I here resigne
> Into hire hond, and with ful humble chere
> Bicome hir man, as to my lady dere.»
>
> (I, 421-34)

The prayer reiterates the themes of service and humility, for these are inextricably tied up with the idea of love as a religious cult. Again the tables are turned as Troilus becomes guilty of the very folly he had mocked in others, as Pandarus is quick to remind him:

> «... thow were wont to chace
> At Love in scorn, and for despit him calle
> 'Seynt Idyot, lord of thise foles alle'.
>
> «How often hastow maad thi nyce japes,
> And seyd that Loves servantz everichone
> Of nycete ben verray Goddes apes.»
>
> (I, 908-13)

Pandarus assumes the role of Love's priest, hearing confession and putting penance on the sinner, in a perfect parody of Christian tradition:

> «Now bet thi brest, and sey to God of Love,
> 'Thy grace, lord, for now I me repente,
> If I mysspak, for now myself I love.'
> Thus sey with al thyn herte in good entente.»
>
> (I, 932-35)

And Troilus submits meekly, without a word of protest:

> ... «A, lord!   I me consente,
> And preye to the my japes thow foryive,
> And I shal nevere more whyle I live.»
>
> (I, 936-38)

Curiously enough, Troilus is more often on his knees before Pandarus
than before Criseyde, who traditionally should be the object of worship.
He prefigures, to some extent, the similar misplacing of adoration on the
part of Calisto, and for the very same reason.   It is Pandarus who will
grant the boon of Criseyde's love through his actions on behalf of Troilus,
just as Celestina has it within her power to accomplish the desires of
Calisto.   The words of praise that Troilus heaps on Pandarus sound far
more like words of adoration directed at the lady.   How much he sounds
like Calisto:

> Tho Troilus gan doun on knees to falle,
> And Pandare in his armes hente faste,
> . . . .
> «Now, Pandare, I kan na more seye,
> But, thow wis, thow woost, thow maist, thow art al!
> My lif, my deth, hol in thyn hond I leye.
> Help now!»
>
> (I, 1044-45, 1051-54)

And Pandarus' response to Troilus' cry for help is, for good or evil, far
more affirmative than Troilus' response to Criseyde's will be.

The narrator also points out that Troilus is conventionally concerned
with maintaining the secrecy of the affair.   This is, as we have seen, the
chief reason he gives for refusing to speak out in parliament.   But from
the beginning Troilus' motives for secrecy have been somewhat less than
noble.   Initially he determines to keep his love for Criseyde secret, not
because it might endanger her reputation if it were known, but because
he is afraid of the mockery of those whom he had earlier derided:

> Out of the temple al esilich he wente,
> Repentynge hym that he hadde evere ijaped
> Of Loves folk, lest fully the descente

Of scorn fille on hymself; but what he mente,
Lest it were wist on any manere syde,
His woo he gan dissimulen and hide.

(I, 317-22)

Indeed this reason for his secrecy is not merely mentioned, but virtually insisted upon by both the narrator and by Troilus himself. Undergoing the love sickness, Troilus, «lest men of hym wende/ That the hote fir of love hym brende» (I, 489-90), feigns a physical illness and chides himself for his foolishness:

«What wol now every lovere seyn of the,
If this be wist? but evere in thin absence
Laughen in scorn, and seyn, 'Loo, ther goth he
That is the man of so gret sapience,
That held us loveres leest in reverence.
Now, thanked be God, he may gon in the daunce
Of hem that Love list febly for to avaunce.'»

(I, 512-18)

And again:

«For, by myn hidde sorwe iblowe on brede,
I shal byjaped ben a thousand tyme
More than that fol of whos folie men ryme.»

(I, 530-32)

But by the time Troilus' pain at the loss of Criseyde has become greater than his shame at becoming love's victim, he throws caution to the winds and sends for Cassandra to interpret his «mysterious» dream in Book V. Her initial smile suggests that she knows quite well what has been going on and does not take the matter too seriously. Her reply seems more like the cruel jibe of a sister jesting at the not-too-serious loss of her brother's sweetheart than the sage reply of a true seer:

«Wep if thow wolt, or lef! For, out of doute,
This Diomede is inne, and thow art oute.»

(V, 1518-19)

59

Troilus has come to the wrong person if he wanted to hear good news, but upon hearing the truth, he lashes out at her with uncontrolled fury:

> «Thow seyst not soth», quod he, «thow sorceresse,
> With al thy false goost of prophecye!
> Thow wenest ben a gret devyneresse!
> Now sestow nat this fool of fantasie
> Peyneth hire on ladys for to lye?
> Awey!» quod he, «ther Joves yeve the sorwe!
> Thow shalt be fals, peraunter, yet tomorwe!»
>
> (V, 1520-26)

We have seen a similar show of temper earlier in the story. Her barbed words, however, have had an affirmative effect on Troilus. For the first time, he springs to action.

> Cassandre goth, and he with cruel herte
> Forget his wo, for angre of hire speche;
> And from his bed al sodeynly he sterte,
> As though al hool hym hadde ymad a leche.
>
> (V, 1534-37)

For the moment he seems cured of inactivity. He rushes about the town making rather indiscreet inquiries for one who is concerned with secrecy. But only four stanzas later, he is again immersed in his woes.

There is a painfully ironic moment developed within these four stanzas. Briefly the narrator breaks away from the tale of Troilus to recount the death of his brother Hector. Then two lines suggest the unspeakable sorrow of Troy at Hector's death, followed swiftly by the renewed sorrow of Troilus:

> And thus this worthi knyght was brought of lyve.

> For whom, as olde bokes tellen us,
> Was mad swich wo, that tonge it may nat telle;
> And namely, the sorwe of Troilus,
> The next hym was of worthynesse welle.
>
> (V, 1561-65)

60

The juxtaposition leads the reader to the conclusion that this time the «sorwe of Troilus» which has, by now, become quite familiar, is directed towards his brother's death. However, the lines that follow suggest that the source of this woe is, mainly, still the loss of Criseyde:

> And in this wo gan Troilus to dwelle,
> That, what for sorwe, and love, and for unreste,
> Ful ofte a day he bad his herte breste.
>
> But natheles, though he gan hym dispaire,
> And dradde ay that his lady was untrewe,
> Yet ay on hire his herte gan repaire.
>
> (V, 1566-71)

The mention of Hector's death juxtaposed with the prolonged description of Troilus' woes is heavily ironic. The easy sliding of Troilus' sorrow from Hector's death to Criseyde's still hypothetical infidelity suggests a painfully superficial hero.

The traditional hero of courtly love romances is customarily described in superlatives. He is the bravest, the best, the finest knight in all the land. It never bothered Chrétien in the least that each of his knights was the bravest and best, though they were all members of the same court. Within their stories, they are unsurpassed. One may, almost at random, find dozens of examples in courtly literature. Marie de France, for example, frequently utilizes this device. Her Eliduc is typically without equal:

> En Bretaine ot un chevalier,
> Pruz e curteiz, hardi e fier;
> Elidus ot nun, ceo n'est vis.
> N'ot si vaillant hume al pais. [31]

Guigemar, hero of the lay of the same name, is also described as peerless:

> En Lorreine, ne en Burguine,
> Ne en Angou, ne en Gascuine,
> A cel tens ne peut hom truver
> Si bon chevalier ne sun per.[32]

---

[31] *Les Lais de Marie de France*, ed. Jeanne Lods (Paris, 1959), 11. 5-8, p. 145.
[32] *Ibid.*, 11. 53-56, p. 4.

One might pile example upon example, but to do so would merely be tedious. Suffice it to say that the hero was traditionally the very best. Troilus, by contrast, is always pointed up as second best, «Ector the secounde». It may be suggested, of course, that Troilus is made second to Hector because Hector is traditionally the finest knight in all Troy. But if Chaucer *did* make Troilus second best only because of tradition, it would surely have been sufficient to mention it once and be done with it. Instead, he returns to the idea again and again. Pandarus even finds occasion to broach the subject of love to Criseyde not in terms of Troilus alone, but in terms of Hector. Criseyde asks news of Hector, and Pandarus takes the opportunity of turning the subject to Troilus. Hector has been wounded in the arm, he tells her,

> «And ek his fresshe brother Troilus,
> The wise, worthi Ector the secounde.»
>
> (II, 157-58)

This is the first and last time we hear of Troilus' being wounded, but it is rather amusing that Pandarus sees fit to make him «Ector the secounde» right down to the flesh wound in the arm. Criseyde acknowledges the remark with «God save hem bothe two!» (II, 163), and then returns to the singular in speaking of the virtues of Hector, «A kynges son» (II, 165). But Pandarus is not to be turned aside from his purpose and he reminds her again:

> «But, by my trouthe, the kyng hath sones tweye,—
> That is to mene, Ector and Troilus.»
>
> (II, 169-70)

He seeks to extol the virtues of Hector once and for all:

> «Of Ector nedeth it namore for to telle:
> In al this world they nys a bettre knyght
> Than he, that is of worthynesse welle;
> And he wel moore vertu hath than myght.
> This knoweth many a wis and worthi wight.
> The same pris of Troilus I seye;
> God help me so, I know nat swiche tweye.»
>
> (II, 176-82)

The superlatives he heaps upon Troilus, once he has Criseyde's full attention, sound rather like an echo. Troilus clearly comes off second best in the tale. It is to Hector that Criseyde goes for help. It is Hector who speaks out in parliament on her behalf. It is Hector who dies first and more heroically at the hand of Achilles. And just as Troilus has earlier received the same wound in the arm, he is later to receive his death blow, like a true «Ector the secounde» at the hands of «the fierse Achille».

As a knight Troilus' reputation is but an echo of Hector's; as a lover his proficiency is dependent upon the practical arrangements of Pandarus. He is like a shadow, devoid of reality without the presence of others. When he does have an idea for action on his own, he lacks the fortitude to carry it through. For example, when he is still uncertain of Criseyde's infidelity he thinks of disguising himself as a pilgrim in order to visit her in the Greek camp. But the idea is short-lived. He knows that he could not disguise himself well enough to deceive discerning people, which speaks poorly for his cleverness, and he knows that if he were discovered, things would not go well for him among the Greeks,

> And ofte tyme he was in purpos grete
> Hymselven lik a pilgrym to desgise,
> To seen hire; but he may nat contrefete
> To ben unknowen of folk that weren wise,
> Ne fynde excuse aright that may suffise,
> If he among the Grekis knowen were;
> For which he wep ful ofte and many a tere.
>
> (V, 1576-82)

His conclusion is typical. It is not a foolproof plan, and Troilus reacts to his own lack of confidence as he has in the past when confronted with a difficult situation. He sits down to cry.

The disguise motif is by no means unprecedented in romance. It occurs in the Tristan legend when the hero becomes a minstrel, a leper, and a beggar in order to see Yseut.[33] In disguise he carries her ashore

---

[33] I am indebted to Professor A. D. Deyermond for pointing out to me a similar use of the disguise motif in the *Primera crónica general* of Alfonso el Sabio. In this prose version of the story based on the lost epic *La condesa traidora*, Garçi Fernández (or Ferrandez) enters France disguised as a pilgrim «pobre et mal uestido» (p. 427b, 11. 35-36) to seek out his unfaithful wife, Argentina, and her lover, «un conde de França», and kill them. See Alfonso X, el Sabio, *Primera crónica general: estoria de España*, ed. Ramón Menéndez Pidal, 2 vols., (Madrid, 1955), II, 427-29.

and is even pointed out by Yseut as the only man besides King Mark who has ever held her in his arms. Yet Tristan is not discovered. Nor does he fear to essay the disguise in spite of the mortal danger should King Mark find him out. Nicolette, as we have seen, also utilizes the disguise in an inverted echo of the Tristan myth. Troilus, on the other hand, is in a situation considerably less explosive than that of Tristan since there is at the moment a truce between the Trojans and the Greeks, yet he lacks the confidence to make the attempt.[34]

All in all Troilus is a tool of parody in essentially the same way as Aucassin. He is a somewhat stylized character, a courtly lover, functioning against the background of a real world which does not pause for the timelessness of love. He loves a real lady who breaks the rules. He obeys a go-between who is most of the time about as courtly as the Wife of Bath. Chaucer has made him obey the courtly conventions. Not one has been overlooked. But he has sometimes obeyed them for the wrong reasons. Or Chaucer has exaggerated the lover's obedience to those rules which possessed built-in absurdities if carried to an extreme. What is lacking in Troilus is equilibrium between action and introspection. As Muscatine has observed, «It is difficult to think of a single hero of French romance who is quite so prostrated by love, so removed from the actual business of courtship, who depends so completely on an intermediary».[35] And while Chaucer puts words of sympathy into the mouth of the narrator, tumbling from the lips of the author himself is the unmistakable sound of gentle laughter. If the twentieth-century reader cannot join in the laughter, it is perhaps because he is all too often preconditioned by a long tradition of prejudice and mis-evaluation concerning the Middle Ages. He is prone to be a bit timid in judging medieval literature, afraid to make the mistake made by the readers of the sixteenth and seventeenth centuries, summed up best, perhaps, by the total condemnation of Boileau—«un temps qui n'a rien produit, qui ne compte pas».[36] He is equally fearful of over-evaluating the eighteenth-century discovery of medieval «naïveté», yet also concerned with avoiding the nineteenth-century error of romanticising the Middle Ages. Too many readers seem afraid to laugh at the humor they think they see in a medieval text, afraid that the desire to laugh

---

[34] In all fairness to Troilus, for a Trojan prince to be found among the Greeks in a time of truce could perhaps be interpreted as treachery and could prove detrimental to the cause of Troy. But his reasons for fearing that he could not «fynde excuse aright» are not indicated. If he is motivated by concern for Troy, Chaucer does not tell us so.

[35] *Chaucer and the French Tradition*, p. 137.

[36] Pauphilet, «Le mythe du moyen âge», *Le Legs*, p. 29.

only bespeaks their unfamiliarity with the convention. And this may be so. But if such knowledge and a thorough examination of the text do not effectively dispel the urge to laugh, then it is very likely that the medieval audience would have chuckled right along. And Troilus is a character who should, and very likely did in the fourteenth century, provoke laughter. There were obviously people of the period who would not have seen the humor, who were, perhaps, much too much like Troilus himself to find the matter in any way amusing. But these are the very people upon whom the joke is played. And lest the realists laugh too hard at their more romantic contemporaries, Chaucer has a built-in check in the form of Pandarus.

But there comes a moment in the text when the laughter is hushed. It is not a moment that comes suddenly, for Troilus is no less inert, no less ineffectual in the waning moments than he was in the beginning. But a moment comes when the reader realizes that his laughter has become hollow, if, indeed, there is still laughter. Many critics have recognized this moment. Alfred David explains it by asserting that Troilus «exhibits symptoms of growth and change and becomes by the end of the poem different from what he was at the beginning».[37] This «change» David explains in terms of increasing wisdom. In his opinion the consummation of Troilus' love for Criseyde «has brought Troilus a new ripeness and assurance that contrasts sharply with his former awkwardness. After this we do not laugh at him any more» (p. 574). Paull F. Baum, too, would fix the moment beyond which we do not laugh. David insists that it is the night of the consummation; Baum would place it the following morning after the «brief serio-comic meeting between Pandarus and Criseyde.... Then comes the remarkable line:

And Pandarus hath fully his entente,

This is in a way the real climax of the poem. After this there is no more laughter.»[38] But the cessation of laughter is not quite so sudden. Both critics seem oblivious of the humor of the scene following Pandarus' «serio-comic meeting» with Criseyde. Shortly afterwards he pays a visit to Troilus, who flings himself to his knees before his benefactor and praises him as one who brought him from «the fery flod of helle» (III, 1600),

[37] Alfred David, «The Hero of the *Troilus*», *Speculum*, 37 (1962), 569.
[38] Paull F. Baum, *Chaucer: A Critical Appreciation* (Durham, N. C., 1958), p. 147.

who «Last in hevene ybrought my soule at reste» (III, 1599). In Christian terms, Pandarus has become Troilus' savior, a role usually reserved for the lady in the religion of love. And as a final indiscretion, hardly consistent with this new-found «wisdom» posited by David, Troilus begins to «telle hym of his glade nyght...Til that the nyght departed hym atwynne» (III, 1646-66). It is equally difficult not to find some absurdity in Troilus' temper tantrum following the parliamentary decision to exchange Criseyde for Antenor in Book IV. Nevertheless, as the Wheel of Fortune begins its downward thrust, the antics of Troilus, so amusing in Books I and II, fail to draw the laughter they once did. I would reject David's idea that we cease to laugh because of any increased wisdom on Troilus' part. I would agree, rather, with John Bayley who, in discussing what he considers to be the «fundamentally untragic» nature of the poem, blames its «artificiality» and «absence of discovery». He goes on to explain: «No one concerned with the poem—neither characters nor author nor reader—finds anything out in the blinding tragic manner: there is no *peripeteia*.»[39] There is no self-discovery on the part of Troilus. He is at the end what he was at the beginning. There are two quite abrupt changes in the character of Troilus, but neither of them is brought about by any wisdom on his part. In the first stage of his development he is, as we have seen, the scoffer, shielding himself from emotion with a shell of cynicism. But the change in the young man is sudden and complete, effected by the arrows of the god of love. As a lovesick swain he continues until his death. The second stage of Troilus' characterization is more fully developed and his emotions vary as he wends his way through the maze of love, but there are no fundamental changes, no real deepening of understanding such as we see in earlier and more serious lovers like Yvain. Troilus bumbles his way through love's garden, experiencing but essentially unchanging. Our final view of Troilus is after his death. He has again been abruptly transformed, this time from the sorrowing lover to the wiser spirit gazing gleefully back from the eighth sphere at the world he has just passed through, a victim of Fortune's mutability—and he laughs. It is significant,

---

[39] John Bayley, *The Character of Love: A Study in the Literature of Personality* (New York, 1963), p. 63. The contrast of Chaucer's treatment of their love with the unquestionably tragic depiction of Robert Henryson in his *Testament of Cresseid* (See *The Story of Troilus*, ed. R. K. Gordon [New York, 1964], pp. 351-67.) is revealing. The meeting between Cresseid, now a leper, and Troilus is one of painful beauty. We do not see the rising into bliss of Troilus at the end. It is, rather, death that delineates the end of Henryson's work. Our last view of their relationship is marked by the tombstone Troilus is said to have had made for Cresseid's grave, the inscription of which emphasizes her tragic undoing and Troilus' brave memory of her as «the flour of womanheid».

I believe, that the story of Troilus' «tragic» love for Criseyde is framed by
the laughter of the protagonist himself. As the scoffer of the first part,
he is mocking what he is to become. And laughing down at the end
from the vantage point of superior vision, he is mocking what he has been.
His final laughter is at himself and at those who grieve for him below,
making the same error of taking it all too seriously. As Howard R. Patch
has suggested, «mirth at this moment in the poem robs it of sentimenta-
lity».[40] Alfred David has concluded that «The first is the laughter of
ignorance; the second of wisdom».[41] But it is a wisdom that has not
come within the context of Troilus' worldly experience.

The very essence of Chaucer's «litel...tragedye» is the unchanging
nature of the characters who live it, and the reader realizes that, in truth,
the prize *has* been «washed away by the same tides that brought it in».
The movement of the Wheel of Fortune is irreversible, turning always in the
same direction. Those who are lifted up today will inevitably be cast
down tomorrow. And Troilus' fall of fortune results from precisely the
same strengths and weaknesses within himself and the other characters
that caused his rise. Only the fact that Criseyde was herself something
of a realist, «a young widow of strongly amorous nature, but circumspect
and modest; of a quick and ready wit and a cool head; without sentimen-
tality, but with a marked ability to face facts which concern her and her
welfare closely»,[42] caused her to yield to Troilus. It is the same «amorous
nature» and «ability to face facts» that cause her to yield to Diomed.
She has never really been the proper sort of courtly lady, never really cool
and disdainful, as are the ladies who usually play opposite the simple,
faithful lover, the role which Troilus overdoes so nicely. He moves more
deeply into the convention with his mourning fidelity while she, «slyding
of corage» (V, 825), moves further away from it. Criseyde's infidelity
and Troilus' doleful incapacity to do anything about it do not represent
any changes in their character. On the contrary, they remain true to
their own natures until the end. By the same token, had Pandarus not
been the sly old fox he is, a realist like Criseyde, faithful to his friend, but
deceptive in his means, and had Troilus not been meekly obedient, the
consummation of the affair might never have been accomplished. It is
highly unlikely that Troilus could have ever found a means of bringing
Criseyde to his bed so deftly as did Pandarus. As long as the Wheel of

[40]   *On Rereading Chaucer*, p. 59.
[41]   «The Hero of the *Troilus*», 570.
[42]   Dodd, p. 167.

6

Fortune is on an upward swing, all of them are joyful, but as the downward motion begins, they cling more closely to that which brought them up. Troilus takes again to his bed; Criseyde accepts the most expedient mode of action; and Pandarus, having done all he can, having suggested a few practical and typical alternatives, but having failed in his friend's affair as he has done all his life in his own, bows out of the story as abruptly as he had entered it. The ultimate pathos of Troilus' position is not fully apparent until one by one his friends abandon him and, at the end, he stands alone. As realists they accept the joyful aspect of love, but reject its sorrow, while for Troilus the romantic, the sorrow is a major and necessary part of the joy. Only he truly understands the paradoxical nature of love, which is not to say that he has grown to this understanding. We must still bear in mind that his first utterance as a lover, the *Canticus Troili*, clearly depicts the paradox:

«If no love is, O God, what fele I so?
And if love is, what thing and which is he?
If love be good, from whennes cometh my woo?»

(I, 400-02)

Baum claims that the joys of love have «made a new Troilus, but when faced with the suffering of Criseyde's desertion he returns to the ineffectual pathos with which he was introduced. Troilus is what Pandarus and Criseyde made him; without them he is uninteresting».[43] It is true that for a brief moment Troilus was kindled by love, but the flame of his earthly joy only flickered and died. It is not so much that he is simply uninteresting without Pandarus and Criseyde. Rather he lacks substance. He almost ceases to exist. What gives reality to Troilus is dependence upon that which is itself insubstantial. The palinode should come as no surprise. And the question of whether or not it is to be taken seriously, so often debated by critics, seems to me a curious one. Chaucer has prepared for it from the beginning. By setting the Wheel of Fortune in motion for Troilus, he has allowed its natural movement to determine both the comic and the tragic elements. Yet by giving us no totally serious character to attach our sympathies to, by making both the realist and the romantic a source of amusement, by condemning neither traitor nor betrayed, he has suggested some higher understanding than that which the characters them-

---

[43] *Chaucer*, p. 156.

selves have been permitted, or, indeed, have sought. Beyond the Wheel of Fortune, which operated exclusively upon this world, is the controlling hand of Providence. The characters themselves have been unable to perceive it. As D. W. Robertson, Jr., has remarked,

> when the human heart is turned toward God and the reason is adjusted to discern the action of Providence beneath the apparently fortuitous events of daily life, the result is the City of Jerusalem, radiant and harmonious within the spirit. But when the will desires its own satisfaction in the world alone, the reason can perceive only the deceptive mutability of Fortune. [44]

The didactic palinode is short. Chaucer, while he is indeed a moral poet, is by no means a moralizing one. The book speaks for itself, and he has little need to belabor his point. It is clearly and more artistically suggested by the laughter of Troilus' «lighte goost» (V, 1808) and the author's choice of words (i.e., «This *litel spot* of erth» [V, 1815]). Fortune has raised Troilus to a height of bliss and it has cast him down to despair. But the final movement of the book is upward. And this time the elevation, not dependent upon Fortune, but on the immutable values of Providence, is permanent. And Chaucer's tale of Troilus and Criseyde remains structurally more a comedy than a tragedy. Undeniably there are elements of pathos, but these are superseded by a final movement to a higher level of understanding. The *Troilus* is closely related to what Northrop Frye has called «the fifth phase of comedy».[45] These «less festive and more pensive» works, he tells us, «do not avoid tragedies but contain them». The fifth phase of comedy which he also identifies with romance ultimately depicts a «redeemed society», «part of a settled order which has been there from the beginning, an order which takes on an increasingly religious cast and seems to be drawing away from human experience altogether» (p. 185). From the point of view of this «higher and better ordered world», we look down on human behavior and «the action or at least the tragic implication of the action is presented as though it were a play within a play that we can see in all dimensions at once» (p. 184). In short, we have arrived at what Muscatine has called the third level of perspective, a wisdom which permits us to see values beyond this world. The function of the parody within this greater context becomes clearly, though not

---

[44] *A Preface to Chaucer*, p. 497.
[45] Northrop Frye, *Anatomy of Criticism* (Princeton, 1957), p. 184.

dogmatically, didactic. The essence of the message is contained in a single stanza of the palinode:

> O yonge, fresshe folkes, he or she,
> In which that love up groweth with youre age,
> Repeyreth hom fro worldly vanyte,
> And of youre herte up casteth the visage
> To thilke God that after his ymage
> Yow made, and thynketh al nys but a faire
> This world, that passeth soone as floures faire.
>
> (V, 1835-41)

The author is closely identified with the narrator at this point. Both are older and wiser than those «yonge, fresshe folkes» to whom the story is directed. The Chaucer of the *Book of the Duchess* has clearly come of age.

CHAPTER IV

CALISTO

The fifteenth-century novel-in-dialogue of Fernando de Rojas, *La tragicomedia de Calisto y Melibea* or, more popularly, *La Celestina*, simultaneously delights and troubles the literary critic. The satisfaction derived from working with this text may be suggested by the titles of some of the major recent critical works devoted to it, notably María Rosa Lida de Malkiel's *La originalidad artística de la Celestina* and Stephen Gilman's *The Art of La Celestina*.[1] It is an artistic masterpiece, unique in kind. Gilman has even gone so far as to say, «Nothing like it has ever been made, and I would almost dare to say, in defiance of Nietzsche, that nothing like it can ever be made again» (p. 194). From its very uniqueness, however, arise the major problems in dealing critically with the *Celestina*. It tends to defy generic categorization, at least that categorization made possible by contemporary critical nomenclature. Gilman goes on, significantly, «It is apparent that on every level of artistry the relationship of the writer to the written word is strangely different from those relationships we have been taught...to recognize as novelistic, lyric, epic, tragic, or comic. In other words, *La Celestina*, by force of its very originality, is without genre.» Even beyond its generic elusiveness it is a curious text in that it confronts the critic with problems which may be dealt with quite simply in most works of literature. Authorship, versions, interpolations, social conventions, philosophical questions—all are fundamentally problematic in terms of the *Celestina*. It is, therefore, not surprising that the significance of courtly love traditions in the work has also been questioned. Much of the controversy has centered upon what is commonly known as the marriage question. Stated quite simply, the problem is

---

[1] María Rosa Lida de Malkiel, *La originalidad artística de la Celestina* (Buenos Aires, 1962); Stephen Gilman, *The Art of La Celestina* (Madison, Wis., 1956).

71

that the question of marriage never arises, although the situation seems singularly ripe for a legal union between Calisto and Melibea. They are apparently of the same social class; both are unmarried; Melibea's father, Pleberio, is already thinking of marriage for his daughter, even going so far as to suggest to his wife the possibility of letting Melibea select her own husband. Several critics, most notably Fernando Garrido Pallardó, Segundo Serrano Poncela and Emilio Orozco Díaz,[2] have argued that Melibea is Jewish and, therefore, unmarriageable for the young Christian Calisto. But few critics writing today treat the Jewish question with much seriousness. It simply never comes up in the text. If it were significant enough to prevent the marriage, then it would be Melibea's Jewishness that was responsible for the tragedy, and it seems unlikely that Rojas, believed to have been a *converso*, would not have been more direct in his suggestions. Surely he could have had little fear of the Inquisition on this point. Had Rojas made Melibea clearly Jewish he could only have been aiding the Inquisition in proving that consorting with Jews could only bring disaster. His work could scarcely have been interpreted as encouraging such relationships any more than it could have been interpreted as actually advocating courtly love. Certainly the Inquisition itself, while it very lightly censored Rojas' work, never found any such elevation of illicit love in it. It remained «untouched by official censorship for one hundred forty-one years, being first mentioned in the Index of Sotomayor (1640)»,[3] and even then only about fifty lines were expurgated. The whole book was not forbidden until 1793. Rojas' contemporaries apparently found no evidence of a Jewish heroine. As Marcel Bataillon has pointed out, this interpretation of Melibea as *conversa* «n'a jamais été avancée ni même insinuée par aucun Espagnol du XVIe ou du XVIIe siècle, époque où l'Espagne était hantée par un impossible 'pureté de sang'».[4] In short, if Melibea and her parents are *conversos*, then neither the author nor his contemporaries, indeed, for two full centuries, his countrymen, attributed the least importance to it.

The emphasis on illicit love in the *Celestina* has been seen by María

---

[2] See Fernando Garrido Pallardó, *Los problemas de Calisto y Melibea y el conflicto de su autor* (Figueras, 1957); Segundo Serrano Poncela, «El secreto de Melibea», *CA*, 17 (1958), 488-510; and Emilio Orozco Díaz, «*La Celestina*, hipótesis para una interpretación», *Insula*, 12, cxxiv (marzo, 1957), 1-10.

[3] Otis H. Green, «*La Celestina* and the Inquisition», *HR*, 15 (1947), 211. See also Henry C. Lea, *Chapters from the Religious History of Spain Connected With the Inquisition* (Philadelphia, 1890), p. 202.

[4] Marcel Bataillon, *La Célestine selon Fernando de Rojas* (Paris, 1961), p. 173.

Rosa Lida de Malkiel to result from the fact that «the only literary pattern then existing for tragic love depicted with artistic sympathy, was the illicit relationship we find in troubadouresque lyric, *roman courtois*, and romances of chivalry».[5] Whether or not the «tragic love» of Calisto and Melibea is treated sympathetically is certainly debatable. But to say that this was the only pattern for tragic love is to dismiss an entire storehouse of classical literature with which Rojas was undoubtedly familiar.[6] Nevertheless, her point is valid, for the romantic love of courtly literature was certainly the most familiar pattern for the era. And most critics, notably A. D. Deyermond, Otis Green, Erna Ruth Berndt, J. M. Aguirre, and even, to a point, Sra. Lida de Malkiel, agree that the love of Calisto and Melibea is well within the tradition.

Significant relationships between Rojas' work and certain courtly love documents have been pointed out in scattered articles. A. D. Deyermond, for example, in his article «The Text-Book Mishandled: Andreas Capellanus and the opening scene of *La Celestina*»[7] suggests that Calisto patterns his first two speeches after three of the *De Amore* dialogues, *loquitur plebeius ad plebeiam*, *loquitur nobilior plebeiae*, and *loquitur nobilior nobili*. The following juxtaposition of the opening scene in Melibea's garden and the speeches from the *De Amore* is made by Deyermond:

[*Loquitur plebeius ad plebeiam*]
Quando te divina formavit essentia, nulla sibi alia facienda restabant: Tuo decori nihil deesse cognosco...

CAL. En esto veo, Melibea, la grandeza de Dios.

[*Loquitur nobilior plebeiae*]
A longinquis retro temporibus diem istam desidaveri et plenarie in mente gessi propositum meam vobis aperire mentem et intentionem et, quanta mihi sit de vogis assidue cogitatio. Temporis tamen inopportunitas usque nunc distulit amantis eloquium.

MEL. ¿En qué, Calisto?

CAL. En dar poder a natura que de tan perfecta fermosura te dotasse, y fazer a mi inmerito tanta merced que verte alcançasse, y en tan conueniente lugar, que mi secreto dolor manifestarte pudiesse.

[*Loquitur nobilior nobili*]
Maiores mihi restant Deo gratiae referendae quam cuiquam in orbe viventi, quia hoc, quod meus animus videre super

Sin dubda, incomparablemente es mayor tal galardon que el seruicio, sacrificio, deuocion y obras pias que por este lugar

---

[5] María Rosa Lida de Malkiel, *Two Spanish Masterpieces* (Urbana, Ill., 1961), p. 65.
[6] Such a pattern exists, for example, in the Hero-Leander, Pyramus-Thisbe love stories.
[7] A. D. Deyermond, «The Text-Book Mishandled: Andreas Capellanus and the Opening Scene of *La Celestina*», *Neophilologus*, 45 (1961), 218-21.

omnia cupiebat, nunc corporali mihi visu est concessum aspicere, et hoc mihi Deum credo praemium concessisse propter nimium desiderii mei affectum, et quia mei voluit exaudire preces importune precantis. Non enim poterat diei vel noctis hora pertransire continua, qua Deum non exorarem attentius, ut corporaliter vos ex propinquo videndi mihi concederet largitatem.[8]

alcançar yo tengo a Dios offrecido.
¿Quien vido en esta vida cuerpo glorificado de ningun hombre como agora el mio? Por cierto, los gloriosos santos, que se deleytan en la vision diuina, no gozan mas que yo agora en el acatemiento tuyo.[9]

There is at least one significant parallel that may be added to Deyermond's observations. Curiously enough, it is a parallel between Melibea's words and those of the woman in the second dialogue, *Loquitur plebeius nobili:*

Mulier ait: Tuo Deus labori digna praemia ferat.[10]

MEL. Pues avn más ygual galardon te daré yo, si perseueras.[11]

Melibea's words, while they appear somewhat ambiguous, carry a thinly veiled insult. First of all, they echo the one dialogue in which the man is scorned as unworthy and in which the situation is left in a somewhat ambiguous state. Further, by utilizing a reminiscence of the second dialogue Melibea puts Calisto in his place, haughtily assuming the position of a woman of the nobility rebuffing a man of what J. J. Parry calls in his translation the «middle class».

Deyermond has hit precisely upon the comic or parodic element of the scene:

> But tragedy and comedy can co-exist, and if the author of Act I is a student writing principally for people like himself, this presentation of the hero who is unexpectedly let down by a standard authority opens up considerable possibilities of comic development for readers who, like Calisto, know the *De Amore*. [12]

Deyermond has not, however, gone on to point out how or why Calisto is let down, where he went wrong in his approach. It is possible, of course,

---

[8] *Ibid.,* 219. Deyermond is quoting from Trojel's edition, pp. 21, 110-111.

[9] *Ibid.* Deyermond is quoting from the *Tragicomedia de Calixto y Melibea*, ed. M. Criado de Val and G. D. Trotter (Madrid, 1958), p. 23.

[10] *De Amore*, Trojel edition, p. 53. All subsequent references are to this edition and will be given within the text.

[11] Fernando de Rojas, *La Celestina*, ed. Julio Cejador y Frauca (Madrid, 1958), I, p. 33. Permission to quote from this Clásicos Castellanos edition has been granted by the editors of Espasa-Calpe. The accentuation has been modernised in accordance with current RAE rules.

[12] «The Text-Book Mishandled», 221.

that the «standard authority» simply does not work.[13]   In any case, the
very title of Deyermond's article, «The Text-Book Mishandled», suggests
that it is Calisto who is doing something wrong.   Careful examination
of the *De Amore* reveals that Calisto is indeed misusing the textbook.
He is in error from his very first words, as he begins bluntly: «En esto veo,
Melibea, la grandeza de Dios.»   But Andreas has cautioned all lovers
against such a direct approach:

> Primitus ipsam suo more salutet; sed haec sunt generaliter dicenda
> et omni credantur amanti, ut post salutationem non statim a
> verbis amoris incipiat, quia pellicibus talia sunt initia facienda.
> Immo et domina salutata quoddam moderatum debet a masculo
> tempus interponi, ut mulier, si velit, primo loquatur.
>
> (p. 20)

If the woman does not speak, the man may begin:

> Primo extrinseca verba proponas, quae ludificum aliquid contineant
> vel illius patriae vel gentis vel personae laudationem.   Nam
> mulieres pro maxima parte in suae personae commendatione
> laetantur, et cuncta, quae suas pertinere videntur ad laudes,
> facile per omnia credunt, plebeiae maxime ac rusticanae.   Post
> illa igitur extrinseca verba tali potes ratione procedere:
> Quando te divina formavit essentia, nulla sibi alia facienda
> restabant.
>
> (pp. 20-21)

From his first words, then, Calisto has insulted Melibea.   He has ap-
proached her, according to Andreas, as men approach only their mistresses.
If, as the reply we have already seen indicates, Melibea also was familiar
with the *De Amore*, it is no wonder that she is furious.   Certainly Calisto
in his love-sick state does not intend to insult Melibea.   Rather, he is like
an eager-to-please young swain who did not do his homework very well.
In each of the dialogues the men approach the ladies by praising them
first for their beauty, but equally for their wisdom, prudence, or virtue.
This is not true, however, in the least successful of the dialogues in which
the man launches into an immediate defense of himself and his right as

---

[13]   It should be noted in this context that J. F. Benton has remarked that «the lovers
in Andreas' book were consistently unsuccessful» («Clio and Venus», p. 30). But it should
also be remembered that there is frequently promise of future success. It is hardly to be
expected that the lover's attainment of his desires should be an easy conquest. Nowhere
in the *De Amore*, however, is the lover rebuffed quite so angrily as he is in the *Celestina*.

a man of the middle class to love a woman of the nobility. Andreas himself has made it quite clear that beauty alone is unworthy of love; beauty, he says, evokes love easily in a simple lover who thinks that the most important aspect of the beloved is a beautiful face and figure. «Simplex enim amans nil credit aliud in amante quaerendum nisi formam faciemque venustam et corporis cultum» (p. 14). Character, he insists, is more important. «Sola ergo probitas amoris est digna corona» (p. 18). Calisto slips easily into the character of Andreas' simple lover who is, Andreas implies, something of a fool.[14] He is lured, not by Melibea's character, but by her beauty. He sees the greatness of God only in nature's endowing Melibea with «tan perfecta fermosura». He emphasizes his joy at *seeing* Melibea, compares seeing her to the «vision diuina» of the saints, and anticipates his own future sorrow, not in losing her love, which he has not yet gained, but in losing her physical presence: «...e yo misto me alegro con recelo del esquiuo tormento, que tu absencia me ha de causar» (I, 33). It is no wonder that Melibea is offended by the gaucherie of his approach. Since he offers praises only to her beauty, and none to those attributes which might cause him to respect as well as desire her, her indignation and her suspicion of his motives are aroused and made manifest in the form of what Otis Green has labelled «la furia de Melibea».[15] On later occasions, as we have seen, when he describes Melibea, he does give a token tribute to her noble family, her wisdom, her virtues.[16] The praise is almost a memory exercise,[17] the stereotyped praises of the day, having its origins as early as Ovid and still catalogued by Castiglione in *Il Cortegiano* some ten years after the completion of the *Celestina*. The ideal lady has essentially the same attributes as the ideal courtier. These ideals Castiglione describes as «non solamente lo ingegno, e bella forma di persona e di volto, ma una certa grazia, e come si dice, un sangue, che lo faccia al primo aspetto a chiunque lo vedo grato ed amabile».[18] There is a remarkable parallel between the ideal lady of Castiglione and Calisto's description of Melibea: «Mira la nobleza e antigüedad de su linaje, el grandíssimo patrimonio, el excelentíssimo ingenio, las resplandescientes virtudes, la altitud e enefable gracia, la soberana hermosura...» (I, 53). Calisto's description is, like

---

[14]   Out of fairness to Calisto, one should remember that it was a common feature of the convention for the lover to be attracted by beauty, though, as Andreas suggests, attraction to beauty *alone* denotes a simple (and foolish) lover.

[15]   Otis H. Green, «La furia de Melibea», *Clavileño*, 4, xx (marzo-abril, 1953), 1-3.

[16]   *Celestina*, II, p. 85.

[17]   See Dorothy Severin, *Memory in «La Celestina»* (London, 1970), for a thorough investigation of the question of memory.

[18]   Baldassare Castiglione, *Il Cortegiano*, ed., Mario Luzi [Milano, 1945], p. 47.

Castiglione's, mere lip service to the convention. But at the thought of Melibea's beauty, Calisto can contain himself no longer: «...la soberana hermosura, de la qual te ruego me dexes hablar vn poco, porque aya algún refrigerio. E lo que te dixere será de lo descubierto...» (I, 53). Enraptured with his topic, he goes on for pages, even past the point where Sempronio moans, «¡En sus treze está este necio!» (I, 55).

But to add insult to injury, Calisto not only approaches her bluntly, as a man might approach his mistress, he approaches her by selecting ideas from *De Amore* dialogues that put her in a position generally below his own. His echo at the beginning places them on the same level, a man of the middle class speaking with a woman of the middle class; then, omitting any allusions to the next two dialogues in which a man of the middle class speaks with a woman of the nobility and of the higher nobility, he suggests rather the fourth and the sixth dialogues in which a nobleman speaks with a woman of the middle class, and a man of the higher nobility speaks with a lesser noblewoman. Melibea has been highly insulted. Calisto has made mistakes at every turn in his seemingly safe opening speech. His intentions are all too clear. It is not surprising that Melibea finally orders him and his lewd hopes out of her garden.

Calisto's intentions may even be symbolically suggested in his original reason for entering the garden—that is, in search of a falcon,[19] an appropriately ambiguous objectification of his desires. According to a twelfth-century bestiary, *Accipiter*, the general name for birds of the falcon family, «gets its name from '*accipiendo*' (accepting), i.e., '*a capiendo*' (from seizing). For it is an avid bird at seizing upon others, whence it is called *Accipiter*, i.e., Raptor—the ravisher, the thief».[20] On the other hand, falconry was a gentleman's sport, appropriate as the courtly lover's pastime. One often sees in drawings or ivories depicting scenes labeled by Raimond van Marle as «la conversation galante» or «promenade d'amoureux»[21] a hawk or falcon resting on the arm of the young lover, even sometimes on the arm of the lady. The scene suggests the ravisher tamed. As such, the falcon strikes me as a singularly ap-

---

[19] See Raymond E. Barbera, «Medieval Iconography in the *Celestina*», *RR*, 61 (1970), 5-13. Barbera's article appeared as the final draft of this study was being prepared for publication. I am pleased to find that his views on the falcon, the walled garden, and the ladder corroborate my own conclusions which were originally expressed in my 1967 doctoral dissertation.

[20] T. H. White, ed. and trans. *The Bestiary: A Book of Beasts* (New York, 1954; reprinted New York, 1960), pp. 138-39.

[21] See Raimond van Marle, *Iconographie de l'art profane au moyen âge et à la renaissance* (La Haye, 1931-32), Vol. I, figures 446 ff.

propriate symbol for the medieval courtier, and, in particular, for the courtly lover with whom it is most often identified. Chained to his master's wrist, he seems an objectification of the «two layers of civilization superimposed, coexisting though contradictory»[22] of which Huizinga speaks in *The Waning of the Middle Ages*. The chained falcon suggests the lover's passion held in check by his submission to his lady, in this respect somewhat like the garden world described in the Introduction. The unusual occurrence of the unleashed falcon in the scene in Melibea's garden suggests, to some extent, Calisto's lack of control in the situation. Maurice Valency has pointed out that the true lover's special virtue was «the quality called *mezura*, measure, that inner restraint which governs the appetites and keeps them subject to the intellect».[23] He does not deny the presence of desire but explains, «The standard of love was...not the degree of its heat, but the degree of its refinement. Through the slow and mysterious operation of the flame of love, whatever was base and gross in the lover's nature was supposedly consumed and dissipated until at last only the pure and noble spirit remained» (p. 177). But what is lacking in Calisto is the *mezura* required to keep himself under control until such refinement could take place. It is an essential quality; without it, the lover is, by courtly standards, doomed to failure. The falcon, who is not chained to Calisto's wrist, but is out of control, suggests Calisto's own ultimately uncontrolled passion for Melibea. In short, in the initial scene in the garden, the most familiar spot for the encounter between the lover and his lady, everything is somewhat awry. Elements of the scene are skillfully combined to make it appear, at first glance, a typical «conversation galante» with an unexpected rebuff of the lover. But closer examination reveals that it is anything but typical, that for Calisto everything goes wrong. He has had his first taste of «aduersa fortuna», whose turning wheel will hurl him downward in the end.

In his article «La furia de Melibea», Otis Green has suggested a parallel between the *Celestina* and another widely-known document of courtly love— the *Roman de la Rose*. He, too, finds the reason for Melibea's fury in the courtly tradition. According to Green, Calisto bypasses the period of *fenhedor*, one of the four divisions of love mentioned by Provençal troubadours. «El *fenhedor* es el que *disimula* su pena, pero dejándola

---

[22] P. 109. Barbera points out that the hawk «appears extensively as a symbol of carnal lust in religious and secular contexts» (p. 5).
[23] Maurice Valency, *In Praise of Love* (New York, 1961), p. 176.

traslucir discretísimamente.»[24]   Implicit in the contrast between the articles of Green and Deyermond is not only the fact that Calisto misused his textbook, but that, indeed, he may even have used the wrong one.   Nevertheless, Calisto's mistake is roughly the same, regardless of his textbook. He is too abrupt, too blunt.   Perhaps the most valuable idea in Green's article is that which calls attention to the relationship between Melibea's reaction and the sudden appearance of Danger in the *Roman de la Rose*. C. S. Lewis has attempted to explain the meaning of the word *Danger*:

> The word, we know, comes from *Dominus* through *Dominarium;* and from the meaning of 'lordship' and 'lordliness' all its other semantic history can be explained. I can well see how a word of this origin could acquire the sense of 'haughtiness' or, in our modern colloquial language, 'stand-offishness', or 'difficulty in granting'; that it should mean *Pudor* would be a grave, though scarcely unparalleled, semantic difficulty. [He is arguing against Langlois' suggestion that *Pudor* and *Danger* correspond to one another.]   Again, if I turn to the *Romance of the Rose*, I find that Danger is a *vilains;* that he is swarthy, huge, and hirsute; that his eyes burn like fire and that he bawls at the top of his voice.   Even if Ovid calls *Pudor 'rustice'*, and even if a rustic is a *vilains*, I cannot but feel that this ogre is a very odd description of womanly modesty.   The most obvious trait of Danger is his conviction that attack is the best form of defence. Is this the character of *Pudor*?   Does not *Pudor* use in this erotic warfare something more like the strategy of Fabius?   I hesitate to give my vote against a great critic; but I cannot help thinking that Danger means something very different from *Pudor:* means rather the rebuff direct, the lady's 'snub' launched from the height of her ladyhood, her pride suddenly wrapped about her as a garment, and perhaps her anger and contempt. [25]

---

[24]   1.   See also the rejoinder of G. D. Trotter, «Sobre 'La furia de Melibea', de Otis H. Green», *Clavileño*, 5, xxv (enero-febrero, 1954), 55-56. Trotter does not agree that the scene depends in any way on the courtly love conventions. «Para mí, pues, el sentido de esta primera escena entre Melibea y Calisto hay que buscarlo en el esquema artístico de la obra entera, y sus orígenes fundamentales en las relaciones tan tibias y estilizadas del *drut* y su *dama* de la culta tradición del *Frauendienst*, pues el amor de los protagonistas de la *Celestina* desconoce ese protocolo complicado. Obedecen ellos solamente a la pasión misteriosa y omnipotente, para el autor y para ellos aniquiladora y fatal, y la 'furia de Melibea' está, al fin y al cabo, tan llena de esta pasión como la entrega completa y sin reservas morales que más tarde hace de sí misma» (p. 56). J. M. Aguirre, in *Calisto y Melibea, amantes cortesanos* (Zaragoza, 1962), does not see any essential contradiction between the two views. He comments: «Green y Trotter se complementan... La nota de Green muestra la realidad de la presencia de las ideas amorosas provenzales en la obra de Rojas; la de Trotter viene a afirmar la realidad humana sobre la que construyen esas ideas medievales» (p. 32).
[25]   *Allegory*, p. 124.

79

That there is indeed a parallel between the appearance of Danger in the *Roman de la Rose* and Melibea's fury in the *Celestina* Green makes quite clear. He carries the parallel no further. However, far from ending here, it seems to continue through much of the text. There is a structural correspondence between the two works, a correspondence not easily recognized because the one is an allegory while the other is marked by its realism. One takes place in the context of a dream; the other, in the real world. While I do not assert the direct influence of the *Roman* on the *Celestina* (though such an influence is, as we shall see, by no means impossible), there does seem to be a structural relationship between the two.

That the *Roman de la Rose* is intended to be, at least by its first author, Guillaume de Lorris, a complete guide to the arts of love is made quite clear from the beginning:

> Qu'Amors le me prie e comande.
> E se nus ne nule demande
> Coment je vueil que li romanz
> Soit apelez que je comenz,
> Ce est le Romanz de la Rose
> Ou l'Art d'Amors est toute enclose.[26]

That it was highly popular is made evident from the striking effect it seems to have had on later courtly literature as well as from the abundance of manuscript versions that have come down to us. Over three hundred extant manuscripts are mentioned by Ernest Langlois in his study *Les Manuscrits du Roman de la Rose*.[27] Of these, seven, all of which date from the fourteenth or fifteenth centuries, are in Spanish libraries. The invention of the printing press in 1440, almost sixty years before the *Celestina* was composed, further aided the dissemination of the *Roman*. The number of printed editions far exceeds the number of manuscripts. In short, it was unquestionably one of the most influential secular works of the Middle Ages. For a work of such importance to have escaped the attention of Fernando de Rojas seems highly unlikely.[28] As for its influence in

---

[26] Guillaume de Lorris and Jean de Meun, *Le Roman de la Rose*, ed. Ernest Langlois. SATF edition (Paris, 1914-24), II. 33-38. All subsequent references will be to this edition and will be indicated within the text.

[27] Ernest Langlois, *Les Manuscrits du Roman de la Rose* (Lille, 1910).

[28] Recent scholarship has tended to question Castro Guisasola's judgments on Rojas' scholarship. Keith Whinnom, in his *Spanish Literary Historiography: Three Forms of*

Spain, F. B. Luquiens contends that the *Roman de la Rose* exerted direct influence on only two Spanish writers, Imperial and Fray Diego, but that it influenced indirectly the nature descriptions that appeared in Castilian *cancionero* poetry in the fifteenth century.[29] Chandler Post agrees that the *Roman* left its impression on the works of Imperial and adds also Ruy Páez de Ribera, the Marqués de Santillana, and, possibly, even Juan Ruiz[30] (though Luquiens has argued against its influence on the *arcipreste*). Pierre Le Gentil has posited a widespread influence particularly on literary depictions of the garden: «En dépit des précédents anciens, dont nous venons de parler, il semble bien que les modèles dont on s'est servi au XVe siècle, en Espagne, soient le *Roman de la Rose* et les *dits* français qui s'en inspirent, ceux de Machaut en particulier.»[31] It seems clear that Rojas was familiar either with the *Roman de la Rose* or works influenced by it,[32] for the garden of the *Celestina* is strongly reminiscent of the thirteenth-century garden styled by Guillaume de Lorris, one that D. W. Robertson, Jr., has called «one of the most elaborate and influential gardens in medieval literature».[33] He has drawn a clear distinction between two essential types of gardens depicted by medieval writers. The first of these is the Garden of *Caritas* in which the symbolic values are directed toward portraying the everliving quality of God's love. The second is the Garden of *Cupiditas* whose imagery suggests carnal delight, the enjoyment of the flesh. The gardens of the *Roman de la Rose* and the *Celestina* both clearly belong to the second category.

Distortion (Exeter, 1967), has even suggested that Rojas «need not have read more than half a dozen books, if one of them were one of those medieval compendia of wise sayings from the philosophers» (p. 7). Even if this were the case, there is certainly evidence that he had indeed read considerably more widely. An inventory of his personal library includes 97 books, 49 of them vernacular, among which have been identified works of Boccaccio, Castiglione, Ovid, Petrarch, Boethius, Guido della Columna —all works which were popular at the time. It seems improbable that the *Roman de la Rose* would have escaped his attention altogether. See Fernando del Valle-Lersundi, «Testamento de Fernando de Rojas, autor de *La Celestina*», *RFE*, 16 (1929), pp. 384-88.

[29] Frederick Bliss Luquiens, «The *Roman de la Rose* and medieval Castilian literature», *RF*, 20 (1907), 284-320. While Luquiens argues primarily against the widespread influence of the *Roman de la Rose* on Spanish literature, it is interesting to note that the influence he does grudgingly admit comes just before and during Rojas' formative period.

[30] Chandler R. Post, *Medieval Spanish Allegory*, HSCL, 4 (Cambridge, Mass., 1915).

[31] Pierre Le Gentil, *La Poésie lyrique espagnole et portugaise à la fin du moyen âge*, i (Rennes, 1949), p. 246.

[32] See Emilio Orozco Díaz, «El huerto de Melibea», *Arbor*, 19 (May/August, 1951), 47-60. Orozco Díaz suggests that this is the first dramatization of nature in Spanish literature. If this is true, the influence may well have come from the *Roman de la Rose*.

[33] «The Doctrine of Charity», p. 40.

In terms of location and enclosure the two gardens are similar. The Jardin d'Amour lies beside a river:

> Jolis, gais e pleins de leece
> Vers une riviere m'adrece
> . . . .
> La praerie grant e bele
> Trés au pié de l'eve batoit
> Clere e serie e bele estoit
> La matinee e atempree;
> Lors m'en alai par mi la pree,
> Contreval l'eve esbaneiant,
> Tot le rivage costeiant.
>   Quant j'oi un poi avant alé,
> Si vi un vergier grant e lé,
> Tot clos de haut mur bataillié,
> Portrait dehors e entaillié
> A maintes riches escritures.
>   (II, 103-4, 122-33)

Pleberio's garden is also located beside a river, as we learn when, near the end of the work, Pleberio suggests that Melibea seek comfort in the cool air from the river bank. «Levántate de ay. Vamos a uer los frescos ayres de la ribera» (II, 190). Melibea agrees, feigning comfort at watching the ships: «Subamos, señor, al açotea alta, porque desde allí goze de la deleytosa vista de los nauíos: por ventura afloxará algo mi congoxa» (II, 190-91). Both gardens are walled around, so high that they cannot be scaled without the aid of a ladder. The dreamer of the *Roman* twice mentions the need of a ladder if one is to scale the wall:

> Hauz fu li murs e toz carrez;
> Si en estoit clos e barrez,
> En leu de haies, un vergiers,
> Ou onc n'avoit entré bergiers.
> Cil vergiers en trop bel leu sist.
> Qui dedenz mener me vosist,
> Ou par eschiele ou par degré,
> Je l'en seüsse mout bon gré;
>   (II, 467-74)

and again:

> Destroiz fui mout e angoisseus,
> Tant qu'au derrenier me sovint
> Qu'onques en nul sen ce n'avint
> Qu'en si bel vergier n'eüst uis,
> Ou eschiele ou quelque pertuis.
> (II, 508-12)

The use of the ladder in the *Celestina* is central. It is the means both of Calisto's sin and of his death. To Melibea it provides a means of assault, perhaps even suggestive of the appropriate phallic symbol. She telescopes the entire act into three short sentences. «Quebrantó con escalas las paredes de tu huerto, quebrantó mi propósito. Perdí mi virginidad» (II, 197). Her repetition of the word *quebrantó* and the paratactic construction suggest that she sees the scaling of the walls and the breaking down of her resistance as a single action, a single assault on her maidenhood. The result is simply stated: «Perdí mi virginidad.»

It is even, perhaps, possible to draw a parallel between the dreamer's admission to the garden by «une pucele, / Qui assez estoit gente e bele» (525-26)—Oiseuse— and Calisto's leisurely wandering into Pleberio's garden in search of a lost falcon.[34] Martín de Riquer has suggested, however, that the original version of Act I had as its setting not a garden at all, but a church.[35] He contends that Rojas «mudó completamente el decorado de esta primera escena» (p. 389), adding the allusions to the garden and the lost falcon to the *argumento*. If such is, indeed, the case, it strengthens the argument in favor of Rojas' deliberate choice of the garden world, as well as his symbolic use of the falcon, for if, as Riquer believes, Calisto's

---

[34] See José Antonio Maravall, *El mundo social de La Celestina* (Madrid, 1964). Maravall contends that such young men, belonging to the «nueva clase ociosa de base burguesa» have adopted many of the forms of life of the old nobility, but with important transformations. Of Calisto, he comments: «Carece de hábitos señoriales ancestrales, de los que no le vemos practicar más que los más exteriores e inertes— levantarse tarde, seguir devociones rutinarias, vestirse con ostentación, etc. Se entretiene en deportes de contenido caballeresco subsidiario, sin otra excepción que la caza, de modo que no hay la menor alusión militar en torno a él... la única referencia a la actividad venatoria del joven señor se reduce a una vaga y tópica noticia de caza de aves» (pp. 43-44). The result might be much the same even with a member of the old nobility who had been displaced for one reason or another from the manor to the city and who found himself involved with an emerging bourgeoisie. The point is that many «hábitos señoriales» which had once been meaningful had become merely empty forms, followed more because of custom or ostentation than because of necessity.

[35] Martín de Riquer, «Fernando de Rojas y el primer acto de 'La Celestina'», *RFE*, 41 (1957), 373-95.

easy access to Melibea's garden is rendered unlikely in view of his subsequent difficult entrances [36] and if «sería raro que Calisto se dedicara a cazar dentro de una ciudad» (p. 384), a point with which I am inclined to agree, although there is no indication that Calisto was actually hunting—the falcon seems, rather, to have escaped from his perch—then Rojas must have chosen the garden setting and the falcon for some very good reason. The one which seems most likely is that the garden setting was more appropriate and more compatible with the overall significance of the text.

The dreamer of the *Roman de la Rose* sees painted on the outside of the garden walls a series of grotesque figures, ten in all, representing Hate, Felony, Villainy, Covetousness, Avarice, Envy, Sorrow, Old Age, Hypocrisy, and Poverty. Relatively little critical attention has been devoted to these figures. They reappear, with others, painted on the walls of the temples of Venus and Mars, particularly the latter, in Chaucer's *Knight's Tale*. There is an interesting difference between these two sets of wall paintings. In the *Roman* they clearly represent «the obverse or *afferre contrarium* of the qualities depicted in the personages within Deduit's garden ... [They] signify what were to the courtly world the most odious of all evils or vices».[37] The fact that they are painted on the outside of the wall insures that they will never be able to gain entrance to the garden where all the company

> sembloient
> Tot por voir anges empenez.
> Si beles gens ne vit on nez.
>
> (II, 724-26)

In the *Knight's Tale* the figures are painted on the *inside* of the walls of the temples. Within the temple of Venus they represent the elements or

---

[36] Riquer's argument is most interesting, but I do not necessarily agree that merely because Calisto must scale the wall at night, he would also have to do so on a chance visit during the day. The garden would, presumably, have a gate which could surely be found open on occasions during the day, but which would undoubtedly be locked at night, with the key safe in Pleberio's keeping. There is even a suggestion in the text that Calisto's first chance entry was a result of his scaling the walls. Already in Act IV Melibea refers to him as «esse loco, saltoparedes» (I, 179). Riquer's suggestion is based on the idea that Rojas is *not* the author of Act I. I do not wish, within the scope of this work, to debate the authorship question. Whatever the case, however, the point remains that Rojas did have control of the text, as the alterations (if that is what they are) concerning the garden and the falcon indicate.

[37] Alan M. F. Gunn, *The Mirror of Love: A Reinterpretation of the Romance of the Rose* (Lubbock, Texas, 1952), p. 106.

the effects, both hopeful and adverse, of love. They are described in the
following way:

> The broken slepes, and the sikes colde,
> The sacred teeris, and the waymentynge,
> The firy strokes of the desirynge
> That loves servantz in this lyf enduren;
> The othes that hir convenantz assuren;
> Plesaunce and Hope, Desir, Foolhardynesse,
> Beautee and Youthe, Bauderie, Richesse,
> Charmes and Force, Lesynges, Flaterye,
> Despense, Bisynesse, and Jalousye,
> That wered of yelewe gooldes a gerland,
> And a cokkow sittynge on hir hand;
> Festes, instrumentz, caroles, daunces,
> Lust and array, and alle the circumstaunces
> Of love, which that I rekned and rekne shal,
> By ordre weren peynted on the wal,
> An mo than I kan make of mencioun.
> For soothly al the mount of Citheroun,
> Ther Venus hath hir principal dwellynge,
> Was shewed on the wal in portreyynge,
> With al the gardyn and the lustynesse.
> Nat was foryeten the porter, Ydelnesse. [38]

When we turn to the temple of Mars, we see painted «upon the wal/ Withinne
the temple of myghty Mars the rede» (1968-69) those figures appropriate to
the countenance of war:

> ... Felonye, and al the compassyng;
> The cruel Ire, reed as any gleede;
> The pykepurs, and eek the pale Drede;
> The smylere with the knyf under the cloke;
> The shepne brennynge with the blake smoke;
> . . . .
> Contek, with blody knyf and sharp manace.
> Al ful of chirking was that sory place.

---

[38] *Works, Knight's Tale*, 11. 1920-40.

The sleere of hymself yet saugh I ther,—
His herte-blood hath bathed al his heer;
The nayl ydryven in the shode a-nyght;
The colde deeth, with mouth gapyng upright.
Amyddes of the temple sat Meschaunce,
With disconfort and sory contenaunce.
Yet saugh I Woodnesse, laughynge in his rage,
Armed Compleint, Outhees, and fiers Outrage.

(1996-2000, 2003-2012)

It would have been no surprise to the medieval audience that while Arcite wins the battle by praying to Mars, he could never hope to win the lady Emelye, though she be the prize of battle. He permits Felonye and Ire, with all their uncourtly retinue, to enter into the drama of love. It is Palamon who must have the fair lady. It is he who puts first things first, and his prayer to the goddess of love brings about the necessary miracle, the trickery of the gods that causes Arcite's horse to bolt. The knight, as a result, «pighte hym on the pomel of his heed» (2689). Calisto makes essentially the same mistake that Arcite has made in that he admits non-courtly qualities into the courtly world. It should be fairly obvious that the figures painted on the outside of the wall of the Jardin d'Amour correspond to Celestina and the servant-prostitute milieu in which she operates. Hate is described as malignant and base, cause of quarrels and jealousy, possessor of an evil passion, with a face marked by spiteful rage, much as the faces of Sempronio and Pármeno must look as they murder Celestina, or as Areusa must appear as she plots her revenge against Calisto and Melibea. Significantly, next to hatred we find Felony who is not described but is distinctly related to Hate. The murder of Celestina, the general actions and occupations of the old *alcahueta* herself belong to this figure. Villainy is next, foul and churlish, yet proud. This ironic mélange of pride and foulness is clearly apparent in Celestina, who recalls with vanity all the maidenheads she has repaired, all the priests who have come to her for their corrupt pleasures. One sees a similar pride emerging in the arrogant Areusa, who gloats over her position as a kept woman, smug in her conscious superiority over Elicia. Covetousness, the next figure on the wall, is clearly a vital element in the intrigue among the servants. She is represented in the prositutes' envy of Melibea, in Sempronio's and Pármeno's covetousness of Celestina's gold. There is an

interesting parallel here between the description of Covetousness and the
precise situation in the *Celestina:*

> C'est cele qui les genz atise
> De prendre e de neient doner,
> E les granz avoirs aüner;
> C'est cele qui fait a usure
> Prester mainz por la grant ardure
> D'avoir conquerre e assembler;
> C'est cele qui semont d'embler
> Les larrons e les ribaudiaus;
> Si est granz pechiez e granz diaus,
> Qu'en la fin maint en covient pendre.
>
> (II, 170-79)

It is covetousness that leads Sempronio and Pármeno to their execution.
«Les larrons e les ribaudiaus» describes quite aptly the characters of the
servant world of the *Celestina.* Celestina's covetousness leads us to the
next figure, for her covetousness becomes Avarice, which ultimately leads
her to her death. The poet of the *Roman* might have been describing
Celestina herself:

> Laide estoit e sale e folee
> Cele image, e maigre e chaitive,
> E ausi vert come une cive;
> Tant par estoit descoloree
> Qu'el sembloit estre enlangoree;
> Chose sembloit morte de fain,
> Qui vesquist solement de pain
> Pestri a lessu fort e aigre.
> E avuec ce qu'ele iere maigre,
> Iert ele povrement vestue:
> Cote avoit viez e derompue,
> Comme s'el fust as chiens remese;
> Povre estoit la cote e esrese
> E pleine de viez paletiaus.
>
> (II, 198-211)

Celestina certainly indulges in a better diet, but she is, like the hag Avarice,
reluctant to spend her own gold for a new cloak. Indeed, she asks Calisto

for a new cloak rather than gold only to avoid sharing it with Sempronio and Pármeno. She laments the condition of her old cloak, which, from Celestina's description, resembles that of Avarice. Calisto, enraptured with the news of Celestina's first encounter with Melibea, expresses the whimsical wish that he had been hidden under her cloak to observe the scene. Celestina replies: «¿Debaxo de mi manto, dizes? ¡Ay mezquina! Que fueras visto por treynta agujeros que tiene, si Dios no le mejora» (I, 211).

Envy is the next image on the wall. It is envy of the joy of Calisto and Melibea that racks the two harlots Areusa and Elicia after their own lovers have been executed. At the beginning their wrath is directed only against Melibea, and Areusa's description of Melibea, which we have already seen, bears witness to the description of Envy on the garden wall:

> Qu'ele fondoit d'ire e ardoit
> Quant aucuns qu'ele regardoit
> Estoit ou preuz ou biaus ou genz
> Ou amez ou loez de genz.
>
> (II, 287-90)

They cannot bear to hear Melibea praised. It is, then, partially their envy of Melibea and partially their envy of the lovers' happiness once their own has been destroyed, that causes them to plot revenge:

> Nule rien ne li puet tant plaire
> Con fait maus e mesaventure.
> Quant el voit grant desconfiture
> Sor aucun prodome cheoir,
> Ice li plaist mout a veoir.
> Ele est trop liee en son corage
> Quant el voit aucun grant lignage
> Decheoir ou aler a honte.
>
> (II, 240-47)

The pleasure Envy feels at seeing men fall is a sort of dual prediction of the fate of Calisto, for his is a double fall, both a physical fall and a fall of fortune. It undoubtedly brings Calisto down in a way intensely satisfying to Areusa and Elicia, for Calisto's death is a strong echo of the deaths of Sempronio and Pármeno.

Sorrow is a curious figure to find here, and a clear distinction must be made between the sorrow that is allowed to penetrate within the wall and the Sorrow that is painted on the outside. The paintings on the wall of the temple of Venus in the *Knight's Tale* had begun with a description of sorrowing figures, sleepless, sick, chilled, weeping, lamenting—in sum, «The firy strokes of the desirynge/ That loves servantz in this lyf enduren». Love's sorrow is acutely painful and may even be fatal if the lady does not act as the lover's physician and cure his malady. But it is not a hopeless sorrow. It is always coupled with Hope and Desire, «the othes that hir covenantz assuren». The Sorrow on the outside of the wall of the Jardin d'Amour, on the other hand, is an unrelenting grief at the loss of things irretrievable—youth, beauty and, consequently, love. It is the secular equivalent of despair. Such sorrow has no place in the courtly world, for Old Age, the next figure on the wall, is clearly barred from the garden. Sorrow for lost youth and joy is a common theme in the Middle Ages. We find it to be the predominant characteristic, for example, of Villon's Belle Hëaulmiere, [39] who has been excluded from a world that was itself a sort of parodic courtly world, apparently very much like that described by Villon in his «Ballade de la Grosse Margot», [40] where the vocabulary has distinctly courtly overtones, but where the situation described is something less than courtly. La Belle Hëaulmiere bitterly regrets her loss of beauty and, consequently, her loss of power over men. Like her, Celestina laments her lost youth and beauty. But she hides her sorrow as much as possible and in precisely the same manner as la Belle Hëaulmiere: She instructs the young in the ways of love, attempting thereby partially to assuage her own appetites.

Next to Sorrow on the wall and clearly related to it stands Old Age, Vieillece, who represents the chief sorrow of hags such as Celestina and la Belle Hëaulmiere. They have lived by their beauty and desirability. Their present state seems even more foul by contrast to what they once were. Old Age is representative of this type:

> Mout estoit sa biauté gastee,
> Mout estoit laide devenue.
> Toute sa teste estoit chenue
> E blanche con s'el fust florie.
> . . . .

---

[39] François Villon, *Oeuvres*, ed. Auguste Longnon, 4e ed. revue par Lucien Foulet (Paris, 1964), pp. 29-30, 11. 533-60.
[40] *Ibid.*, pp. 63-64, 11. 1591-1610.

Les oreilles avoit mossues,
E toutes les denz si perdues
Qu'ele n'en avoit mais nes une.
. . . .
Ele avoit esté sage e entre,
Quant ele iert en son droit aage;
Mais je cuit qu'el n'iere mais sage,
Ainz estoit tout rassotee.
Ele ot d'une chape forree
Mout bien, si con je me recors,
Abrié e vestu son cors.
Bien fu vestue chaudement,
Car ele eüst froit autrement:
Ces vieilles genz ont tost froidure;
Bien savez que c'est lor nature.
                    (II, 344-47, 355-57, 396-406)

Again the cloak is mentioned. Possessions have become for Old Age, as they have for Celestina, a substitute for the warmth of the flesh that time has forced them both to renounce.

Hypocrisy comes next, and its connection with Celestina herself is surely evident as she goes about her affairs, praying to God in public, to the Devil in private:

C'est cele qui en recelee,
Quant nus ne s'en puet prendre garde,
De nul mal faire n'est coarde;
El fait dehors le marmiteus,
Si a le vis simple e piteus
E semble sainte creature,
Mais soz ciel n'a male aventure
Qu'ele ne penst en son corage.
                    (II, 410-17)

Last of all the figures comes Poverty. It is the motivation of all the servants of the *Celestina*. While their *cupiditas* is the central factor in their demise, it is ultimately born of poverty.

Much time and space have been taken in pointing up the somewhat obvious parallels between the figures on the outside of the wall of the Jardin d'Amour and the characters who populate the servant world of the *Celestina*. However, it may well prove to be one of the most significant

points in determining why Calisto ultimately fails as a courtly lover. As
we have already noted, these are the attributes that can never be permitted
to enter the domain of love. They are opposed within the garden by such
figures as Courtesy, Beauty, Wealth, Largesse, Franchise, Idleness, and
Youth. Yet in many instances Calisto rashly ushers into the garden the
very figures that are forever forbidden entrance. The intrusions introduced
or permitted by Calisto will be made clearer as we trace a little further the
structural parallel between the *Celestina* and the *Roman de la Rose* (discussed
more fully later in this chapter).

Once inside the walls the dreamer of the *Roman* is struck by Cupid's
arrow and falls in love with the rose. As one would expect, the arrow of
Cupid pierces the heart of the lover by entering through his eye:

> Il [Cupid] entesa jusqu'a l'oreille
> L'arc, qui estoit forz a merveille,
> E traist a moi par tel devise
> Que par mi l'ueil m'a ou cuer mise
> La saiete par grant roidor.
>   (II, 1691-95)

Henceforth, the lover, a victim of the sickness of love, agrees to become
Love's vassal. Calisto, by the same token, describes his falling in love
with Melibea in these same allegorical terms: «¡O mis ojos! Acordaos
cómo fuistes causa e puerta, por donde fue mi coraçón, llagado, e que aquel
es visto fazer daño, que de la causa» (I, 222). He, too, suffers from the
lover's malady caused by what he refers to as the «crudo caxquillo» and
its «aguda punta» (I, 224) with which Melibea's beauty has wounded him.
The lover of the *Roman*, approaching the rose, is welcomed by Bialacoil
(or Fair-Welcome) who offers him assistance, but when he proposes to
pluck the rose, Danger rises up in ugly wrath and chases them both away.
This scene, as we have already noted, parallels the opening scene of the
Celestina. The lover laments his misfortune in being chased away from
the rose's enclosure. Calisto, too, expresses grief at his adversity and
expulsion from the garden as he sings:

> ¿Qual dolor puede ser tal,
> que se yguale con mi mal?
>   (I, 39)

As the lover of the *Roman* laments his expulsion from the presence of the
rose, he is confronted by Reason who counsels him to turn aside from

91

following Love. The role of Reason in the *Celestina* is curiously assumed by Sempronio, who is himself a victim to the folly of love. Both Reason and Sempronio fail in their attempts to dissuade the lovers from their amorous pursuits. Reason bemoans the fact that «quant juenes on fait folie» (II, 3016). Sempronio philosophizes similarly: «No es este juyzio para moços, según veo, que no se saben a razón someter, no se saben administrar» (I, 51-52). Sempronio's advice must be accepted ironically as it is by Calisto who knows of his carryings on with Elicia and taunts him with them, but Sempronio answers calmly: «Haz tú lo que bien digo e no lo que mal hago» (I, 43). In the *Roman de la Rose* the voice of Reason is overcome, and in the *Celestina* Sempronio soon realizes that, with his master so bent upon his folly, it is more profitable to aid him than to dissuade him. Rejecting the role of Reason, he becomes the agent of Love, and it is in this guise that he recommends the services of Celestina. The god of love in the *Roman* suggests at this point that the lover seek out a friend for aid and solace. The code of morality advocated by Friend, the use of bribery, corruption, deception and hypocrisy, is remarkably like that of Celestina. The lover of the *Roman* recoils in horror. Calisto, by contrast, asks no questions. But the lover, too, is eventually won over. The god of love joins in the attack on the castle. The plan of siege is, in some cases, identical to Celestina's. Franchise and Pity are to overcome Danger. By the same token, Celestina uses Melibea's pity and generosity to calm her fury at the name of Calisto by explaining that his difficulty is a toothache that only she can alleviate. In the *Roman* Courtesy and Generosity do away with the Duenna who guards Fair-Welcome by bribing her. Celestina, in turn, declares love for Lucrecia and promises her bleach to make her hair like gold and something to stop her bad breath.

Pleasure and Hidewell are sent to attack Shame, and Constrained Abstinence and False Seeming deal with Evil Tongue. The reappearance of Danger corresponds to Melibea's fury at the mention of Calisto's name. There is a skillful portrayal of the soothing of this *danger* in the *Celestina*. It is accomplished in the scene just mentioned by evoking Melibea's pity, but we must bear in mind also that Celestina is a witch [41] who casts a spell over the girl. When her spell has taken hold of Melibea, she is summoned

---

[41] See Julius Berzunza, «Notes on Witchcraft and Alcahuetería», *RR*, 19 (1928), 141-50; P. E. Russell, «La magia como tema integral de *La Tragicomedia de Calisto y Melibea*», *Studia Philologica: Homenaje ofrecido a Dámaso Alonso*, III (Madrid, 1963), 337-54; and M. J. Ruggerio, *The Evolution of the Go-Between in Spanish Literature Through the Sixteenth Century*, UCPMP, 78 (Berkeley and Los Angeles, 1966), chapter 2, pp. 24-43.

by Lucrecia to her mistress' side to heal the sting of love's arrow, darted into the flesh, in a sense, by Celestina herself who is acting as Love's agent, however displaced from her courtly counterpart she might be.[42] The following scene recalls the intervention of Venus in the *Roman de la Rose*, her arrow of flame shot into the ivory tower setting it on fire and causing Danger, Fear, and Shame to flee, leaving the tower in flames, open to the attack of the forces of Love and to the lover who, as a result, comes to possess the rose.

In her first visit, Celestina has set a small spark aflame in Melibea, and having taken her girdle, has, through her magic, fanned the spark into a burning fire. Her medicine is half-innoculation, half incantation. There is a tripartite structure in the scene of Celestina's second visit to Melibea's house. When Celestina has arrived, Melibea asks her three times to help her, not to delay, and each time there is some mention of her honor. She begs for a cure, the first time closing her plea with «tal que mi honrra no dañes con tus palabras» (II, 55). Celestina delays talking of Melibea's pains. Again Melibea chides her, asking for an immediate diagnosis, «pues te pido le muestres, quedando libre mi honrra» (II, 56). Celestina continues to delay, warning Melibea to hold her tongue and be patient. But Melibea's will is broken. Her suffering is too great as she indicates at last her willingness to sacrifice everything, even her honor:

> Agora toque en mi honrra, agora dañe mi fama, agora lastime mi cuerpo, avnque sea romper mis carnes para sacar mi dolorido coraçón, te doy mi fe ser segura e, si siento aliuio, bien galardonada.
> (II, 56)

Now it is Celestina's turn to attack, Melibea's to resist, in a triple echo of the scene just played. Celestina says that she must bring medicine from the home of Calisto. At the instant his name is uttered Melibea bursts out: «Calla, por Dios, madre. No traygan de su casa cosa para mi prouecho ni le nombres aquí» (II, 58). Celestina urges her to restrain herself, saying that this is but the first *punto* of the treatment. Again she mentions the name of Calisto and this time she manages to get four words beyond the name before she is, once again, interrupted by Melibea:

> CEL.—...tan virtuosa como Calisto, que si conocido fuesse...
> MELIB.—¡O por Dios, que me matas! ¿E no te tengo dicho que no me alabes esse hombre ni me le nombres en bueno ni en malo?
> (II, 58)

---

[42] Ruggerio contends that Venus is transformed by stages from a goddess «into a type of contemporary society—that of the procuress» (p. 25). In the personage of Celestina she becomes «the ally of the devil (that is, a witch) who turns her power to evil» (p. 35).

This was the second *punto*. Then a third time Celestina mentions his name. This time she is allowed to complete her sentence and even go one sentence beyond as Melibea delays her denunciation:

> CEL.—...tú quedrás sana e sin debda e Calisto sin quexa e pagado. Primero te auisé de mi cura e desta inuisible aguja, que sin llegar a tí, sientes en solo mentarla en mi boca.
> MELIB.—Tantas vezes me nombrarás esse tu cauallero, que ni mi promesa baste ni la fe, que te di, a sofrir tus dichos.
>
> (II, 58-59)

Melibea's hesitation belies her words and gives Celestina the courage to name her malady: «Amor dulce» (II, 59).[43] Melibea asks for a further explanation and Celestina complies in the paradoxical language worthy of a Provençal troubadour:

> Es vn fuego escondido, vna agradable llaga, vn sabroso veneno, vna dulce amargura, vna delectable dolencia, vn alegre tormento, vna dulce e fiera herida, vna blanda muerte.
>
> (II, 59)

Cejador points out in a note that this particular passage is a borrowing from Petrarch. But the use of antithesis in describing that love we call courtly dates back, of course, to the troubadours. Le Gentil describes the typical attitude toward love in Spain at the end of the Middle Ages:

> On ne peut pas dire que l'antithèse soit ici un simple procédé de développement; les oppositions, les contradictions sont dans la nature même de l'amour et dans les effets qu'il produit. C'est un sentiment où la joie se mêle à la souffrance, l'espoir au désespoir; les obstacles, loin de diminuer sa force, l'augmentent au contraire; c'est un mal auquel on prend plaisir, qui exalte. [44]

In the face of such a paradox Melibea expresses a (feigned?) despair that she may never find a cure for such a disease of contradictions. But Celestina has an answer:

> No desconfíe, señora, tu noble juuentud de salud. Que, quando el alto Dios da la llaga, tras ella embía el remedio. Mayormente que sé yo al mundo nascida vna flor que de todo esto te dé libre.
>
> (II, 60)

---

[43] There is an interesting parallel to this scene in Chrétien de Troyes's *Cligés*, 11. 3011-62, where Thessala, who claims to be an expert in charms, potions, and enchantments (an influence, of course, from the Tristan legend), diagnoses the cause of her mistress' sorrow as love and promises to help her in her desires.
[44] *La Poésie lyrique*, pp. 126-27.

Celestina's metaphorical language is highly significant here. A flower is blossoming that will free Melibea from her pain. The flower is, of course, the flower of carnal love, that love to which Melibea is about to succumb. We must remember at this point that in the *Roman de la Rose*, the rose is not to be taken as an allegorical representation of the lady herself but of her love, or more precisely, her body given in love. Possession of the rose, as the sexual connotations of its description clearly indicate, represents the physical act of love.

When Celestina names the cure for Melibea's illness, «Calisto», Melibea swoons. It is made clear in the text that this swoon marks the end of her modesty, her *danger*, her shame—those same elements that flee from the tower when Venus fires her flaming arrow. Their departure is sudden, as Melibea herself indicates:

> Quebróse mi honestidad, quebróse mi empacho, afloxó mi mucha vergüença, e como muy naturales, como muy domésticos, no pudieron tan liuianamente despedirse de mi cara, que no lleuassen consigo su color por algún poco de espacio, mi fuerça, mi lengua e gran parte de mi sentido...

(II, 61)

It is at this point, at last, that the lover is able to make his way into the tower, for Fair-Welcome has offered him the rose that he may pluck it at leisure. The actual plucking of the rose is not unlike the deflowering of Melibea in some respects. Fair-Welcome requests that the lover perform no outrageous act, no act beyond what he, Fair-Welcome, might wish. And the lover, in contrast to the eager Calisto, agrees. Melibea makes the same demand of Calisto who has completely lost control of his courtly demeanor. The lover of the *Roman* is gentle, carefully loosening the bud:

> Toutes en fis par estouveir
> Les branches croler e mouveir,
> Senz ja nul des rains depecier,
> Car n'i voulaie riens blecier,
> E s'i m'en couvint il a force
> Entamer un po de l'escorce;
> Qu'autrement aveir ne savaie
> Ce don si grant desir avaie.
> (V, 21711-18)

95

Calisto's crude haste, his refusal to yield to Melibea's demands, his single self-directed desire, contrast sharply with the tender solicitude of the lover. Yet in spite of the lover's gentleness, the bud reprimands him:

> Si m'apele il de couvenant,
> E li faz grant desavenant,
> E sui trop outrageus, ce dit.
>
> (V, 21737-39)

Like Melibea, as Tristán and Sosia point out, the rose makes the usual complaint when it is too late. Well over two centuries later, Melibea echoes the rose, as she, too, complains in the garden:

> ¡O mi vida e mi señor! ¿Cómo has quisido que pierda el nombre e corona de virgen por tan breue deleyte?
>
> (II, 119)

The attack on the tower which separates the lover from his rose near the end of Jean de Meun's portion of the *Roman* is suggested in the language of Calisto as he bemoans the difficulties in winning Melibea:

> ¡O desdichado! Que las cibdades están con piedras cercadas e a piedras, piedras las vencen; pero esta mi señora tiene el coraçón de azero. No ay metal, que con él pueda; no ay tiro, que le melle. Pues poned escalas en su muro: vnos ojos tiene con que echa saetas, vna lengua de reproches e desuíos, el asiento tiene en parte, que media legua no le pueden poner cerco.
>
> (I, 221)

But when love's forces in the *Roman de la Rose* win the tower, and the lover, in turn, wins the rose, the poem is at an end. In the *Celestina*, as in the *Roman*, events happen up to this point as they should in a comedy. As Northrop Frye has described it, «a young man wants a young woman, ...his desire is resisted by some opposition, ... and ... near the end of the play some twist of the plot enables the hero to have his will».[45] Here the reader expects the marriage between the two lovers, or, at the very least, the inevitable happy ending. But the *Celestina* does not end here. The dream world described by Frye, where everything happens not as it would but as it should, becomes suddenly demonic, and murder is followed by execution,

---

[45] Frye, *Anatomy*, p. 163.

accidental death by suicide. What is lacking is the permanence implied by a comic ending «manipulated by a twist in the plot».[46] Comedy may be defined as tragedy that does not quite happen, tragedy prevented by some contrived *anagnorisis*. But the *Celestina* presses relentlessly forward to its most logical conclusions. The characters remain, as they do in the *Troilus*, true to themselves, and their various fates are a direct result of what they have been and done throughout the story. The *Celestina* fulfills the dire prediction made by Reason in the *Roman*, where, perhaps, its fulfillment is avoided only by its termination at precisely this point. Reason states the physical and moral results of this sort of love in unmistakably clear terms:

> Car, en l'amour ou tu t'entrapes,
> Maint i perdent, bien dire l'os,
> Sen, tens, chatel, cors, ame, los.
>
> (II, 4626-28)

Up to this point, however, it should be clear to the reader that the two love stories are built as parallel constructions.[47] I do not, as I stated above, insist upon any direct influence of the *Roman* upon the *Celestina*; to do so would surely require more evidence than I have presented here. Yet the structural similarity is difficult to escape. It seems almost ludicrous that those critics whom we have already noted deny the presence of the courtly love element in the *Celestina* when it is clearly composed on a pattern essentially the same as that of the most influential courtly love poem of the Middle Ages.

Any doubts that critics may still have had concerning the presence of

---

[46] *Ibid.*, p. 170.

[47] Since the completion of my original study in 1967, which included the preceding comparison (now revised) of the *Celestina* with the *Roman de la Rose*, I have come across the following paragraph by Dorothy Clotelle Clarke in her *Allegory, Decalogue, and Deadly Sins in La Celestina*, UCPMP, 91 (Berkeley and Los Angeles, 1968):

> At the end of the century in which Spanish medieval allegory reached the peak of its development and popularity, it is not surprising to find that a potential lover has found a means of entering a walled garden, is overwhelmed by the sight of a beautiful creation, is attempting to «pluck the rose» (allegorically speaking), is discovering that the rose is thorny (proud and angry), and is being banished from the garden. That potentiality becomes a reality, that the lover is confined virtually helpless and ill in a dark enclosure (cf. prisons of love), and suffering untold torture (cf. hells of love), that the lover despairs of removing from between himself and his beloved the separation caused by her sublimity and his humble state come not as a surprise either. That the lover's hope should be rekindled and feebly maintained by the services of a love messenger is all part of the literary game as it had been played for some three centuries (p. 3).

courtly love elements in the *Celestina* should have been, for the most part, dispelled by J. M. Aguirre's book *Calisto y Melibea, amantes cortesanos*, the stated intention of which is «demostrar que Calisto y Melibea son ejemplos típicos del galán y la dama cortesanos, y que el drama de Rojas es la obra capital de la literatura anticortés española» (p. 10). Following a definition of courtly love derived primarily from Denomy, Aguirre seeks to present Calisto as a more or less ideal courtly lover, breaking only the law of secrecy by confiding his love to «extraños» (p. 35). The love of Calisto and Melibea, Aguirre contends, is «amor cortés» while the love among the servants is «amor impuro» (p. 22). Even though he presents Calisto's and Melibea's love as true, courtly, and of a generally higher type than that of the servants who enjoy sex for the sake of sex (pp. 22-23), Aguirre claims, Rojas' work is «anticortés», and Rojas clearly disapproves of courtly love.

If we accept, then, the notion that the *Celestina* is indeed written within the conventions of courtly love, the principal question raised by Aguirre's book is whether or not Calisto is to be taken as a serious treatment of the courtly lover, as Aguirre himself contends, or whether he is treated as parody. If the latter, how is the parody achieved? And what ends does it serve? I have argued in the Introduction that effective parody requires a fundamental similarity to the original, whether it be an individual work or a convention that is being parodied, yet it must in some significant way depart from the original. One may parody an author's style by emptying it of weighty content. Or one may parody poor style, by transferring the content of a good work into the style of a poor one. One may parody an idealized convention by placing it in the midst of the real world. In each case, some essential element has been altered to show up a convention, a style, etc., in a humorous, often didactic, light.

Within most of his speeches, Calisto retains the style of the courtly lover. As we have already seen, he has utilized the approach set forth by Andreas Capellanus in the *De Amore*. He suffers from the characteristic love sickness; he addresses his beloved in the most courtly of language. And yet, as a courtly lover, he emerges in the course of the work as an absurdity. Why? What is missing? How does Calisto differ from the ideal courtly lover? He errs in precisely the same way that the Wyf of Bath errs as a Christian. He follows the letter of the law, at least most of the time, but ignores (or is ignorant of) its spirit. From its inception courtly love had been considered a potentially ennobling phenomenon. Guillaume IX of Poitou sees it as a powerful, but contradictory force:

Per son joy pot malautz sanar,
E per sa ira sas morir
E savis hom enfolezir
E belhs hom sa beutat mudar
E.l plus cortes vilanejar
E totz vilas encortezir.[48]

As the convention grew and developed the affirmative aspects of the paradox were stressed over the negative ones, and love became the source of virtue with the power to make a man generous, brave, kind, and, above all, wise. But from the beginning, while Calisto professes a certain ennoblement, his actions belie his words. His first encounter with Melibea appears courtly enough, but, as close examination has revealed, he handles the whole thing in a rather fumbling manner. His departure, however, he takes like a true gentleman: «Yré como aquel contra quien solamente la aduersa fortuna pone su estudio con odio cruel» (I, 34). The courtliness of his tone is in striking contrast with his opening words in the next scene as he calls out for his servant: «¡Sempronio, Sempronio, Sempronio! ¿Dónde está este maldito?» (I, 34). Who could imagine such language from a perfect, gentle knight like Lancelot? Or even Aucassin? Upon finding Sempronio, Calisto continues to curse him:

> ¡Assi los diablos te ganen! ¡Assi por infortunio arrebatado perezcas o perpetuo intollerable tormento consigas, el qual en grado incomparablemente a la penosa e desastrada muerte, que espero, traspassa. [sic] ¡Anda, anda, maluado! Abre la cámara e endereça la cama.
>
> (I, 35)

Yet in his next speech he is again the courtly lover disconsolate at the loss of his lady:

> Cierra la ventana e dexa la tiniebla acompañar al triste y al desdichado la ceguedad. Mis pensamientos tristes no son dignos de luz. ¡O bienauenturada muerte aquella, que desseada a los afligidos viene! ¡O si viniéssedes agora, Hipocrates e Galeno, médicos, ¿sentiríades mi mal? ¡O piedad de silencio, inspira en el Plebérico coraçón, porque sin esperança de salud no embie el espíritu perdido con el desastrado Píramo e de la desdichada Tisbe!
>
> (I, 35-36)

---

[48] Quoted from *Anthology of the Provençal Troubadours*, ed. Raymond Thompson Hill and Thomas Goddard Bergin (New Haven, 1941), p. 8.

8

If Calisto's repetitious language (for example, his much-used *desdichado*) seems unimaginative, this should not, perhaps, bother the reader so much. Nowhere do the traditional courtly love works state that the lover must exhibit originality in his lovemaking. What should strike the reader, however, is Calisto's shifting from the courtly idiom to the curses and maledictions he directs almost casually toward his servant and back again to courtly speech.[49]   Calisto is attempting to play a role for which he is ill suited.   Somewhat like Molière's M. Jourdain, who is not born to be an *honnête homme* but seeks through all available means to learn and ape his characteristics, Calisto is clearly not born to be a courtly lover.   He moves in a world of essentially bourgeois values and virtues.   His world is so totally unlike that of Lancelot that the two may seem at first to have almost no relationship to one another.   Even if Calisto has been born within the proper social class, Castiglione's tract *Il Cortegiano*, begun about nine years after the *Celestina* and probably reflecting a fairly widespread attitude of the period, makes it quite clear that lovers are not lovers merely by virtue of their noble birth.   Being a courtier alone will not suffice to make a man courteous.   And for Calisto the world of *courtoisie* is clearly an adoptive world.   He moves much more freely among his servants, barking orders, cursing them in the language they understand, than he does in the garden he is trying to mold into the garden of love.

One cannot claim for Calisto, as one could for Aucassin and Troilus, that a large part of his problem is derived from the unsuitable nature of the lady for her role as *domna*.   Melibea gives the impression that she is at least trying to act the part of a courtly lady.   Only occasionally does she confuse her role as sovereign over her lover with the masculine role of servility, as she does in contradicting Calisto who has just called her «mi señora»: «Es tu sierua, es tu catiua, es la que más tu vida que la suya estima» (II, 116).   While she may not be in all instances the perfect courtly lady, Melibea emerges from the work relatively unscathed by the whip of parody.   One may smile occasionally at her naïveté, but whatever she lacks in *savoir-faire*, she makes up for in sincerity.   She clearly loves Calisto, whatever his shortcomings, with a consuming passion.   To some critics,

---

[49]   Carmelo Samonà, in his *Aspetti del retoricismo nella «Celestina»* (Roma, 1953), comments, concerning such sudden changes of style: «Questa *mutatio*, generalmente improvvisa, puo avvenire all'interno del discorso di un personaggio, e indica con effetto preciso il cambiamento di un'attitudine o un pensiero che sopravviene... Frequenti sono gli essempi in quasi tutti i monologhi, com'è naturale per lo stato psicologico che questi vanno gradatamente esprimendo» (p. 183).

notably Rachel Frank,[50] she rises at the end to near-tragic heights. While this seems to me to be imposing upon Melibea more stature than she merits in the text, she nonetheless approaches the dimensions of tragedy far more closely than does Calisto. She is perhaps naïve and foolish, but if she reduces herself sometimes to the level of Calisto's slave, if she assumes the masculine role, it is because this is the way she feels. She *does* adore Calisto. She *is* ready to die for him. One may well question whether or not Calisto would have thrown himself off the tower had their roles at the end been reversed. If Rojas were to remain true to the psychological portrayal of his characters, it is highly unlikely.

Calisto's essential problem lies within his own nature, and the constantly shifting tone of his language is a clue to a certain baseness in his character. His words lack the sincerity essential to the ideal courtly lover. His love lacks the power to ennoble him. And desire, rather than being refined as it grows stronger, tends to become coarser. As though attempting to conceal the base nature of his desire for Melibea, he relies heavily on the love religion. His worship appears almost from the beginning excessive. After their first meeting he exclaims in answer to Sempronio's question concerning whether or not he is a Christian, «¿Yo? Melibeo so e a Melibea adoro e en Melibea creo e a Melibea amo» (I, 41). But in spite of his enthusiastic «Melibeanism» and his implicit renunciation of Christianity because of it, there is a curious inversion in his words. The problem with Calisto's «worship» of his lady is that he seems given to worship a bit too facilely. If one examines the first scene of physical love between Calisto and Melibea, it is easy to see precisely how sincere his adoration is. According to the precepts of courtly love, the knight's adoration of the lady led him to obey without question or hesitation any command she might make, no matter how difficult or absurd it might seem. Guenevere, for example, orders Lancelot who is triumphing in a tournament in the kingdom of Gorre, all for the purpose of rescuing her from her abductor, to perform as badly as he can. In unquestioning obedience, he permits himself to be unhorsed by his next opponent. He has already tasted Guenevere's wrath at his hesitation to mount the shameful cart earlier in the story. Calisto, by contrast, is callously disobedient to Melibea's requests, which may or may not be intended to be taken seriously. The seriousness of the request is

---

[50] Rachel Frank, «Four Paradoxes in *The Celestina*», *RR*, 38 (1947), 53-68. Américo Castro has commented in *La Celestina como contienda literaria* (Madrid, 1965) that «Unos amores logrados por medio de una alcahueta no podían ser un tema trágico» (p. 146).

unimportant. The simplest, most capricious whim of the lady is to be accepted by the lover as his solemn duty. As C. S. Lewis explains it, «The lover is always abject. Obedience to his lady's lightest wish, however whimsical, and silent acquiescence in her rebukes, however unjust, are the only virtues he dares to claim.»[51] Melibea makes the unfortunate mistake of placing demands on Calisto when his desire has reached a peak. It is not difficult to see upon which he places most importance—his love service to his lady or his own wilful desire. Melibea entreats him:

> ... no quieras perderme por tan breue deleyte e en tan poco espacio. Que las malfechas cosas, después de cometidas, más presto se pueden reprehender que emendar. Goza de lo que yo gozo, que es ver e llegar a tu persona.
>
> (II, 116-117)

But Calisto's desire is too strong:

> Señora, pues por conseguir esta merced toda mi vida he gastado, ¿qué sería, quando me la diessen, desechalla? Ni tú, señora, me lo mandarás ni yo podría acabarlo comigo. No me pidas tal couardía. No es fazer tal cosa de ninguno, que hombre sea, mayormente amando como yo.
>
> (II, 117)

Again Melibea begs him, «Bástete, pues ya soy tuya, gozar de lo esterior, desto que es propio fruto de amadores; no me quieras robar el mayor don que la natura me ha dado...» (II, 117). Calisto does not reply with an explanation of the distinctions between pure and mixed love and a gentle rational persuasion that mixed love is best, as does one of the lovers of the *De Amore*. Indeed, he has forgotten those ill-learned lessons in the art of love. Rather, he responds with a series of questions that are almost impudent:

> ¿Para qué, señora? ¿Para que no esté queda mi passíon? ¿Para penar de nueuo? ¿Para tonar el juego de comienço? Perdona, señora, a mis desuergonçadas manos, que jamás pensaron de tocar tu ropa con su indignidad e poco merecer; agora gozan de llegar a tu gentil cuerpo e lindas e delicadas carnes.
>
> (II, 117-18)

Like «hende» Nicholas of the *Miller's Tale*, Calisto cries «mercy», but the reader has every reason to believe that, if Melibea refuses to submit, he would have little compunction in taking her by force.

---

[51] *Allegory*, p. 2.

At this point he makes a suggestion so far removed from the precepts of courtly love that, to the reader anticipating the courtly climax as the lover wins the lady by sweet persuasion and humility, it seems shocking. Melibea, realizing that the moment has come for her to send her servant away, that she can control Calisto no longer, orders Lucrecia to leave. Again, Calisto questions his lady's commands: «¿Por qué, mi señora? Bien me huelgo que estén semejantes testigos de mi gloria» (II, 118). The scene seems even more debasing when one recognizes that it contains a strong echo of an earlier scene enacted between a servant and a prostitute in Areusa's bedroom. Yet in spite of Calisto's clearly carnal orientation, he still exhibits an excessive external adoration for Melibea. However, without the corresponding reverence and emotion for the beloved, without a sincere perception of his lady as superior, all his rhetoric becomes calculating and foolish. He eternally overweights the scales on the side of physical love and then attempts to make up the balance by an excessive rhetorical adoration.[52] But the words are empty, weightless; the scales never attain a proper balance. And Calisto appears all the more absurd for his efforts. As an example, let us examine Calisto's first words upon entering the garden on the evening he first possesses Melibea:

> ¡O angélica ymagen! ¡O preciosa perla, ante quien el mundo es feo! ¡O mi señora e mi gloria! En mis braços te tengo e no lo creo. Mora en mi persona tanta turbación de plazer, que me haze no sentir todo el gozo que poseo.
>
> (II, 116)

Calisto's ecstatic *exclamatio* «¡O!» precedes most of his effusive praise. Ironically, he chooses here the images of an angel and a pearl to describe Melibea. The angel clearly evokes the idea of God-like purity, of something other-worldly; the pearl suggests that Melibea is an object of enormous value. The idea of angelic otherworldliness is strengthened by the fact that before Melibea, «el mundo es feo». He continues in the most courtly tone, «O mi señora y mi gloria». The next sentence of the text suggests an almost religious awe at her earthly presence, «En mis braços te tengo e no lo creo». But this sentence serves as a sort of bridge between the quasi-religious implications of «angélica» and «gloria» and the suggestions

---

[52] For a full discussion of the use of rhetoric in the *Celestina*, see Samonà, *Aspetti del retoricismo*. One of his observations concerning Rojas' attitude toward rhetoric and courtly love is of particular interest: «La posizione di Rojas dinanzi al retoricismo el alla tradizione dell'amore cortese suggerisce in qualche punto un presentimento di quella cervantina dinanzi alla letteratura cavalleresca» (p. 220).

of the sentence that follows, spiced by more carnally-oriented words, «turbación de plazer», «sentir», «el gozo», and the verb «poseer». The reader can almost see Calisto as he pounds his breast at the beginning of the speech; but when he reaches the line, «En mis braços te tengo e no lo creo», there is a sudden realization that she is indeed in his arms and that he is aware of it. At this point, Calisto's high-sounding courtly praise of Melibea takes on false colors. The reader is forced to remember the earlier words of Sempronio when he explains why he considers Calisto more sinful than the Sodomites: «Porque aquellos procuraron abominable vso con los ángeles no conocidos e tú con el que confiessas ser Dios» (I, 44). Rather than being shocked by Sempronio's impious suggestion, Calisto laughs. The image of the pearl calls to mind a well-known passage from the Bible, Matthew 7:6: «Nolite dare sanctum canibus: neque mittatis margaritas vestras ante porcos, ne forte conculcent eas pedibus suis, et conversi dirumpant vos.» If Melibea is the pearl, Calisto is the swine; if she is the holy thing, then he is the dog; if she is an angel, then he is an evil man of Sodom, city of the devil. The irony is further strengthened when one remembers that these are the exact words used by Celestina upon her first encounter with Melibea: «¡O angélica ymagen! ¡O perla preciosa, e como te lo dizes!» (I, 172). And her motives are clearly devious. Calisto's actions belie his words. His rhetoric turns on him to reveal the essential carnality of his desires. As the scene progresses we see, similarly, the word *gloria* used in another context, as Calisto avows that he would enjoy having «testigos de mi gloria». In view of its later sexual context and the meaning that Calisto himself ultimately gives to the word, it becomes heavily ironic as an epithet for Melibea.[53]

To substantiate the idea that Calisto uses words carelessly and that the meaning he gives to them at other points in the text renders them ineffective as praise and laughable as courtly adoration, one may point out that he often uses the same style, indeed, the same words of address in lauding both Melibea and Celestina. In most cases, his words are reminiscent, as was much courtly love terminology, of the praise to the Virgin of the sort found in medieval lyrics. Of Melibea he says: «¡O señora mía, esperança de mi gloria, descanso e aliuio de mi pena, alegría de mi coraçón!» (II, 85). They clearly echo the earlier joyful cry directed to Celestina: «¡O joya del mundo, acorro de mis passiones, espejo de mi vista! El

---

[53] Keith Whinnom in his *Spanish Literary Historiography* comments that «the word *gloria*—in Juan del Encina, in the *Celestina*, in the *Comedia Thebaida*...is a euphemism for sexual possession» (p. 22).

coraçón se me alegra en ver essa honrrada presencia... ¿Qué dizes, gloria e descanso mío?» (II, 67). Such repetition weakens the force of Calisto's words. Melibea's honor is reduced to that of Celestina. His praise is cheapened. His encomium is revealed as pompous and meaningless, inadequate to balance the scales already so heavily weighted, as we have seen, on the side of carnality.

Equally self-conscious and empty, though followed to the letter, is the love sickness in which Calisto indulges. Sempronio berates his master:

> Tu temor me aquexa; tu soledad me detiene. Quiero tomar consejo con la obediencia, que es yr a dar priessa a la vieja. ¿Mas como yré? Que, en viéndote solo, dizes desuaríos de hombre sin seso, sospirando, gimiendo, maltrobando, holgando con lo escuro, deseando soledad, buscando nueuos modos de pensatiuo tormento. Donde, si perseueras, o de muerto o loco no podrás escapar, si siempre no te acompaña quien te allegue plazeres, diga donayres, tanga cançiones alegres, cante romances, cuente ystorias, pinte motes, finja cuentos, juegue a naypes, arme mates, finalmente que sepa buscar todo género de dulce passatiempo para no dexar trasponer tu pensamiento en aquellos crueles desuíos, que rescebiste de aquella señora en el primer trance de tus amores.
>
> (I, 115-16)

But Calisto knows the rules he, as courtly lover, is supposed to follow. He replies haughtily and, characteristically, confuses his courtly knowledge with his baser manner:

> ¿Cómo?, simple. ¿No sabes que aliuia la pena llorar la causa? ¿Quanto es dulce a los tristes quexar su passión? ¿Quanto descanso traen consigo los quebrantados sospiros? ¿Quanto relieuan e disminuyen los lagrimosos gemidos el dolor? Quantos escriuieron consuelos no dizen otra cosa.
>
> (I, 116-17)

But while the conventional groaning, sighing, paleness, and sleeplessness are all a part of Calisto's malady, it is characterized most strongly by the pain of fire. Reflecting his master's «sickness», Sempronio, in reply to Calisto's request that he sing the saddest song he know, sings:

> Mira Nero de Tarpeya
> a Roma cómo se ardía:
> gritos dan niños e viejos
> e el de nada se dolía.
>
> (I, 40)

But Calisto interrupts: «Mayor es mi fuego e menor la piedad de quien agora digo» (I, 40). The analogy of the consuming fire and lust is made earlier by Saint Paul and later misquoted by the Wyf of Bath,[54] who takes it as a license for unrestrained lust: «Dico autem non nuptis, et viduis: bonum est illis si sic permaneant, sicut et ego. Quod si non se continent, nubant. Melius est enim nubere, quam uri» (I Corinthians 7: 8-9). Fire was in the Middle Ages, as it still is, a common euphemism for lust. And the extreme burning symptom of Calisto's love sickness overshadows all others. Indeed, he claims that his burning is greater than that of pagan Rome itself.

Almost from the beginning, then, it is evident that the courtliness of Calisto is but a shell concealing his base desires, his lust for Melibea. He has a curious lack of contact with reality, a phenomenon which María Rosa Lida de Malkiel connects with egoism:

> La nota básica del carácter de Calisto es su egoísmo. No un egoísmo limitado al solo aspecto moral de su personalidad, como en el protagonista de la novela de Meredith, sino total, pues condiciona a la vez su concepción de la realidad, su juicio ético y su conducta social. Calisto es el héroe egoísta o ensimismado en el sentido etimológico de esos términos: el soñador introspectivo absorbido en su yo. [55]

She blames his symptoms ultimately on a prolonged adolescence. «Pero la inadaptación a la realidad, con su alternativa entre exaltación y depresión, son sí notas típicas de la adolescencia que, significativamente, Calisto ha retenido fuera de su término común» (p. 354). She is correct, I believe, in seeing Calisto as an egotist. But it is significant to recognize that Calisto's symptoms are precisely those used in Christian theology to describe a man overcome by lust:

> Du côté de l'intelligence, c'est d'abord l'aveuglement, caecitas mentis. L'esprit du luxurieux est affaibli, il ne saisit plus dans toute leur clarté les vérités de la vie morale et chrétienne et, sous l'influence de sa passion, il se laisse parfois entraîner au rejet de la foi. [56]

---

[54] See the Prologue to the tale of the Wyf of Bath, 11. 51-52:
> He seith that to be wedded is no synne;
> Bet is to be wedded than to brynne.

[55] *Originalidad*, p. 347.
[56] *Dictionnaire de théologie catholique*, ed. A. Vacant, E. Magenot, E. Amann (Paris, 1926), v. IX, col. 1354.

One could not hope to find a more apt description of Calisto, whose increasing mental ineptitude can perhaps be said to find a culmination in his death when his brains are quite literally scattered—all over the walls and street around Melibea's garden.

Such descriptions of the lustful man were constant almost from the beginnings of Christianity. The very earliest literary conflicts between the virtues and the vices depict *luxuria* as having a weakening effect on man, cutting off his contacts with the real world. The fifth-century *Psychomachia* of Prudentius, for example, depicts *luxuria* as a woman, riding in a chariot and using flowers and narcotic scents to rout and overcome the courage of her enemies.[57] Prudentius' description already makes it clear that *luxuria's* effect on man is precisely one that drugs his senses, that impedes his clear perceptions of reality. It is not particularly unusual for this imperception to take the form of physical or spiritual blindness. Perhaps the most constant of blind figures is that of Cupid,[58] but such blindness comes up from time to time in other characters such as Chaucer's January in the *Merchant's Tale*, the story of the lecherous old man and his young wife May. As Charles A. Owen, Jr., has expressed it, January's «lust for pleasure and his desire for salvation combine in the first consultation scene to blind him to the danger inherent in taking a young wife».[59] In justifying his marriage in old age in the first place he describes woman as man's helpmate:

> His paradys terrestre, and his disport.
> So buxom and so vertuous is she
> The moste nedes lyve in unitee.
> O flesshe they been, and o flessh, as I gesse
> Hath but oon herte, in wele and in distresse.[60]

According to Owen,

> The 'unitee' and 'o flessh' receive an ironical fulfillment in the
> blind old man's constant clutch on his buxom and perforce

---

[57] See Adolf Katzenellenbogen, *Allegories of the Virtues and Vices in Medieval Art*, trans. Alan J. P. Crick (New York, 1964), pp. 1-13.

[58] For a discussion of Blind Cupid, see Panofsky, pp. 95-128.

[59] Charles A. Owen, Jr., «The Crucial Passages in Five of the *Canterbury Tales*: A Study in Irony and Symbol», *JEGP*, 52 (1953), 298.

[60] *Merchant's Tale*, IV (E), 1332-1336.

virtuous May, and an additional twist in the line from his invitation to the garden,

'No spot of thee ne knew I al my lyf,'

IV (E) 2146

where the irony of the contrast between his ugly passion and the romantic imagery and sacred associations of the Song of Songs matches the irony of his being as unconscious of the physical spot he is even then touching as he will later be of the moral spot—adultery—when he is looking at it with miraculously unblinded eyes.

(p. 229)

Calisto is blind only in a spiritual sense; but his physical perceptions are obviously dimmed as he missteps in the darkness and falls from the ladder, a graphic representation of his spiritual fall from the Ladder of Virtue.[61]

Gregory the Great has listed as the consequences of *luxuria* «caecitas mentis, inconsideratio, inconstatis, praecipitatio, amor sui, odium Dei, affectus praesentis, saeculi, horror autem vel desperatio futuri generantur».[62] Rojas might almost have had a list of these characteristics before him as he created the character of Calisto. Perhaps the most significant point that arises from Gregory's list is that what Sra. Lida de Malkiel names as Calisto's chief characteristic—egoism—*(amor sui)*—is a symptom and consequence, according to Gregory, of *luxuria*, lust. The fact that Calisto exhibits the other characteristics as well, mental weakness, inconsideration, inconstance, precipitation in his actions, a rejection of God, and so forth, reinforces the idea that the motivating force behind Calisto's behavior is lust. As Bataillon has stated it, «A aucun moment il [Rojas] n'a haussé l'amour de Calisto au-dessus du niveau de l'obsession sensuelle».[63] Bataillon points out several instances that indicate the carnal quality of Calisto's «love» for Melibea. For example, his reaction to Melibea's girdle, brought to him as a sort of ritual promise by Celestina, gives evidence of Calisto's sensual orientation, while the seduction scene in the garden where Calisto is unable and unwilling to control himself in obedience to Melibea's will serves to confirm it. He is reduced at this point to the pseudo-courtly level of one of Chaucer's *fabliau* figures; he is the blood brother to Nicholas in the *Miller's Tale*, who, in response to Alison's cry, so like that of Melibea, «Do wey youre handes, for youre courteisye»,[64]

---

[61] See Katzenellenbogen, pp. 22ff. The motif of the ladder is also discussed by Barbera in «Medieval Iconography in the *Celestina*».

[62] *PL*, LCCVI, col 621.

[63] *La Célestine*, p. 113.

[64] *Miller's Tale*, 1. 3286.

cries for «mercy», frequently a courtly euphemism for sexual favors.[65] In effect, Calisto is a good deal like «hende» Nicholas. When examined closely, each of the characteristics of his lust is revealed to be but an exaggerated, inverted, or misunderstood element of the courtly world and its affections.

His lack of touch with reality may suggest a similar attribute in Don Quixote and in Aucassin, who, as we have seen, has been judged by one critic as «un fou au pays des sages». Auerbach has commented that:

> The world of knightly proving is a world of adventure... Nothing is found in it which is not either accessory or preparatory to an adventure. It is a world specifically created and designed to give the knight opportunity to prove himself... Such idealization takes us very far from the imitation of reality. [66]

But Calisto, like Don Quixote and Aucassin, lives in a world not especially prepared for the aspiring young knight and courtly lover, a world that José Antonio Maravall has characterized as materialistic, urban, and essentially pragmatic.[67] Unlike them, however, Calisto seems at home in his world; he accepts it more or less for what it is and knows how to function quite well, at least in the beginning, among the prostitutes, rogues, and procuresses who populate it. For Aucassin or Don Quixote to behave or to discourse in a lower mode is unthinkable, not because they are pre-

---

[65] The term *mercy* has sexual connotations in the *Miller's Tale:*

> This Nicholas gan mercy for to crye
> And spak so faire, and profred him so faste,
> That she hir love hym grannted atte laste.
> (3288-90)

These lines are followed by a discussion of plans to deceive her husband and set up an assignation. Calisto uses the term *merced* in an obviously sexual context, mentioned above. Melibea asks him to be content with seeing her and being with her, but he refuses, beginning his argument, «Señora, pues por conseguir esta merced toda mi vida he gastado...» Similar sexual connotations are suggested occasionally in troubadour lyrics. For example, in a *tenso* by Lanfranc Cigala, quoted in the *Anthology of the Provençal Troubadours* (ed. Hill and Bergin, p. 196), we find false lovers asking *merce* of their ladies:

> Senz, vos e.1 cor failletz, al mieu parer,
> Qe.1 faillimenz mou totz de leuiaria
> Dels amadors, qi son fals e chamian,
> E car domnas i trobon pauc de fe
> Si fan preiar e loingnon lur merce
> Per conoisser lo leial del truan...

[66] *Mimesis*, p. 119.
[67] See Maravall, especially pp. 50-67.

tentious, but because they simply do not understand the painful fact of fathers who refuse to keep their promises or taskmasters who beat their servants. Their loss of touch with reality results from a conflict of idealism with reality. For Calisto, however, it results from an increasing moral blindness. He closes his eyes to his false use of the courtly tradition. He is able to adapt himself with remarkable facility from one mode to the other, leading the reader to the inevitable conclusion that he is an *arriviste*[68] to the courtly world and that he lacks a number of its essential qualifications. He swears at his servants with ease. He knows well how to use to its greatest advantage the courtly virtue *largesse* and is quick to understand Celestina's mumbled words which complain that idle words pour forth from Calisto's mouth instead of money from his purse. He is equally quick to cross her palm with silver, the only key that will permit him entrance, he has apparently concluded, to Melibea's garden. Upon hearing Celestina's complaint, he turns to Sempronio:

> CAL.—¿Qué dezía la madre? Parésceme que pensaua que le ofrescía palabras por escusar galardón.
> SEMP.—Assí lo sentí.
> CAL.—Pues ven comigo: trae las llaues, que yo sanaré su duda.
> SEMP.—Bien farás e luego vamos. Que no se deue dexar crescer la yerua entre los panes ni la sospecha en los coraçones de los amigos; sino alimpiarla luego con el escardilla de las buenas obras.
> CAL.—Astuto hablas. Vamos e no tardemos.
>
> (I, 93)

While Calisto's loss of touch with reality takes the form of moral blindness, even he can scarcely be unaware of the role he is playing in this parody of «buenas obras». There is a world of difference between a lover's showing *largesse* to someone in need and his paying a procuress to help him satisfy his own needs. It is essentially the difference between the idealized world of courtly love and the near-picaresque world, steeped in material considerations, in which Calisto seems to belong. He knows how to buy his way, how to drop flattery in such a way that it will fall, as though unintentionally, on the right ears. His adeptness in the more materialistic world and his ineptness within the garden world strike a sharp contrast to the reverse condition in Aucassin and Quixote, who, upon meeting felons, transform them mentally into knights and ladies.

---

[68] See *Ibid.*, pp. 27-49. According to Maravall, Calisto «responde fielmente a la figura del joven miembro de la clase ociosa... No sólo es rico, sino que lo ostenta» (p. 32).

It is precisely this difference that sets the tone of the parody in the *Celestina*. Because Don Quixote and Aucassin are misplaced courtly figures, forced to function in a world not specifically prepared for them, the reader tends to view their escapades with humor, perhaps, but nonetheless with sympathy. They are misfits in a cruel and unsympathetic world. Calisto, on the contrary, whose *modus operandi* fits only too well into the world of his servants, seems ridiculous and almost conniving as he seeks to emulate the courtly lover. The parody takes on a harsher note, a more serious corrective or didactic tone.

Calisto's loss of touch with reality has been discussed at some length by Sra. Lida de Malkiel and Bataillon;[69] there is, consequently, no need to point out again the various examples from the text. It has been made sufficiently clear that Calisto lives his life according to a misconception of reality, an essential miscalculation of truth. His misunderstanding seems to increase in direct proportion to his lust. And his moral blindness and self-deception gradually make him ineffectual even in the servant world in which he seems so at home in the beginning. He is, as we have seen, shrewd enough at first in understanding Celestina's mental processes. He is also reasonably clever at finding flaws in Sempronio's arguments against love:

> CAL.—¿Qué te paresce de mi mal?
> SEMP.—Que amas a Melibea.
> CAL.—¿E no otra cosa?
> SEMP.—Harto mal es tener la voluntad en vn solo lugar catiua.
> CAL.—Poco sabes de firmeza.
> SEMP.—La perseuerancia en el mal no es constancia; mas dureza o pertinacia la llaman en mi tierra. Vosotros los filósofos de Cupido llamalda como quisiérdes.
> CAL.—Torpe cosa es mentir el que enseña a otro, pues que tú te precias de loar a tu amiga Elicia.
> SEMP.—Haz tú lo que bien digo e no lo que mal hago.
>
> (I, 43)

He is even able to laugh at his own foolishness when Sempronio confronts him with it:

> CAL.—¿De qué te ríes?
> SEMP.—Ríome, que no pensaua que hauía peor inuencion de pecado que en Sodoma.

---

[69] See Lida de Malkiel, *Originalidad*, pp. 353ff.; and Bataillon, *La Célestine*, pp. 121ff.

CAL.—¿Cómo?

SEMP.—Porque aquellos procuraron abominable vso con los ángeles no conocidos e tú con el que confiessas ser Dios.

CAL.—¡Maldito seas!, que fecho me has reyr, lo que no pensé ogaño.

(I, 44-45)

But his laughter is shortlived as he gradually convinces himself of his own sincerity in his apotheosis of Melibea. As his self-deception progresses, he becomes less and less capable of distinguishing, first of all, metaphysical truth, right from wrong, then of understanding psychological truth. He has lost much of his rapport with his servants by the time he is finally permitted to enter the garden. Just as he has totally miscalculated the courage and loyalty of Sempronio and Pármeno when he tells Melibea in answer to her question «¿Son muchos los que traes?» that while his men are few they are, indeed, capable of protecting them well: «No, sino dos; pero, avnque sean seys sus contrarios, no recebirán mucha pena para les quitar las armas e hazerlos huyr, según su esfuerço. Escogidos son, señora, que no vengo a lumbre de pajas» (II, 91), so he completely misjudges the valor of Sosia and Tristán. Hearing noises outside the garden walls, Calisto in precipitate haste leaps, as he would have us believe, to the rescue. But as he is taking leave of Melibea, Sosia's voice is heard: «¿Avn tornays? Esperadme. ¿Quiçá venís por lana?» (II, 183). His words clearly indicate that he and Tristán have driven off the first «attack» and are ready with stout hearts for the second. Calisto is not needed. Yet he rushes to the «battle» which is already won. His actions strongly suggest the symptoms of the lustful man:

> Puis viennent la précipitation, l'inconsidération et l'inconstance dans le jugement, car les impressions sensuelles ou charnelles le dominent. On ne prend plus le temps de réfléchir, de délibérer, d'arrêter un jugement fondé. [70]

At this point Calisto's inability to interpret correctly metaphysical truth and psychological reality melts into an equal inability to interpret physical reality. Just as he misjudges the entire situation, so he misjudges his footing on the ladder, stumbles, and plunges to his death.

Calisto's baseness, glossed over by a thin layer of courtly learning, leads one to the conclusion that it is perhaps in this enormous gap between

---

[70] *Dictionnaire de théologie catholique*, vol. IV, col. 1354.

what Calisto is and what he pretends to be that the parody lies. And it
is at precisely this point that my views differ sharply from those of Aguirre.
What Rojas is attacking is not so much the true courtly lover, but the
false—he who pretends to be what he is not. Aguirre contends that
Rojas distinguishes between the *amor cortés* of Calisto and the *amor
impuro* of the servants. On the contrary, all Rojas' devices for stripping
the mask from Calisto result in reducing the characters, regardless of
their social rank, to a single level. Marcel Bataillon has suggested this
leveling influence in his discussion of the use of maxims and proverbs
in the *Celestina:*

> Si, partant de l'idée que *La Célestine* est oeuvre réaliste, on
> s'attendait à voir les proverbes populaires et 'positifs' plus spé-
> cialement invoqués par la vieille, les prostituées et les valets, les
> maximes élevées des philosophes étant réservéees à des person-
> nages de plus haut niveau comme les parents de Mélibée, ou à
> la rigueur à un Sempronio que sa verve de 'figura del donaire'
> peut faire classer comme un clerc manqué, on s'apercevrait, au
> plus rapide examen, qu'une telle ligne de démarcation n'existe pas.
> A cet égard comme à tant d'autres, *La Celestina* n'est pas réaliste.
> Les personnages de cette moralité comique font flèche de tout
> bois. Et l'originalité de son art en cette matière est la parfaite
> désinvolture avec laquelle les personnages les moins sages et les
> moins vertueux s'approprient le double trésor. [71]

Bataillon is certainly right in pointing out this lack of stylistic differentiation between the «high» and the «low» worlds of the *Celestina,* and,
more specifically, «les dissonances entre la noblesse des maximes et la
bassesse des pensées» (p. 106). But the leveling influence goes much
further than the use of maxims and proverbs alone. It is a fundamental
technique of Rojas, who, here and there throughout the text, with a few
swift strokes of the pen, reduces virtually all of the characters, with the
possible exception of Melibea's parents, to the same basic level. They
are men; they are mortal; they are sinners.

Calisto lives on the moral level of his servants. Like them, he is guilty
of the sin of *cupiditas,* which carries meanings of both greed and lust.
It has been interpreted both ways as it appears, for example, in the familiar
passage from I Timothy 4:10: «Radix enim omnium malorum est cupiditas: quam quidam appetentes erraverunt a fide, et inseruerunt se dolo-
ribus multis.» Aquinas has interpreted it in connection with this passage

---

[71] *La Célestine,* p. 100.

as the love of money.[72]   Augustine gives the word a considerably broader meaning—an inordinate desire for any worldly thing.[73]   It is this latter meaning which seems to have prevailed during most of the medieval period.   For example, in the Middle English translation of the *Roman de la Rose*, commonly attributed to Chaucer, the idea of *cupiditas* as it occurs in this passage from Timothy is given as lust:

> For of ech synne it is the rote,
> Unlefull lust, though it be sote,
> And of all yvell the racyne.[74]

Inordinate desire, of which lust is one manifestation, is also the interpretation which comes down to us in Catholic theology:

> Le mot *cupiditas* présente dans l'Ecriture des sens assez divers, mais dont la note essentielle se situe dans un désir très vif... Quand la cupidité place l'amour porté à la chose convoitée, elle est péché mortel et détruit la charité. [75]

Cupiditas was, for medieval man, an inordinate desire for anything that would cause him to turn his vision away from God.   In these terms, Calisto is guilty of the sin of *cupiditas* from the moment he utters «Melibeo so», if, indeed, not before.   It is also *cupiditas*, this time an inordinate desire for money, that brings Pármeno and Sempronio to murder Celestina. And Celestina herself, who plots her illicit intrigues as she says her rosary, unquestionably places the love of money before the love of God.   It is the same sin, then, that brings about the deaths of Celestina, the two servants, and Calisto—the mortal sin of *cupiditas*, of lust after this world.

Along with their common sins, Rojas has given them, as Bataillon suggests, a common language.   The lack of stylistic differentiation between the speeches of the servants and their master is a problem that has long bothered *Celestina* scholars and translators.   The problem is not so much that two levels of style do not exist in the *Celestina*.   One might

---

[72]   See *Summa Theologica*, I-II, Qu. 84, art. 1. Aquinas is correct in his interpretation. The Greek text reads *philargyria* (i.e., love of money), but it is translated *cupiditas* in the Vulgate Bible.

[73]   *On Christian Doctrine*, trans. D. W. Robertson, Jr. (New York, 1958), Book III, x, 16, p. 88.

[74]   *Romance of the Rose*, *Works*, Robinson edition, 11. 4879-81.

[75]   *Dictionnaire de théologie catholique*, Tables générales, Bernard Loth et Albert Michel (Paris, 1955), col. 883.

well distinguish, as I have attempted to do to some extent, between the courtly style and the base style. The difficulty is, rather, that the courtly style is not reserved for those characters of higher social level; nor is the base style exclusively used among the servants. On the contrary, depending on the occasion upon which a character is speaking, depending upon his psychological makeup at the time, the language is either in a high style or a low style. It is a daring technique. One need only compare the style of the medieval *fabliau*, which approximates the world one would expect such characters as Celestina, Sempronio, and Areusa to inhabit, with the style of the romance, a more appropriate world for the «courtly» love of Calisto and Melibea, to realize just how daring it is.

The problem of style is intimately related, as we shall see, to the problem of love. Just as in the late medieval motif of the *danse macabre*, all men, regardless of rank, are reduced through death to a single level, so in the *Celestina* are they all reduced to a single level through love, «that olde daunce», as Chaucer styles it.[76] The leveling influence of love works in two directions, lowering Calisto through his obsessive lust, raising the servants through their occasionally sublime and courtly language. But the very fact that everyone, regardless of class or sentiment, can pour forth the courtly formulas already serves to point up the essential emptiness to which the convention has been reduced. While Calisto is, himself, a parody of the true courtly lover, the servants, in turn, are parodies of Calisto and other young men like him. With Calisto the altered element is nobility of sentiment; with the servants it is nobility of sentiment plus social position. Thus, they are one step further removed from the true convention. The parody reaches its most extreme point in the person of Sosia, the little stable boy who pays court to Areusa after the death of Pármeno. He, too, knows the courtly idiom, and his tribute to Areusa curiously fills in one of the elements missing from Calisto's use of the Andreas dialogues. He praises not only her beauty, but also her gentility, graciousness, and wisdom:

> Señora, la fama de tu gentileza, de tus gracias e saber buela tan alto por esta ciudad, que no deues tener en mucho ser de más conoscida que conosciente, porque ninguno habla en loor de hermosas que primero no se acuerde de ti que de quantas son.
> (II, 157-58)

---

[76] See «The General Prologue» to *The Canterbury Tales*, 476; *Troilus and Criseyde*, III, 695; *Romance of the Rose*, 4300.

9

In one sense, such a courtly encomium directed towards the whore Areusa makes it painfully obvious that the convention has become a mere form, a language of love of any sort, an attribute formerly of the nobility, but now sunk so low as to take place between a stableboy and a prostitute. One might say of Rojas' work essentially the same thing that E. T. Donaldson has said of the *Miller's Tale*, «Beneath the Miller's remorseless criticism the Blanchefleurs and even the Emilys of Middle English romance degenerate into the commonplace targets of a lewd whistle».[77] From one point of view we have reached the nadir of the degeneration of courtly love. On the other hand, we are almost working toward a revitalization of the convention, for here, in the youthful innocence of Sosia, we have, in contrast to Calisto, one who is sincere, or as sincere as he can be under the circumstances, in his love for Areusa. We see him later telling Tristán about his encounter with his lady. He is truly humble as he recounts how sweetly she smelled by contrast to his own odor of manure. He tells of his longing and his shyness. But when Tristán suggests that Areusa may be trying to use him and trick him, how unlike Calisto's reaction to wise counsel is that of Sosia!

> ¡O Tristán, discreto mancebo! Mucho más me has dicho que tu edad demanda. Astuta sospecha has remontado e creo que verdadera.
>
> (II, 176)

Yet Sosia, too, remains a parody, thrice removed from the convention itself.

More significant, however, than the mere similarity of stylistic levels among characters of the different social classes, is the presence of rough, uncourtly speech within a generally courtly rhetorical framework. We have already seen some indications of crude speech within the courtly context, in the *malditos* of Calisto to Sempronio. Even the language he uses in his adoration of Melibea suggests, as we have found, the coarser base from which he operates. From time to time in the garden the courtly mask slips off completely, and we see Calisto's intentions clearly revealed in his vulgar idiom. Melibea's garden again provides the setting for what is probably the most offensive of his uncourtly errors. He is, as

---

[77] E. Talbot Donaldson, «Idiom of Popular Poetry», p. 134.

usual, praising Melibea in those same conventional terms he has used for her elsewhere, as well as for Celestina:

> Pues, señora e gloria mía, si mi vida quieres, no cesse tu suaue canto. No sea de peor condición mi presencia, con que te alegras, que mi absencia, que te fatiga.
>
> (II, 180-81)

But when Melibea chides him for his shamelessness («¿Qué prouecho te trae dañar mis vestiduras?»), he replies with a proverb in rather poor taste:

> Señora, el que quiere comer el aue, quita primero las plumas.
>
> (II, 181)

Less strong, certainly, is the courtly flavor of the servant milieu. Nevertheless, the conventional praise, so often juxtaposed with crude language, continues to jolt the ear. Sempronio, for example, soothes Elicia's wrath with such sweet and gentle language:

> ¡Calla, señora mía! ¿Tú piensas que la distancia del lugar es poderosa de apartar el entrañable amor, el fuego, que está en mi coraçon? Do yo vó, comigo vás, comigo estás. No te aflijas ni me atormentes más de lo que yo he padecido.
>
> (I, 61-62)

But only a moment before he has been mocking her fury: «¡Hy! ¡Hy! ¡Hy! ¿Qué has, mi Elicia? ¿De qué te congoxas?» (I, 61).

Rojas uses a similar leveling device in the broader framework of scenic composition. Quite often a scene played by Calisto and Melibea will be reflected in a similar scene enacted among the servants. There is a sort of double plot which keeps the readers continually aware of the essential foolishness of the entire situation. Of double plot William Empson has said: «...the device sets your judgment free because you need not identify yourself firmly with any one of the characters...; a situation is repeated for quite different characters, and this puts the main interest in the situation not the characters.»[78] On the secondary plot he comments, «Usually it provides a sort of parody or parallel in low life to the serious parts ...This gives an impression of dealing with life completely...» (p. 29).

---

[78] William Empson, *English Pastoral Poetry* (New York, 1938), p. 54.

These statements may well be made of the use of the double plot in the *Celestina*. The parodying of certain scenes on the servant level that have been played or will be played by the more aristocratic lovers keeps the reader from becoming truly involved in the love story. At a distance, one is much more capable of seeing Calisto for the fool he is. Even Melibea is not above a certain foolishness revealed through the parodies of her by the whore Areusa. The malady from which Areusa suffers in Act VII, for example, is clearly revealed, as the plot runs its course, to be the same malady which causes Melibea such pain. They have the same diagnostician, Celestina, who offers a single cure for virtually everything— «amor dulce». The triple love story, guided by the witch Celestina, is like a three-fold mirror, each panel reflecting the others. The scene in the garden when Calisto wants Lucrecia to stay and witness his *gloria* echoes an earlier scene played in Areusa's bedroom. She, like Melibea, protests the presence of a third person, in this case Celestina. «Ay, señor mío, no me trates de tal manera; ten mesura por cortesía...» (I, 259). The «por cortesía» only serves to remind the reader of the lack of *cortesía* in the scene. Areusa adds, «Assí goze de mí, de casa me salga, si fasta que Celestina mi tía sea yda a mi ropa tocas» (I, 259). Like Calisto, Celestina sees no reason why there should not be spectators at the event. Unlike Melibea, Areusa gives in and agrees to allow Celestina to stay, but now Celestina demurs on the basis that it will only arouse her appetites. Calisto's desire that he have witnesses to his *gloria* is echoed again in Pármeno's monologue in the morning after his possession of Areusa: «¡O alto Dios! ¿A quién contaría yo este gozo? ¿A quién descubriría tan gran secreto? ¿A quién daré parte de mi gloria?» (II, 8-9).

These scenes also serve to *confirm* the essential baseness of Calisto's sentiments so like those of Celestina and Sempronio. They also suggest that the humility, so integrally a part of the makeup of the courtly lover, is replaced in Calisto by a somewhat adolescent boastfulness about his erotic adventures. But such pride, particularly about his obtaining «mercy» from his lady, has no place in the courtly design. On the contrary, its stress is on secrecy. According to Maurice Valency, «It was the lover's duty to see that no breath of scandal should touch his lady, no matter how careless she herself might become.»[79] Calisto seems, from time to time, when he is in better control of himself, at least aware of the courtly stress on secrecy, although other factors may well be responsible for his actually

---

[79]   Valency, *In Praise of Love*, p. 171.

abiding by it.   On their first evening together, when Calisto and Melibea are separated by the garden wall, Melibea, in a sense demanding her own downfall, curses the doors and their strong locks.   Calisto, eager in this instance to please her since her wishes are so close to his own desire, replies:

> ¡O molestas e enojosas puertas!   Ruego a Dios que tal huego os abrase, como a mí da guerra: que con la tercia parte seríades en vn punto quemadas.   Pues, por Dios, señora mía, permite que llame a mis criados para que las quiebren.
>
> (II, 86)

No thought for her reputation crosses his mind until Melibea reminds him with a reprimand:

> ¿Quieres, amor mío, perderme a mí e dañar mi fama?
>
> (II, 87)

But he remembers the lesson well when Pármeno warns him that someone is coming.   Calisto flees with his servants after a few parting words to Melibea, which justify his departure by the courtly code of secrecy but which may also reveal the real cause of his flight:

> ¡O mezquino yo e como es forçado, señora, partirme de tí! ¡ Por cierto, temor de la muerte no obrara tanto como el de tu honrra!
>
> (II, 91)

Calisto apparently uses the courtly code however and whenever he chooses. The fact that he seemed so little concerned earlier in the scene for Melibea's reputation suggests that there may be a certain degree of insincerity in his sudden change of heart, particularly when it occurs so conveniently as soon as danger threatens.

Calisto's suspect courage coupled with his lack of true concern for Melibea's honor point toward an egotism that belies his claim of humility and ennoblement in the elegant speech he delivers earlier on that same evening.   Reinforcing the irony of the speech is the fact that he begins by praising Melibea in those terms, previously mentioned, that he has used in tribute to Celestina:

> ¡O señora mía, esperança de mi gloria, descanso e aliuio de mi pena, alegría de mi coraçón!   ¿Qué lengua será bastante para te dar yguales gracias a la sobrada e incomparable merced que

119

en este punto, de tanta congoxa para mí, me has quesido hazer
en querer que vn tan flaco e indigno hombre pueda gozar de tu
suauíssimo amor? Del qual, avnque muy desseoso, siempre me
juzgaua indigno, mirando tu grandeza, considerando tu estado,
remirando tu perfeción, contemplando tu gentileza, acatando mi
poco merescer e tu alto merescimiento, tus estremadas gracias,
tus loadas e manifiestas virtudes. Pues, ¡o alto Dios!, ¿cómo te
podré ser ingrato, que tan milagrosamente has obrado comigo
tus singulares marauillas? ¡O quántos días antes de agora
passados me fue venido este pensamiento a mi coraçón, e por
impossible le rechaçaua de mi memoria, hasta que ya los rayos
ylustrantes de tu muy claro gesto dieron luz en mis ojos, encen-
dieron mi coraçón, despertaron mi lengua, estendieron mi mere-
cer, acortaron mi couardía, destorcieron mi encogimiento, dobla-
ron mis fuerças, desadormescieron mis pies e manos, finalmente,
me dieron tal osadía, que me han traydo con su mucho poder a
este sublimado estado en que agora me veo, oyendo de grado tu
suaue voz.

(II, 85)

Yet in spite of his avowals of humility and concern for Melibea's reputation,
it is only of himself that he thinks the next morning when Sosia brings
him the news of the ignoble end of Pármeno and Sempronio, both beheaded
in a public square. Not a single thought of Melibea's honor passes through
his mind. Nor does he express any real concern at the deaths of those
three who have been closest to him as he sought to win the love of Melibea.
Rather, his reaction is one of self-interest and that alone. Sosia, attempting
to comfort his master, tells him that because they were already so injured
by their jump from a high window, Pármeno and Sempronio probably
felt no pain. Calisto replies, with typical self-concern and self-pity:

Pues yo bien siento mi honrra. Pluguiera a Dios que fuera yo
ellos e perdiera la vida e no la honrra, e no la esperança de conseguir mi començado propósito, que es lo que más en este caso
desastrado siento. ¡O mi triste nombre e fama, cómo andas al
tablero de boca en boca! ¡O mis secretos más secretos, quán
públicos andarés por las plaças e mercados! ¿Qué será de mí?
¿Adonde yré?

(II, 110-111)

Not only is his reaction egotistical and cowardly. It is also a startling
echo of four centuries of medieval ladies distressed at the thought of
losing their good names. It also suggests that he consciously realizes
he has inextricably entangled his own fate with that of his servants.

The scene is extremely important in the work as a whole. For Calisto, as Bataillon points out, it is a singularly low point of his honor,[80] an extreme manifestation of his self-concern, and a complete revelation of the superficiality of his courtly countenance. The mask has slipped away completely, and we see Calisto naked and cowardly, openly plotting his self-preservation without the slightest apparent concern for that lady to whom, only the evening before, he had avowed her reputation to be more important to him than his own life. Now he speaks only of «*mi* honrra». The comic structure is beginning to give way to naked irony; the concatenation of deaths has already begun. For Calisto, it represents the beginning of the end. Already, before his *gloria* is attained, his fall has begun, as he himself suggests:

> ¡O mi gozo, cómo te vas diminiendo! Prouerbio es antigo, que de muy alto grandes caydas se dan. Mucho hauía anoche alcan-çado; mucho tengo oy perdido... ¡O fortuna, quánto e por quántas partes me has combatido!
>
> (II, 111-12)

The gap between Calisto's words and his actions has, in this scene, diminished. He has placed himself on the level of his own cowardly servants who, on the previous evening, had revealed their cowardice, their greed and their malice. Not unlike them, Calisto expresses here his own sort of cowardice, lust, and ill-feeling.

The author keeps the reader constantly aware of Calisto's failure as a courtly lover by continually permitting non-courtly elements to enter, figuratively at least, into the garden of love. As we have already seen, the figures painted on the outside walls of the Jardin d'Amour are those who are never allowed to enter, yet these same characters, portrayed in the *Celestina* by the various servants, are woven into the garden scenes along with their aristocratic counterparts to produce a tapestry of carnal love. While Lucrecia is the only servant who physically enters Pleberio's garden, the presence of the others is felt in many ways. We have already seen those verbal echoes («O señora mía, esperança de mi gloria...») that call to mind Celestina. Scenes played out by the servants and reenacted by Calisto and Melibea, also previously discussed, suggest equally well the symbolic presence of the servants. Perhaps the most significant intrusions are those caused by the juxtaposition of scenes within the garden where

---

[80] *La Célestine*, pp. 118ff.

Calisto is wooing Melibea in his most bombastic manner, with the scene outside the garden wall, where the servants listen and comment on the action.   In the first such instance Calisto has not yet been wholly admitted into the garden itself, and he and Melibea are engaged in a conversation through the closed gates.   There is a contrapuntal structure in the proximity of the two scenes, moving between Calisto's bravado in claiming he would gladly tear down the gates to reach his lady, and the servants' terror that he might, indeed, do such a thing in his madness.   Melibea, as we have already noted, pleads for secrecy.   The servants discuss the possibility of flight at the very moment that Calisto is boasting of their boldness. This hodgepodge of bravado and cowardice and the irony of both Calisto's words and his actions turn what should be a tender love scene into high comedy.   Nor do the comic intrusions end with the execution of Pármeno and Sempronio.   On the night Calisto possesses Melibea for the first time, as the moment of fulfillment approaches, Melibea, eager, as we have seen, to be rid of onlookers, orders Lucrecia to leave.   The scene shifts suddenly to Sosia and Tristán who listen outside the walls.   Whether Melibea wishes it or not, Calisto has arranged, however inadvertently, to have witnesses to his *gloria*.   When the action moves to the garden, Melibea is lamenting the loss of her maidenhood.   But the «noble sorrow» of her speech is undercut by Sosia's ironic comment that reduces Melibea's complaint to a commonplace:

> ¡Ante quisiera yo oyrte esos miraglos!   Todas sabés essa oración después que no puede dexar de ser hecho.   ¡E el bouo de Calisto, que se lo escucha!
>
> (II, 119)

In the final scene in the garden, while Sosia and Tristan are outside fending off the pseudo-assassins, the crippled Traso and his two friends, Lucrecia is inside envying the lovers and commenting on Melibea's coyness:

> Mala landre me mate si más los escucho.   ¿Vida es esta? ¡Que me esté yo deshaziendo de dentera y ella esquiuándose porque la rueguen!
>
> (II, 181)

The reader is never permitted to be caught up in the love story; he is forced by these constant intrusions to keep his distance, for he is continually aware of the ridiculousness of the situation, the inherent foolishness of Calisto who has pretensions to. being a courtly lover but who is continually being unmasked both by his servants and himself. The reader is, at this point, still only slightly prepared by the earlier deaths for the sudden demonic twist of the story, its final irony whereby one of the comic intrusions viciously propels Calisto to his death. That intrusion is, of course, the «attack» by the crippled Traso (and the reader must bear in mind that in medieval literature cripples were sometimes comic figures) and his friends, hired by Centurio, who had been hired, in turn, by Areusa, to avenge the deaths of Pármeno and Sempronio. The very complexity of the situation directs the reader's expectations toward a comic conclusion, but his anticipations are deceived and the story ends, if not in real tragedy, at least in bitter irony.

The final leveling factor, directed toward reducing Calisto's role as lover to the level of that of his servants, is Celestina herself. Throughout the book she acts as a sort of high priestess for a false religion of inverted values. She deceives not only Calisto and Melibea, but also Pármeno and Sempronio. At the same time they are belittling Calisto's foolishness, they are indulging in their own, as Sempronio himself finally admits when Pármeno comes to him with news of his love for Areusa:

> ¿Ya todos amamos? El mundo se va a perder. Calisto a Melibea, yo a Elicia, tú de embidia has buscado con quien perder esse poco de seso que tienes.
>
> (II, 10)

And Pármeno replies with a proverb that indicates that he, too, places himself with the others, within Celestina's power:

> ¿Luego locura es amar e yo soy loco e sin seso? Pues si la locura fuesse dolores, en cada casa auría bozes.
>
> (II, 10)

Sempronio warns Calisto away from love and women, yet Celestina maintains control of him largely through his own desire for Elicia. Pármeno warns Calisto not to trust Celestina, yet he, too, falls prey to her wiles and for precisely the same reason as Calisto. But Celestina does not stop at merely controlling the individual characters who populate the world of the work. She goes much further by putting them to work to control and corrupt others. Certainly the role that Sempronio and Pármeno play in Calisto's and Melibea's downfall is clear enough. What is perhaps not so clear is the fact that Calisto, too, is unwittingly involved

123

in Celestina's diabolical game of corrupting the innocent on at least three occasions. The most obvious of these is, of course, the seduction of Melibea. Almost as clear is the involvement of Calisto in the corruption of Pármeno. Celestina attempts, in her own way, promising a false paradise of love, to bring the young servant to her side. Her approaches to him recall the flattery of Sir Renard to Chantecleer in Chaucer's *Nun's Priest's Tale*.[81] She tells him of her closeness to his mother; she flatters him. But his corruption is ultimately brought about by her promise that Areusa will be his. For all of Celestina's life, sex has been her chief weapon, and now that she can no longer promise herself, use her own body to corrupt, she promises those firmer, younger bodies of her protégées. Calisto's role in the corruption of Pármeno is more subtle. At the beginning of the play Pármeno is faithful and clear-sighted. He sincerely tries to dissuade Calisto from his project:

> Señor, flaca es la fidelidad, que temor de pena la conuierte en lisonja, mayormente con señor, a quien dolor o afición priua e tiene ageno de su natural juyzio. Quitarse ha el velo de la ceguedad, passarán estos momentáneos fuegos: conoscerás mis agras palabras ser mejores para matar este fuerte cáncre, que las blandas de Sempronio, que lo ceuan, atizan, tu fuego, abiuan tu amor, encienden tu llama, añaden astillas, que tenga que gastar fasta ponerte en la sepultura.
>
> (I, 123)

His clearsightedness is prophetic. It extends beyond Calisto to the general result of being in Celestina's debt. He knows clearly the consequences: «...a quien dizes el secreto, das tu libertad» (I, 120). And yet, he, too, is overcome by the same temptation of lust as Calisto. He, too, is finally willing to give his soul to Celestina. Not, however, without some help from Calisto, who accuses Pármeno of being disloyal, of not understanding the finer points of love, who belittles him and alienates him as no gentle knight would ever do. And it is Calisto's treatment that finally causes Pármeno to break. He succumbs with a bitter outcry:

> ¡O desdichado de mí! Por ser leal padezco mal. Otros se ganan por malos; yo me pierdo por bueno. ¡El mundo es tal! Quiero yrme al hilo de la gente, pues a los traydores llaman discretos, a los fieles nescios. Si creyera a Celestina con sus seys dozenas de años acuestas, no me maltratara Calisto. Mas esto me porná

---

[81] *The Canterbury Tales*, 3295-3321.

escarmiento d'aquí adelante con él. Que si dixiere comamos, yo
también; si quisiere derrocar la casa, aprouarlo; si quemar su
hazienda, yr por fuego. ¡Destruya, rompa, quiebre, dañe, dé a
alcahuetas lo suyo, que mi parte me cabrá, pues dizen: a río
buelto ganancia de pescadores. ¡Nunca más perro a molino!
(I, 125-26)

The final dual effort at corruption between Calisto and Celestina
involves Lucrecia, the servant-companion of Melibea. She is bribed by
Celestina who will give her rinse to brighten her hair and a potion to
sweeten her breath, but more than that, who permits her to observe, as
Bataillon has pointed out, the «joys» of those in love. It is, in reality,
Areusa who taunts Lucrecia with the attractions of the life of a prostitute.
With a message from her mistress Lucrecia enters Celestina's house, and
upon learning of her arrival, Areusa begins a harangue against the slavery
of domestics, against servants of ladies. Bataillon describes the effect of
Areusa's discourse upon its victim:

> Si nous pouvions douter de l'effet cherché, l'impression pro-
> duite sur Lucrèce par l'accueil et les révélations que lui ménage
> savamment cette demeure devrait suffire à nous édifier. Écoutons
> l'aveu qu'en fait la servante. Le paradis évoqué par Célestine
> lui faisait oublier le message dont elle est porteuse. [82]

Celestina reinforces the impact of Areusa's words by reminiscing about
her happy life, the honor paid to her by gentlemen of all ranks, the money
she has received, the wines she has drunk. Lucrecia's reply reveals the
extent of her attraction to this world:

> Por cierto, ya se me hauía oluidado mi principal demanda e
> mensaje con la memoria de esse tan alegre tiempo como has con-
> tado e assí, me estuuiera vn año sin comer, escuchándote e pen-
> sando en aquella vida buena, que aquellas moças gozarían, que
> me parece e semeja que estó yo agora en ella.
> (II, 49)

One clearly sees an unspoken banding together of Celestina and her young
followers in an attempt to corrupt Lucrecia.

Calisto's role in the matter is principally one of example. His thoughts
are not of Lucrecia but of himself as he suggests that she remain in the

---

[82] *La Célestine*, p. 159.

garden to observe his possession of Melibea. But the suggestions of Areusa and Celestina coupled with what Sra. Lida de Malkiel has called his «curioso exhibicionismo» have had a profound effect on Lucrecia. We even see her pawing over Calisto until Melibea stops her:

> Lucrecia, ¿qué sientes, amiga? ¿Tórnaste loca de plazer? Déxamele, no me le despedaces, no me le trabajes sus miembros con tus pesados abraços. Déxame gozar lo que es mío, no me ocupes mi plazer.
>
> (II, 180)

It is, perhaps, an indication of just how far Melibea herself has fallen when she deigns to quarrel with her own servant over a lover. Lucrecia's corruption follows the same essential pattern as Pármeno's — from clearsighted fidelity to envious onlooking, until finally, both seek to be active participants in the game of love. The extent of Lucrecia's desires is suggested in her frustrated words berating Sosia and Tristán for their lack of initiative in attempting to seduce her, words spoken while she waits in the garden, listening to the sounds of Calisto and Melibea's lovemaking:

> ¡Que me esté yo deshaziendo de dentera y ella esquiuándose porque la rueguen! Ya, ya apaziguado es el ruydo: no ouieron menester despartidores. Pero también me lo haría yo, si estos necios de sus criados me fablassen entre día; pero esperan que los tengo de yr a buscar.
>
> (II, 181-82)

Calisto's part in the corruption of these three young people—all virtuous at the outset—places him morally on the level of the servants and prostitutes. He has, like Sempronio, allied himself with the forces of evil, with Celestina, that high-priestess of *cupiditas*. He is not a true courtly lover, despite his protestations of ennoblement and concern for honor, despite his claims of servitude to his lady and his verbal obedience to the rules of love. Aguirre has taken these statements at face value, without considering fully the actions and implications that encompass them. It is true that Calisto apes the courtly lover, that he is garbed in his clothes and affects his manners. But his elegant exterior is but a useful deceit covering over his carnal desires, and, thereby, rendering them more acceptable.

Earlier in this chapter the question was posed: What end does the parody of the courtly lover, if that is, indeed, what we are dealing with, serve within the work? The answer should, by now, be clear. The parody is a functional element, and a very successful one, of the overall didactic framework. The author is proving carnal love, *cupiditas*, sex for itself alone, frivolous and insubstantial as a source of happiness. And in so doing, he has dealt with the problem on several levels and in several disguises. Aguirre has asserted that Rojas distinguishes between the higher, more noble *amor cortés* of Calisto and the sex-for-the-sake-of-sex *amor impuro* of the servants. He further asserts that Rojas' work is «específicamente escrita contra las doctrinas del amor cortés».[83] There seems to me a curious contradiction in these two assertions. If one accepts, as does Aguirre, Denomy's definition of courtly love with its ennoblement of the lover and if one sees Calisto as an attempt to portray a truly ennobled courtly lover, then the didactic element of the work is weakened, and Calisto's fate seems somewhat arbitrary. If, on the other hand, Rojas considers, as I believe he does, *amor cortés*, as he portrays it in terms of Calisto, merely a useful disguise for *amor impuro*, if, in fact, he is attempting to unmask the «courtly» lover by showing him to be but a lustful man, no better than a Sempronio courting an Elicia, then the didactic element is strengthened. Lust masked by the refinements of courtly love deserves the same fate as any other form of *cupiditas*. And it is, thus, that Calisto is punished, in essentially the same way as Sempronio, Pármeno, and Celestina.

The reader is never permitted to take Calisto seriously as a lover nor to feel sympathy for him. Only if the reader maintains an objective viewpoint well outside the character can he judge him as Calisto is apparently intended to be judged. And Rojas, with his repeated interruptions of the love scenes, the continual mockery of Calisto's poetry and love sickness on the part of his servants, never permits the reader to identify with the protagonist. The double plot mentioned above is also a guarantee against reader identification. The objective viewpoint, as well as many of Rojas' literary techniques and the essential structure of the work, are fundamentally comedic as its author apparently recognized in calling it originally *La comedia de Calisto y Melibea*. Yet the story ends unhappily. How, then, is one to deal generically with the work? As the form of the *Celestina* troubles the modern reader, who has no neat category in which to place it, so it seems to have troubled its contemporary readers. In the 21-act version, the author announces:

> Otros han litigado sobre el nombre, diziendo que no se auia de llamar comedia, pues acabaua en tristeza, sino que se llamasse

[83]   *Calisto y Melibea*, p. 83.

tragedia. El primer auctor quiso darle denominación del principio, que fue plazer, e llamóla comedia. Yo viendo estas discordias, entre estos extremos partí agora por medio la porfía, e llaméla tragicomedia.

(Prólogo, 25)

This term —tragicomedy— is, at least in the twentieth century, both apt and awkward. It neatly implies an inclusion of both tragic and comic elements, but these elements are virtually undefined. In view of certain other dramatic works that are labeled tragicomedies, the term seems to be a catchall for any play with tragic and comic elements. How different, for example, is *En attendant Godot* from the *Celestina*! In Beckett's play we find an essentially pathetic situation which, in its unfolding, employs a few Bergsonian comic techniques for provoking laughter. But the play begins unhappily and ends in the same way, with precisely the same scene with which it opened. The *Celestina*, on the other hand, has, as was mentioned above, a fundamentally comedic structure.[84] And Calisto functions primarily as a comic figure. Usually, however, at the end of comedy, even one in an ironic mode as is the *Celestina*, the hero is permitted to arrive at that «kind of self-knowledge which releases a character from the bondage of his humor».[85] But for Calisto there is neither release nor self-knowledge. Rather, his bondage to desire increases his self-deception, leading ultimately to his death. Thus, while the term «tragicomedy» [86] may have a certain potential value, its lack of definition makes it somewhat ineffective in categorizing the *Celestina*.

Edwin Morby agrees with Bataillon, albeit with some reservations, that the *Celestina* may be called a morality,[87] but this seems to me a particularly unsuitable term. Moralities are defined by David Bevington as «those plays, exemplified by *Everyman*, which aimed at moral edification through the medium of allegory».[88] The *Celestina* does, indeed, aim at moral edification, but this didactic element, which is in large part responsible for the entire problem because it requires the unhappy ending, is by no means unique to the moralities. Virtually every medieval genre was used, in

---

[84] See Northrop Frye, *A Natural Perspective: The Development of Shakespearean Comedy and Romance* (New York, 1965), pp. 72ff. See also *Anatomy*, pp. 163ff.

[85] Frye, *A Natural Perspective*, p. 79.

[86] For a discussion of tragicomedy, see Marvin T. Herrick, *Tragicomedy: Its Origin and Development in Italy, France, and England*. ISLL, 39 (Urbana, Ill., 1955).

[87] Edwin Morby, The *Celestina* as a Morality Play», *RP*, 16 (1963), 323-31.

[88] David Bevington, *From «Mankind» to Marlowe* (Cambridge, Mass., 1962), pp. 8-9.

some sense, as a didactic vehicle. The predominant characteristic of a morality play is, then, not its didacticism, but its allegory, which is conspicuously absent in the *Celestina*. The unmodified terms of «tragedy» and «comedy» are no better. Sra. Lida de Malkiel claims that the *Celestina* belongs historically to the genre known as humanistic comedy,[89] while Stephen Gilman has called it «ageneric».[90] One might better borrow a term which Frye uses in a rather pejorative manner but which may also suggest a play like our *Tragicomedia*, that is, moral comedy or didactic comedy.[91] Whatever term one chooses, one must account for at least two aspects of the book—its essential comedic structure and its unhappy, heavily didactic, ending.

Fernando de Rojas seems to have hit upon an excellent vehicle in choosing the novel-in-dialogue form for the *Celestina*. In such a form, the characters are allowed to reveal themselves with a verve that would have been almost impossible with editorial intervention on the part of the author. Even the *argumentos* seem not only to be unnecessary, but actually to weaken the structure. Given such a dialogue form, the choice of an essentially comedic tone would seem to be inevitable. Tragedy allows the audience (or in this case, the reader or listener) to get too close to the characters. When one sees *Oedipus Rex* or *Hamlet*, one participates in the tragic experience by becoming emotionally involved with the protagonist, an involvement which Aristotle has described as one of Pity and Fear. In comedy, however, as Bergson has indicated, one is not involved emotionally but intellectually. As Georges Poulet has stated it:

> Loin d'entrer dans son [the character's] être, il s'agit d'«entrer dans son ridicule». Et entrer dans le ridicule, c'est précisément le contraire d'entrer dans l'être, c'est s'écarter de lui: c'est poser l'être comme un objet qu'on voit, et non comme un être qu'on sent; c'est poser un objet, au lieu d'*être* un sujet. [92]

Even on a second reading of the *Celestina*, when one knows that Calisto is to die, one can laugh at him. The laughter is perhaps somewhat different, somewhat more ironic, for the reader has become aware of the almost sinister foreshadowings that were not evident at first, «the ironic incompatibility between the meaning which the characters give to the action and

---

[89] See *Two Spanish Masterpieces*, pp. 56-57; see also *La originalidad*, pp. 37-50.
[90] *The Art of La Celestina*, p. 194.
[91] *Anatomy*, p. 167.
[92] Georges Poulet, *Études sur le temps humain*, EUPLL, 1 (Edinburgh, 1949), p. 116.

the meaning it holds for the authors and readers».[93]   Although the unhappy
ending is an important didactic element in the story, the choice of the
comedic structure reinforces the ending, for comedy is inherently didactic.
One laughs, according to Bergson, at that which is foolish or obsessive;
since man does not like to be the source of such laughter in others, he
will make an effort to avoid such behavior in himself.   Frye claims that
comedy tends to appeal to the younger members of society, while the
older members tend to find something subversive about it, and that
«something» is inevitably didactic—an element directed toward reforming
the old society.   In the *Celestina*, however, there is not so much an appeal
to youth as a warning, one based on the moral standards of the existing
society.   This is the «jugement de convenance» [94] that the audience imposes
upon the character, a judgment which condemns the character's behavior
as absurd because he does not conform to an accepted standard.   Thus,
we seem to have two traditions functioning side by side in the *Celestina*,
one which would normally make an appeal to youth and one which would
warn them against yielding to that appeal—that is, the courtly love tradition
and the Christian moral tradition.

The ending can leave no doubt as to the moral implications of the
work.   The consistent greed of Celestina turns upon her in the form of
Sempronio and Pármeno, who have learned their lesson from her too well.
The two servants are, in turn, beheaded in the public square.   One can
easily see how these deaths grow out of the plot, how the death of each
one is somehow connected with his crime.   But there is some debate
about whether or not Calisto's death is an artistic slip on the part of the
author.   Sra. Lida de Malkiel insists that it is a poorly chosen end for
Calisto:

> ... ese azar, inconexo con la obra, no sólo es ajeno a su estructura
> dramática, sino que merma lamentablemente su resonancia moral,
> propia de toda tragedia.   Como tropezar y caer de una escalera
> puede sucederle al más virtuoso, nos hallamos con el viejo chiste
> del fumador empedernido a quien su vicio lleva a la muerte...
> en un accidente de tránsito.   En todas las épocas ha existido la
> vaga creencia de que la muerte accidental puede ser, en el fondo,
> castigo divino pero, porque la creencia ha sido siempre vaga y
> porque testimonia lo inescrutable de las vías de la Providencia
> y no su justicia, no es suficiente como motivación dramática. [95]

---

[93] Lida de Malkiel, *Two Spanish Masterpieces*, pp. 56-57.
[94] Poulet, p. 118.
[95] *Originalidad*, pp. 231-32.

Bataillon disagrees. He contends that «C'est une maxime banale qu'on est souvent puni par où l'on a péché. Quelle matérialisation plus claire et plus sobre de cette 'vérité' que l'échelle d'où Calisto fait une chute mortelle? N'est-ce pas Mélibée elle-même qui l'a qualifié de 'fou sauteur de murailles' la première fois que Célestine est venue lui parler du jeune homme qui avait un jour envahi son jardin à la recherche d'un faucon?» [96] He sees Calisto's death as a punishment for his sins, as a warning, not a martyrdom. Thus, in spite of the comic form of the work, the rather grim nature of the didactic element requires that the protagonist die. I would agree with Bataillon that the way in which each character dies seems singularly appropriate. It is, I believe, significant that four of the five deaths are a result, at least in part, of a fall. These deaths suggest the falling motion of the Wheel of Fortune. Boethius has described it in *De Consolatione Philosophiae:* «Rotam volubili orbe versamus, infima summis, summa infinis mutare guademus. Ascende, si placet, sed, es lege, ne uti, cum lucicri mei ratio poscet, descendere injuriam putes.» [97] Here we have an abstract idea encased in concrete terms. Just as Calisto rises to the top of the Wheel of Fortune, the Wheel turns and the fall occurs. Even more appropriate, perhaps, in view of the fact that Calisto uses a ladder to scale the wall of Melibea's garden, is the depiction of the Ladder of Virtue which appears in the twelfth-century *Hortus Deliciarum.* Each rung of the ladder which stretches from heaven to earth represents a virtue. Many people are making the ascent, while below them beckon the Vices, symbolized by such manifestations as a bed, a woman, gold, food, horses, and shields. (One will recognize among the symbols those vices which caused the four falls in the *Celestina.)* Those who cannot resist the temptation, though they know the right way is the way of virtue, fall backwards to the earth. It seems that the critic should be aware of this iconographic ladder in judging the appropriateness of the death of Calisto. [98] Like the deaths of Celestina, Pármeno, Sempronio, and Melibea, Calisto's is quite consistent with both his character and his crime.

Five deaths in quick succession hammer home the moral point of the

---

[96] *La Célestine*, pp. 130-31.
[97] Boethius, *De Consolatione Philosophiae*, ed. B. G. Teubner (Lipsiae, 1871), Book II, Presa II.
[98] See Barbera, «Medieval Iconography», pp. 11-13. He comments: «Whereas the ladder was supposed to have been used by man to reach God, we know that Calisto, who so persistently deifies Melibea beyond the mere courtly convention, reaches his deity via a ladder, only ironically to fall headlong to his death. Presumably, his ladder possessed rungs of the vices rather than the virtues» (p. 12).

story, concisely expressed in Romans 6:23: *Stipendia enim peccati, mors.*
The wages of sin is death. Salvation is open to the sinner until death,
which may perhaps explain why such delightful sinners as the Arcipreste
de Hita or the Wyf of Bath, for whom salvation is still possible, can be
treated as almost purely comic figures, while the antics of Celestina and
Calisto, which begin as comedy, are suddenly transformed into acts of
damnation. Celestina, Calisto, Pármeno, and Sempronio—all have
willfully placed themselves in positions where violent deaths may be expected,
and violent death may well mean death without the possibility of repentance.
It is important to note that both Celestina and Calisto cry out for confession,
but too late. And the jump from the window in an attempt to escape the
punishment for their crime has left Pármeno and Sempronio already
too near death to think of repentance. Only Melibea is left in a position
to seek salvation. But her thoughts are not of God, nor of any forgiveness
she might receive in the next world; they are of herself and Calisto, thoughts,
as A. D. Deyermond has described them, of «a place where she can rejoin
him, a pagan erotic heaven»,[99] not unlike, one might add, that heaven of
courtly love described in the *De Amore.* Although she is aware of the pain
she will cause her parents, whose only error is their trust in her, she willfully
heaps sin upon sin. She asks no forgiveness; she does not repent. Yet
in her final audacity of commending her soul to God, she escapes that
worst of all sins—despair. In some aspects, Melibea's sins are the greatest
of all. Calisto's death was accidental. Nor did any other character
willfully take his own life. But Melibea's suicide is a calculated gesture,
aimed at joining Calisto in his symbolic fall from grace.

That the work is morally didactic is abundantly clear. That it is written
within the Christian tradition we have the author's word:

> No trae sentencia, de donde no mana
> Loable a su auctor y eterna memoria,
> Al qual Jesucristo resciba en su gloria
> Por su passion santa que a todos nos sana.

> Amonesta a los que aman que siruan a Dios
> y dexen las malas cogitacion(e)s e vicios de amor.

> Uos, los que amays, tomad este enxemplo
> Este fino arnés con que os defendays:

---

[99] A. D. Deyermond, *The Petrarchan Sources of La Celestina* (Oxford, 1961),
p. 117, n. 1.

Bolued ya las riendas, porque no os perdays;
Load siempre a Dios visitando su templo.
Andad sobre auiso; no seays d'exemplo
De muertos e biuos y propios culpados:
Estando en el mundo yazeys sepultados.
Muy gran dolor siento quando esto contemplo.

(El autor, I, 13)

And the insistent echoes of Petrarch, particularly of Book I of the *De Remediis* of which the central theme is the insubstantial quality of all earthly happiness, tend to confirm Rojas' words.[100] In his depiction of Christian moralism, however, Rojas paints for us a dim picture. The emphasis is upon God's wrath with no glimmer of joy and forgiveness. It is in this respect that Rojas uses Book I of the *De Remediis* out of proportion to the rest of Petrarch's work. According to Deyermond, «He might, for example, have made Pleberio seek religious consolation in Act XXI. This would, after all, have been in accord with Petrarch's general plan in *De Remediis,* and the fact that Rojas did not follow this course is due to his individual outlook (reinforced by the lesser power and attractiveness of Book II), not to lack of Petrarchan precedent» (p. 109). Rojas' position is entirely understandable, of course. The end of the fifteenth century was marked by philosophical pessimism. His Jewish background may, perhaps, have led him to a more Old Testament Jehovah-judge interpretation of God. And his role as *converso* under the Inquisition could scarcely have given him reason to put much stock in the forgiveness of the Christian God. Deyermond has commented:

> He seems, from what we know of his later life, to have become at least a conforming and probably a devout Christian; certainly there is no reason to believe that he was ever a secret Judaizer; but it would hardly be surprising if such a reconciliation to Christianity, in a sensitive man cut off from the religion of his ancestors, were effected only at the cost of great suffering, and after a period in which neither the old religion nor the new had any success as a defence against profound pessimism. It would not be surprising if that suffering and pessimism left its mark on anything such a man wrote.
>
> (p. 119-20)

Indeed, it would have been surprising had it *not* left a mark.

---

[100] See Deyermond, *Petrarchan Sources,* pp. 109ff.

In short, the *Celestina* has come down to us as the deeply pessimistic work of a man who looks dimly upon the joys of this world, but who has not yet learned to trust completely in those of the next. It is no wonder that the novel-in-dialogue ends on the profoundly moving lament of Pleberio for his dead daughter. It is no wonder that he closes upon that agonizing question that man has posed for centuries when he finds himself faced with the uncertainty of this world and the stony silence of the next— *¿Por qué?* In a series of six questions that terminate his lament, this one question is wrenched out of context by force of its repetition and is left at the end reverberating in the reader's mind— *¿Por qué?* Pleberio, probably like his creator in this respect, has not yet found an answer.

CHAPTER V

CONCLUSION

The major purpose of this study, as it was stated at the outset, has been to determine whether the male protagonist in each of the three works considered is a serious or parodic treatment of the courtly lover. Overwhelming evidence indicates, as we have seen, that all three are parodies, though of different sorts. Curiously enough, it became necessary from time to time to justify the choice of the work by proving that the courtly love tradition was, indeed, operative within it. It was, perhaps, the *Celestina* that called for the most extensive justification. There is good reason for this. The other two works were more clearly written for a courtly audience, though their popular appeal is undeniable. The *Celestina*, on the other hand, is somewhat further removed from the courtly world. Written as the bourgeoisie began to recognize itself as a distinct social class, it is composed for and about people who may no longer be called truly courtly.[1] While Calisto is perhaps a young nobleman, he is more like a wealthy bourgeois, as is Melibea, whose father is a shipbuilder. Indeed, most courtly lovers beyond the thirteenth century function, to borrow a term from Northrop Frye, as «displacements»[2] of the ideal courtly lover of romance, who is, himself, one step removed from the archetypal or mythical. The hero of romance, Frye tells us, is, like the hero of epic, though perhaps to a somewhat lesser extent, «superior in *degree* to other men and to his environment». He «moves in a world in which the ordinary laws of nature are slightly suspended: prodigies of courage and endurance,

---

[1] See Maravall, *El mundo social*. P. E. Russell's review of Maravall's book in *BHS*, 43 (1966), 125-28, expresses some doubts about the bourgeois elements of the work. In any case, there is a displacement from the purely courtly milieu. I would agree with A. D. Deyermond that «Calisto and Melibea are courtly (or semi-courtly) lovers in a non-courtly situation». See his review of J. M. Aguirre's *Calisto y Melibea, amantes cortesanos*, in *BHS*, 41 (1964), 68.

[2] *Anatomy*, p. 136ff.

unnatural to us, are natural to him, and enchanted weapons, talking animals, terrifying ogres and witches, and talismans of miraculous power violate no rule of probability once the postulates of romance have been established» (p. 33). While the courtly lover of romance may share this role with the epic hero, he goes beyond him in that he has a new emotional dimension which permits us to identify more closely with him and which, thus, propels him rapidly away from romance to works in a lower key, toward what Frye calls the high mimetic mode, and even beyond, to the low mimetic, and ultimately, and inevitably, to the ironic.

In a sense, the three works we have dealt with suggest this gradual displacement. In the *Aucassin*, we still have some evidence of the world of romance, nowhere more evident, perhaps, than in the imaginative land of Torelore. But there are indications that movement away from the fantastic to the ordinary is beginning to take place. The traditional ogre is but an ugly herdsman. Aucassin kills only ten knights and wounds only seven—all ordinary men—in his escape from the forces of Count Bougar, a modest feat when it is compared to the prodigious deeds of more traditional and more mythical heroes. The entrance to the «otherworld» of Torelore is by ship, rather than by some conventionally perilous route.

Still less remains in the *Troilus* of the world of romance. Nothing truly extraordinary occurs, and those elements in the story that would have lent themselves nicely to romance (i. e., Cassandra's gift of prophecy, the marvellous deeds of the Greek and Trojan warriors) tend to be played down by Chaucer. Troilus himself is far removed from the hero of romance. He shares some characteristics with the hero of the high mimetic mode who, says Frye, «has authority, passions, and powers of expression far greater than ours, but what he does is subject both to social criticism and to the order of nature» (p. 34). The description would be more apt if Troilus were depicted in a totally serious manner. However, as a parody, he has much in common with the hero of the low mimetic mode, who, Frye tells us, is the hero of «most comedy and of realistic fiction» (p. 34). Chaucer undermines Troilus'«superior» powers of expression by striking him dumb from time to time and by enlisting Pandarus' aid in Troilus' behalf. His authority is weakened by his ineffective role within the parliament. In short, he is essentially a high mimetic hero with tendencies toward the low mimetic mode.

Calisto is displaced one step further, in that he bridges the low mimetic and the ironic. Calisto is still more like us, his world more marked by realism. Yet, at the same time, the reader has the sense of looking down on him as he acts out his scenes of frustration and absurdity. And the reader is aware, while Calisto, perhaps, is not, that his destiny is worked out, to a great extent, by forces beyond his control, that he is, like the ironic hero, a man in bondage.

Thus, while externally all three heroes preserve vestiges of the ideal courtly lover, they are moving away from that ideal. They live in a different world. And in their roles as courtly lovers they are inevitably incongruous figures within their more pragmatic worlds. They have two alternatives: either they remain misfits and function ineffectively or they adapt themselves and sacrifice the courtly ideal. Interestingly enough, it is this new element of realism which brings the three works into focus as variations on Frye's definition of comedy. He has pointed out that the action of comedy «tends to become probable rather than fantastic, and it moves toward realism and away from myth and romance».[3] We have noted at several points that the traditional courtly world tends to be a fantasy world, populated by giants, dwarfs, and *fée* figures, and in which the action centers around otherworldly adventures, magic rings, perilous beds, sword bridges, and so forth. The parodies that we have examined tend to take the lover out of this fantasy world and place him, rather, in the middle of a world of practical considerations, where the other characters involved tend to be realistic in their approaches to life. There is, clearly, a link between Count Garin, Pandarus, and Celestina and her *entourage*. They approach life pragmatically, not idealistically. They know what they want and they set out to gain it by the most expedient means possible. Honor is no real consideration, though they may speak of it on occasions. And like them, to some extent, the ladies to whom our lovers direct their attentions are somewhat uncourtly and, with the possible exception of Melibea, practical in their attitudes toward life and love.

That the three works under consideration do follow an essentially comedic structure, the basic structure of classical New Comedy which Frye has described on various occasions, should by now be quite clear. Obviously *Aucassin et Nicolette* follows the form most closely. Frye might almost have been describing the *chantefable* as he outlined in «The Argument of Comedy» the Menandrine tradition from which most comedy as we know it has derived:

> Its main theme is the successful effort of a young man to outwit
> an opponent and possess the girl of his choice. The opponent

---

[3] Northrop Frye, «The Argument of Comedy», in *English Institute Essays, 1948* (New York, 1949), p. 60.

137

is usually the father (senex)... The girl is usually a slave or court-esan, and the plot turns on a *cognitio* or discovery of birth which makes her marriageable.

(p. 450)

This is essentially the story of Aucassin, whose father forbids his marriage to the slave girl Nicolette, who turns out to be, quite predictably, daughter of the King of Carthage. She is, therefore, not only marriageable, but extremely desirable since her social rank is superior to that of Aucassin, the son of a mere count.

Formally, the *Troilus* and the *Celestina* are variations of this type of comedy. Frye points out that «tragedy is really implicit or uncompleted comedy» while «comedy continues a potential tragedy within itself».[4] In the case of both Chaucer's and Rojas' works the formal movement goes beyond its comic conclusion so that the «potential tragedy» is fulfilled. The rising motion of comedy becomes the falling motion of tragedy. The *Troilus*, however, is ultimately denied its tragic potential by the rising motion as Troilus' spirit ascends to the eighth sphere. And Calisto lacks the dignity of the true tragic hero. But within both works the structural movement of comedy is apparent. It may best be described through the following diagrams where the comedic structure is represented by the broken arrow:

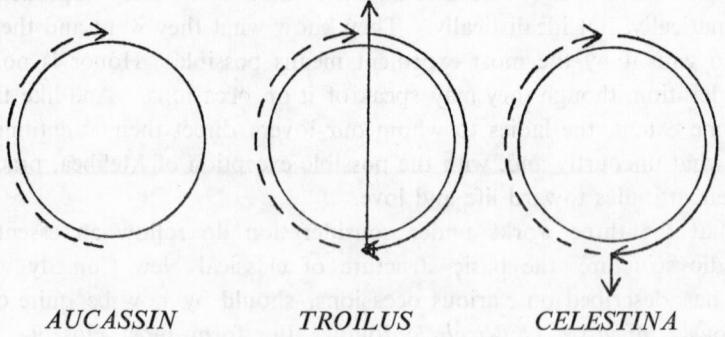

AUCASSIN   TROILUS   CELESTINA

The structural simplicity of the *Aucassin* is evident within the more complex designs of the *Troilus* and the *Celestina*. The rising motion at the end of the *Troilus* propels the hero out of the sphere of Fortune into the realm of Providence. With Calisto the movement is reversed. His fall is a total one. There is no «eighthe spere» for him, only damnation.

---

[4] *Ibid.*, p. 455.

138

It is interesting to note that in the latter two cases, it is not the father who is the opposing factor to the marriages. In the *Troilus* it is a social concern not unlike that of the opposing father; it is presumably Troilus' position as prince of the realm while Criseyde is the daughter of a traitor. With Calisto, as we have seen, there is no apparent reason for his not marrying Melibea at the beginning, aside from the fact that he envisages himself romantically as a lover, not a husband. As Denis de Rougemont has pointed out in connection with the *Tristan*, where no obstruction exists, it is created by the lovers themselves.[5] Interestingly enough, he interprets this self-imposed obstruction as a death-wish —one that is well fulfilled for Calisto and Melibea.

The three works clearly have a common base in the courtly love tradition and in their fundamentally comic form. And all three are in some sense parodies. There the similarity ends. The parodies function in different ways and for different purposes. As part of our definition of parody we concluded that it must reveal the potential weaknesses of the original. It is significant, in pointing out just how the parodies work, to review precisely what weaknesses each of the parodies underlines. Aucassin's behavior points up quite clearly the tendency of courtly love to emasculate the male, thereby permitting the female to assert herself as, if I may coin a term, the «lordly lady». (Indeed, it was a painful mistake that has plagued the masculine world ever since!) The author's method is quite simple. He utilizes the tendency, exaggerates it by permitting Nicolette to accomplish feats that Aucassin has been unable to achieve, by making her the active force in the relationship, by describing Aucassin in traditionally feminine epithets, the result of which suggests a total inversion of the male-female roles in society. He tops it all off with the Torelore episode where the king, having totally assumed the role of the female, goes one step further, and becomes a mother.

In the *Troilus* Chaucer underscores the foolishness of the stylized behavior of the courtly lover by exaggerating certain features, most notably the love sickness, which causes Troilus to hop in and out of bed far more often than does the fulfillment of his heart's desire, and by revealing the rule-bound hero to be virtually incapable of action. Again contrast is used to show up the hero in his most foolish light. Criseyde is lively and practical, at times impatient with the languishing Troilus. In the *Aucassin* it is Nicolette who, assuming the active role, prevents the *chantefable* from

---

[5] Denis de Rougemont, *Passion and Society*, trans. Montgomery Belgion, revised edition (London, 1962), pp. 42-46.

becoming a tragedy fulfilled. She manages to return to her lover and, thereby, become his bride. Criseyde is cast in a similarly active role. Troilus' inactivity forces her to promise to return. But Criseyde, being weaker of character than her counterpart Nicolette, does not keep her promise. She is realistic, and just as she has yielded to Troilus partly out of practicality, so she yields to Diomede. Along with Criseyde is another contrasting figure, the ever-active Pandarus. It is he who is truly the foil for Troilus, and it is in scenes played between Troilus and Pandarus that the weaknesses of the former become most apparent.

But it is Fernando de Rojas who deals the most cruel blow to the courtly convention by revealing its potential for concealing common lust. He shows the rules, the rhetoric, all its «niceness», would-be sublimation, and elegance to be for Calisto but an empty form, a meaningless euphemism for base desires. Rojas' technique is a fairly complex one. He permits Calisto to reveal himself slowly as he shifts from the courtly tone to low speech, as he moves easily, from his garden of romance into the world inhabited by Celestinas and Sempronios.

All three works have didactic messages in these critical barbs which are driven home with varying degrees of seriousness and humor. I offered at the end of Chapter II the possibility that humor and didacticism exist in inverse proportions within a parody. This is not to say that parody may be all humor or all didacticism. It must, by definition, include both elements. But the humor may be of many sorts, from the hilarity of the adventures of the inept Aucassin to the satiric irony resulting from the activities of Calisto. And the didactic element may range from an amused «tsk tsk» to bitter denunciation. The tone of the parody is, to a great extent, controlled by the various philosophical bases from which the characters operate. The *Aucassin*, for example, tends to be what might be called *humorous parody*. The author has no philosophical bones to pick. He is neither arguing in favor of nor attacking any philosophy. There is a single moment that could, perhaps, be interpreted as a confrontation with Christianity— that is, Aucassin's comments on Heaven, which he condemns as a rather dull place, preferring, himself, to go to Hell where all the really interesting people will be. But the comment cannot be taken seriously, except as a farcical suggestion of the basic conflict between courtly love and Christianity. In short, the *Aucassin* is the least overtly philosophical of the three works. It is a light, amusing fantasy, aimed at poking fun at the overworked hero of courtly romance. Its didactic element is of a negative sort. There is a barb of literary criticism in that we have no desire to emulate the rather ridiculous hero; on the other hand, there is no counter ideal to which the reader can turn. The society in which Aucassin finds himself is, if anything, less admirable than he. And Nicolette, while she may appear acceptable to the modern reader as a spirited and self-sufficient young woman, is hardly the ideal medieval heroine. Yet despite the author's casting Aucassin in the role of buffoon, he ultimately permits him to defeat his father and come to terms with society. And by permitting him to succeed without changing, without becoming less of a fool, the author softens the impact of the didactic element of his work. A happy ending, while it does not make Aucassin less ludicrous in any significant way, does give sanction to his foolishness and to the new society which will grow up around him. In short, at the risk of incurring the wrath of those who condemn the intentional fallacy in critical studies, I would suggest that the intention of the parodist-author of the *Aucassin* was primarily to amuse, to have a rollicking good time at the expense of a conventional character whom he considered too absurd to be taken seriously. While there *is* inherent criticism of the conventional hero (and of those who take him seriously), it is of only secondary importance. That this «trifle», as Grace Frank has spoken of it, has survived is a tribute to both the good taste and good humor of medieval man who could accept the amusing mockery of an Aucassin alongside the more serious treatments of a Lancelot or a Tristan.

The tone of the parody in the *Troilus* is quite different. It is, in essence, *sympathetic parody*.[6] Its mockery is amusing but gentle. There is a touch of wistfulness in Chaucer's portrayal of Troilus, as though the mature poet were smiling at the foolishness of the sort of young man he used to be. But beneath the gentle humor of the *Troilus* lies a serious foundation in the teachings of Boethius, in particular his doctrines of Fortune and Providence. The philosophical position determines the rise and fall of our young hero. The movement of the Wheel of Fortune is shown in its entirety. Troilus rises to the top and is cast down again. His foolishness is punished within this world for fixing his eyes on Fortune and not on Providence. And the moral lesson is brought into focus by the author himself who issues a warning to all the «yonge, fresshe folkes» to turn their eyes to God where enduring happiness lies rather than to this world «that passeth soone as floures faire». A fundamentally Christian poet, Chaucer is not satisfied with merely condemning Troilus' actions. His concern is, rather, with salvation. Troilus, while he is a foolish young man, is not

---

[6] The similar term «sympathetic irony» has been used before in connection with the *Troilus*. See H. R. Patch, *On Rereading Chaucer* (Cambridge, Mass., 1939), p. 67.

fundamentally evil. And in the Christian doctrine of grace Chaucer finds a framework whereby he may lift his hero up again and permit him a final amused look at the pitfalls of fortune.

Calisto, on the other hand, is treated unsympathetically. There is a dual philosophy at work here—Rojas' innate pessimism coupled with his Petrarchan point of view. There is no grace for Calisto, and we see his death as final, a symbolic fall from grace. The *Celestina* comes closest of the three works to presenting us with what may be called *didactic parody*. There is humor in the work, but much of what appears to be, on first reading, quite amusing, becomes, when one has learned the final outcome, bleak and terrifying irony. The admonition to lovers is unmistakable, almost apocalyptic. And the world Rojas presents to us is demonic. He is heavyhanded as he hammers home his point that to sin is to be damned. And as though the didactic point had not been made quite clear within the action of the play, it is stated quite explicitly at the beginning:

SIGUESE

La comedia o *tragicomedia* de Calisto y Melibea, compuesta en reprehensión de los locos enamorados, que, vencidos en su desordenado apetito, a sus amigas llaman e dizen ser su Dios. Assí mesmo fecha en auiso de los engaños de las alcahuetas e malos e lisonjeros siruientes.

(I, 27)

The most humorous of the works is, therefore, the least didactic; and inversely, the most didactic, the least humorous. The author of the *Aucassin* seeks primarily to amuse; Rojas, to teach. Chaucer presents us with a work which lies well balanced between the two, as he maintains a delicate equilibrium between his attitudes of satire and sympathy. Unlike Rojas who condemns his hero utterly, Chaucer remains fundamentally optimistic. And while both men employ the structural framework of the Wheel of Fortune, Chaucer introduces the optimistic doctrine of grace, so that the end results of the two works are quite different. Troilus' salvation softens the blow of his worldly defeat. And unlike Calisto, he is not ultimately condemned for his participation in the follies of love.

Such parodies of the courtly lover and, indeed, of the whole tradition, were, I believe, inevitable and, perhaps, necessary. That it was, to some extent, inherently foolish is undeniable. But that it was also, in its purest form, a gracious tribute to medieval sensibilities is equally true. The

Middle Ages is often accused of being a cruel and barbaric period, and the criticism is justifiable. But there was another side to medieval man, that aspect of him that recognized the harshness of life and sought means of making it more beautiful. Courtly love, despite its falseness and artificiality, persisted to the end of the Middle Ages and even beyond in various displaced forms. It survived in spite of, perhaps even because of, the continual mockery of parody, which permitted within the flights of fantasy some contact with reality. The ideal was necessary, but its mockery was equally necessary. And somehow equilibrium was maintained. Thus, medieval man mocked his own ideal. Having composed his dream of love from all his resources of beauty, order, and fantasy, he considered that life was not so fine after all—and he smiled.

BIBLIOGRAPHY

Abrams, M. H. *A Glossary of Literary Terms.* Based on the original version by Dan S. Norton and Peters Rushton. New York, 1957.

Adinolfi, Giulia. «*La Celestina* e la sua unità di composizione.» *FilR*, 1 (1954), 12-60.

Adler, Alfred. «Sovereignty in Chrétien's *Yvain.*» *PMLA*, 62 (1947), 281-305.

Aguirre, J. M. *Calisto y Melibea, amantes cortesanos.* Colección Almenara i. Zaragoza, 1962.

Alfonso X, el Sabio. *Primera crónica general: estoria de España.* Ed. Ramón Menéndez Pidal. 2 vols. Madrid, 1955.

Andreas Capellanus. *De Amore libri tres.* Ed. E. Trojel. Havniae, 1892; reprinted Munich, 1964.

—. *The Art of Courtly Love.* Trans. John Jay Parry. New York, 1941.

Anzoátegui, Ignacio B. «Calixto o el amante.» In *Tres ensayos españoles.* Madrid, 1944. Pp. 79-124.

apRoberts, Robert P. «The Central Episode in Chaucer's *Troilus.*» *PMLA*, 77 (1962), 373-85.

—. «The Boethian God and the Audience of the *Troilus.*» *JEGP*, 69 (1970), 425-36.

Arntz, Sister Mary Luke. «That Fol of Whos Folie Men Ryme.» *ANQ*, III (1965), 151-52.

Atkins, J. W. H. *English Literary Criticism: The Medieval Phase.* Cambridge, Eng., 1943.

Aucassin and Nicolette. Trans. Edward Francis Moyer and Cary DeWitt Eldridge. Introduction by Urban Tigner Holmes, Jr. Chapel Hill, 1937.

Aucassin et Nicolette: Chantefable du XIIIe siècle. Ed. Mario Roques. 2e ed. Paris, 1963.

Aucassin und Nicolette. Ed. Hermann Suchier. 10th ed. Paderborn, 1932.

Auerbach, Erich. *Mimesis: The Representation of Reality in Western Literature.* Trans. Willard Trask. Princeton, 1953; reprinted Garden City, New York, 1957.

Augustinus, Aurelius, Saint, Bishop of Hippo. *De Doctrina Christiana.* liber qvartvs. Ed. Sister Thérèse Sullivan. Washington, D. C., 1930.

—. *On Christian Doctrine.* Trans. D. W. Robertson, Jr. New York, 1958.

Ayllón, Candido. «Death in *La Celestina.*» *Hispania*, 41 (1958), 160-64.

—. «Negativism and Dramatic Structure in *La Celestina.*» *Hispania*, 46 (1963), 290-95.

—. *La visión pesimista de la Celestina.* Colección Studium, 45. México, 1965.

Bar, F. «Sur un épisode d'*Aucassin et Nicolette.*» *Romania*, 67 (1942-43), 369-70.

Barbera, Raymond E. «Calisto; The Paradoxical Hero.» *Hispania*, 47 (1964), 256-57.

—. «A Harlot, A Heroine.» *Hispania*, 48 (1965), 790-99.

—. «Medieval Iconography in the *Celestina.*» *RR*, 61 (1970), 5-13.

—. «Sempronio.» *Hispania*, 45 (1962), 441-42.

Basdekis, Demetrius. «Romantic Elements in *La Celestina.*» *Hispania*, 44 (1961), 52-54.

Bataillon, Marcel. *La Célestine selon Fernando de Rojas.* Paris, 1961.

—. «La originalidad artística de *La Celestina.*» *NRFH*, 17 (1963-64), 264-90.

Baugh, Albert C. *Chaucer's Major Poetry.* New York, 1963.

Baum, Paull F. *Chaucer: A Critical Appreciation.* Durham, N. C., 1958.

—. *Chaucer's Verse.* Durham, N. C., 1961.

Bayley, John. *The Character of Love: A Study in the Literature of Personality.* New York, 1960; reprinted New York, 1963.

Bechtel, Robert B. «The Problem of Criseide's Character.» *SUS*, 6-7 (1963), 109-18.

Beckson, Karl, and Arthur Ganz. *A Reader's Guide to Literary Terms.* New York, 1960.

Bédier, Joseph. «Les Fêtes de mai et les commencements de la poésie lyrique au Moyen Age.» *RDM*, 135 (mai, 1896), 146-72.

Benton, John F. «Clio and Venus: An Historical View of Medieval Love.» In *The Meaning of Courtly Love*. Ed. F. X. Newman. Albany, 1968. Pp. 19-42.

—. «The Court of Champagne as a Literary Center.» *Speculum*, 36 (1961), 551-91.

—. «The Evidence for Andreas Capellanus Re-examined Again.» *SP*, 59 (1962), 471-78.

Bergson, Henri. «Laughter.» In *Comedy*. Ed. Wylie Sypher. Garden City, New York, 1956. Pp. 61-190.

—. *Le rire, essai sur la signification du comique*. Paris, 1938.

Bernart de Ventadorn. *The Songs of Bernart de Ventadorn*. Ed. Stephen G. Nichols, Jr. and John A. Galm. UNCSRLL, 39. Chapel Hill, 1962.

Berndt, Erna Ruth. *Amor, muerte, y fortuna en «La Celestina.»* Madrid, 1963.

Bernheimer, Richard. *Wild Men in the Middle Ages: A Study in Art, Sentiment and Demonology*. Cambridge, Mass., 1952.

Béroul. *Le Roman de Tristan*. Ed. Ernest Muret. Paris, 1903.

Berryman, Charles. «The Ironic Design of Fortune in *Troilus and Criseide*.» *ChauR*, 2 (1967-68), 1-7.

Berzunza, Julius. «Notes on Witchcraft and Alcahuetería.» *RR*, 19 (1928), 141-50.

Bethurum, Dorothy. «Chaucer's Point of View as Narrator in the Love Poems.» *PMLA*, 74 (1959), 511-20; reprinted in *Chaucer Criticism*, II: *Troilus and Criseyde and the Minor Poems*. Ed. Richard J. Schoeck and Jerome Taylor. Notre Dame, 1961. Pp. 211-31.

Bevington, David. *From «Mankind» to Marlowe: Growth of Structure in the Popular Drama of Tudor England*. Cambridge, Mass., 1962.

Bezzola, Reto R. «Guillaume IX et les origines de l'amour courtois.» *Romania*, 66 (1940-41), 145-237.

—. *Les origines et la formation de la littérature courtoise en occident (500-1200)*. 3 Vols. in 5. Paris, 1958-1966.

—. *Le Sens de l'aventure et de l'amour*. Paris, [1947].

Bloch, Marc. *La Société féodale*. 2 Vols. L'Evolution de l'Humanité, Synthèse Collective, 34. Paris, 1949.

Bloomfield, Morton W. «Distance and Predestination in *Troilus and Criseyde*.» *PMLA*, 72 (1957), 14-26.

—. «Symbolism in Medieval Literature.» *MP*, 56 (1958-59). 73-81.

Boethius. *De Consolatione Philosophiae*. Ed. B. G. Teubner. Lipsiae, 1871.

Bond, Richmond P. *English Burlesque Poetry 1700-1750*. HSE, 6. Cambridge, Mass., 1932.

Boughner, David C. «Elements of Epic Grandeur in the *Troilus*.» *ELH*, 6 (1939), 200-10; reprinted in *Chaucer Criticism*, II. Ed. Schoeck and Taylor, pp. 185-95.

Bowra, C. M. *Mediaeval Love-Song*. London, 1961.

Brenner, Gerry. «Narrative Structure in Chaucer's *Troilus and Criseyde*.» *AnM*, 6 (1965), 5-18.

Brewer, D. S. *Chaucer*. London, 1953.

—, ed. *Chaucer and Chaucerians: Critical Studies in Middle English Literature*. University, Ala., 1966.

Briffault, Robert S. *The Troubadours*. Ed. Lawrence F. Koons. Bloomington, Ind., 1965.

Broadbent, J. B. *Poetic Love*. London, 1964.

Bronson, Bertrand H. *In Search of Chaucer*. Toronto, 1960.

Calderwood, James L. «Parody in *The Pardoner's Tale*.» *ES*, 45 (1964), 302-09.

Camproux, Charles. *Le 'joy d'amour' des troubadours. Jeu et joie d'amour*. Montpellier, 1965.

Castiglione, Baldassare. *Il Cortegiano*. Ed. Mario Luzi. [Milano, 1945].

Castro, Américo. *La Celestina como contienda literaria*. Madrid, 1965.

Castro Guisasola, Florentino. *Observaciones sobre las fuentes literarias de «La Celestina.»* RFE anejo V. Madrid, 1924.

Chaytor, H. J. *The Troubadours*. Cambridge, England, 1912.

Chrétien de Troyes. *Cligés*. Ed. Wendelin Foerster. Halle/Saale, 1901.

—. *Erec und Enide*. Ed. Wendelin Foerster. Halle/Saale, 1934.

—. *Guillaume d'Angleterre*. Ed. Maurice Wilmotte. Paris, 1927.

—. *Le Chevalier au lion (Yvain)*. Ed. Mario Roques. Paris, 1960.

—. *Le Chevalier de la charrette.* Ed. Mario Roques. Paris, 1958.
—. *Le Roman de Perceval ou le conte del graal.* Ed. William Roach. Geneva, 1956.
Chute, Marchette. *Geoffrey Chaucer of England.* New York, 1946.
Cipriani, Lisa. «Studies in the Influence of the *Roman de la Rose* upon Chaucer.» *PMLA*, 22 (1907), 552-95.
Clark, John W. «Dante and the Epilogue of *Troilus.*» *JEGP*, 50 (1951), 1-10.
Clark, Kenneth. *The Nude: A Study in Ideal Form.* Bollingen Series, 35. Washington, 1956.
Clarke, Dorothy Clotelle. *Allegory, Decalogue, and Deadly Sins in La Celestina.* UCPMP, 91, Berkeley and Los Angeles, 1968.
Coghill, Nevill. *Geoffrey Chaucer.* New York, 1959.
—. *The Poet Chaucer.* London, 1947.
—. «Love and 'Foul Delight': Some Contrasted Attitudes.» *Patterns of Love and Courtesy: Essays in Memory of C. S. Lewis.* Ed. John Lawler. London, 1966. Pp. 141-56.
Cohen, Gustave. *Chrétien de Troyes et son oeuvre.* Paris, 1931.
Cohn, Norman. *The World-View of a Thirteenth-Century Parisian Intellectual: Jean de Meun and the Roman de la Rose.* Durham, England, 1961 [inaugural lecture].
Colby, Alice M. *The Portrait in Twelfth-Century French Literature: An Example of the Stylistic Originality of Chrétien de Troyes.* Genève, 1965.
Collas, J. P. «The Romantic Hero of the Twelfth Century.» *Medieval Miscellany Presented to Eugène Vinaver.* Ed. F. Whitehead, A. H. Diverres, and F. E. Sutcliffe. New York, 1965. Pp. 80-96.
Conner, Wayne. «The *Loge* in *Aucassin et Nicolette.*» *RR*, 46 (1955), 81-89.
Cook, Albert S. «The Character of Criseyde.» *PMLA*, 22 (1907), 531-47.
Cook, Robert G. «Chaucer's Pandarus and the Medieval Ideal of Friendship.» *JEGP*, 69 (1970), 407-24.
Cope, Jackson I. «Chaucer, Venus, and the 'Seventhe Spere.'» *MLN*, 67 (1952), 245-46.
Coppin, Joseph. *Amour et mariage dans la littérature française du Nord au moyen-âge.* Paris, 1961.
Corsa, Helen Storm. *Chaucer, Poet of Mirth and Morality.* Notre Dame, 1964.
—. «Is This a Mannes Herte?» *LP*, 16, iii-iv (1966), 184-91.
Covella, Sister Francis Dolores. «Audience as Determinant of Meaning in the *Troilus.*» *ChauR*, 2 (1967-68), 235-45.
Criado de Val, M. *Índice verbal de La Celestina. RFE anejo 64.* Madrid, 1955.
Croce, Benedetto. *Poesia antica e moderna.* Bari, 1939.
—. «La Celestina.» *La Critica*, 37 (1939), 81-91.
Cross, Tom Peete, and William A. Nitze. *Lancelot and Guenevere: A Study on the Origins of Courtly Love.* Chicago, 1930.
Curry, Walter Clyde. *Chaucer and the Mediaeval Sciences.* London, 1926; revised and enlarged, New York, 1960.
—. «Destiny in Chaucer's *Troilus.*» *PMLA*, 45 (1930), 129-68.
Curtius, Ernst Robert. *European Literature and the Latin Middle Ages.* Trans. Willard R. Trask. New York, 1953; reprinted New York and Evanston, 1963.
Daly, Saralyn R. «Criseyde's Blasphemous Aube.» *NQ*, 10 (1963), 442-44.
Damon, Phillip. «Courtesy and Comedy in *Flamenca.*» *RP*, 17 (1963-64), 608-15.
David, Alfred. «The Hero of the *Troilus.*» *Speculum*, 37 (1962), 566-81.
Dempster, Germaine. *Dramatic Irony in Chaucer.* Palo Alto, Calif., 1932; reprinted New York, 1959.
Denomy, Alexander J. «Courtly Love and Courtliness.» *Speculum*, 28 (1953), 44-63.
—. «The *De Amore* of Andreas Capellanus and the Condemnation of 1277.» *MS*, 8 (1946), 107-49.
—. «Fin' Amors: the Pure Love of the Troubadours, Its Amorality, and Possible Source.» *MS*, 7 (1945), 139-207.
—. *The Heresy of Courtly Love.* New York, 1947.
—. «An Inquiry into the Origins of Courtly Love.» *MS*, 6 (1944), 175-260.
—. «*Jois* Among the Early Troubadours: Its Meaning and Possible Source.» *MS*, 13 (1951), 177-217.
—. «*Jovens:* The Notion of Youth Among the Troubadours, Its Meaning and Source.» *MS*, 11 (1949), 1-22.

147

—. «The Two Moralities of Chaucer's *Troilus and Criseyde*.» *Transactions of the Royal Society of Canada*, 44, Ser. III, sec. 2 (June, 1950), 35-46; reprinted *Chaucer Criticism*, II. Ed. Schoeck and Taylor, pp. 147-59.

de Rougemont, Denis. *Passion and Society*. Trans. Montgomery Belgion. London, 1940; revised ed. 1962.

Deyermond, A. D. *The Petrarchan Sources of La Celestina*. Oxford, 1961.

—. «El hombre salvaje en la novela sentimental.» *Actas del Segundo Congreso Internacional de Hispanistas*. Nimega, 1967.

—. «The Index to Petrarch's Latin Works as a Source of *La Celestina*.» *BHS*, 31 (1954), 141-49.

—. Review of J. M. Aguirre, *Calisto y Melibea, amantes cortesanos*. *BHS*, 41 (1964), 67-68.

—. «Some Aspects of Parody in the 'Libro de buen amor.'» *Libro de buen amor Studies*. Ed. G. B. Gybbon-Monypenny. London, 1970. Pp. 53-78.

—. «The Text-Book Mishandled: Andreas Capellanus and the Opening Scene of *La Celestina*.» *Neophilologus*, 45 (1961), 218-21.

Dictionnaire de théologie catholique. Ed. A. Vacant, E. Mangenot, E. Amann. Paris, 1926.

—. Tables générales. Ed. Bernard Loth et Albert Michel. Paris, 1955.

Dodd, William George. *Courtly Love in Chaucer and Gower*. HSE, i. Cambridge, Mass., 1913; reprinted Gloucester, Mass., 1959.

—. *Chaucer's Poetry*. New York, 1958.

Donaldson, E. T. «The Ending of Chaucer's *Troilus*.» *Early English and Norse Studies Presented to Hugh Smith*. Ed. Arthur Brown and Peter Foote, London, 1963. Pp. 26-45.

—. «Idiom of Popular Poetry in the *Miller's Tale*.» *English Institute Essays, 1950*. Ed. Alan S. Downer. New York, 1951. Pp. 116-40.

—. «The Myth of Courtly Love.» *Ventures: Magazine of the Yale Graduate School*, 5, ii (1965), 16-23.

—. *Speaking of Chaucer*. London, 1970.

Dronke, Peter. «The Conclusion of *Troilus and Criseyde*.» *MAe*, 33 (1964), 47-52.

—. *Medieval Latin and the Rise of European Love Lyric*. 2 vols. Oxford, 1965-66.

—. Review of Felix Schlösser, *Andreas Capellanus: seine Minnelehre und das Christliche. Weltbild um 1200*. *MAe*, 32 (1963), 56-60.

Dunning, T. P. «God and Man in *Troilus and Criseyde*.» *English and Medieval Studies Presented to J. R. R. Tolkien*. Ed. Norman Davis and C. L. Wrenn. London, 1962. Pp. 164-82.

Durham, Lonnie J. «Love and Death in *Troilus and Criseyde*.» *ChauR*, 3 (1969), 1-11.

Earle, Peter G. «Love Concepts in *La cárcel de amor* and *La Celestina*.» *Hispania*, 39 (1956), 92-96.

Elbow, Peter. «Two Boethian Speeches in *Troilus and Criseyde* and Chaucerian Irony.» In *Literary Criticism and Historical Understanding: Selected Papers from the English Institute*. Ed. Phillip Damon. New York, 1967. Pp. 85-107.

Empson, William. *English Pastoral Poetry*. New York, 1938.

Erzgraber, Willi. «Tragik und Komik in Chaucers *Troilus and Criseyde*.» *Festschrift für Walter Hübner*. Ed. Dieter Riesner and Helmut Gneuss. Berlín, 1964. Pp. 139-63.

Everett, Dorothy. «*Troilus and Criseyde*.» *Essays on Middle English Literature*. Ed. Patricia Kean. New York, 1955; reprinted Oxford, 1964. Pp. 115-38.

Falk, Robert P., ed. *The Antic Muse: American Writers in Parody*. New York, 1955.

Fansler, Dean Spruill. *Chaucer and the Roman de la Rose*. New York, 1914; reprinted Gloucester, Mass., 1965.

Faral, Edmond. *Les Arts poétiques du XIIe et du XIIIe siècle: recherches et documents sur la technique littéraire du moyen âge*. Paris, 1924.

—. *Recherches sur les sources latines des contes et romans courtois du moyen âge*. Paris, 1913.

Farnham, Anthony E. «Chaucerian Irony and the Ending of the *Troilus*.» *ChauR*, 1 (1967), 207-16.

Ferguson, George. *Signs and Symbols in Christian Art*. Oxford, 1961.

Fisher, J. H. «Tristan and Courtly Adultery.» *CL*, 9 (1957), 150-64.

—, ed. *The Medieval Literature of Western Europe, a Review of Research Mainly 1930-1960*. New York, 1966.

Fleming, John V. «The Moral Reputation of the *Roman de la Rose* Before 1400». *RP*, 18 (1964-65), 430-35.

—. *The Roman de la Rose: A Study in Allegory and Iconography*. Princeton, 1969.

Foster, David William. «Some Attitudes Towards Love in the *Celestina*.» *Hispania*, 48 (1965), 484-92.

Foster, Kenelm. *Courtly Love and Christianity*. Aquinas Paper no. 39. London, 1963.

Fothergill-Payne, Louise. «*La Celestina* como esbozo de una lección maquiavélica.» *RF*, 81 (1969), 158-75.

Frank, Donald K. «The Corporeal, the Derogatory and the Stress on Equality in Andreas' *De Amore*.» *MH*, 16 (1964), 30-38.

—. «On the Troubadour *Fin'Amors*.» *RomN*, 7 (1965-66), 209-17.

—. «On the Troubadour Sense of Merit.» *RomN*, 8 (1966-67), 289-96.

—. «Some Rational Considerations of Andreas Capellanus.» *RomN*, 8 (1966-67), 121-27.

—. «Twelfth-Century Naturalism and the Troubadour Ethic.» *DA*, 3071-2, v. 21, nos. 9-10 (1960-61).

Frank, Grace. «*Aucassin et Nicolette*, Line 2.» *RR*, 40 (1949), 161-64.

—. *Medieval French Drama*. Oxford, 1954.

—. «The Distant Love of Jaufré Rudel.» *MLN*, 57 (1942), 528-34.

Frank, Rachel. «Four Paradoxes in *The Celestina*.» *RR*, 38 (1947), 53-68.

Frappier, Jean. *Chrétien de Troyes, l'homme et l'oeuvre*. Paris, 1957.

—. *Le Roman breton: introduction des origines à Chrétien de Troyes*. Paris, 1959.

—. *Le Roman breton: Yvain ou le chevalier au lion*. Paris, 1958.

French, J. Milton. «Defense of Troilus.» *PMLA*, 44 (1929), 1246-51.

French, Robert D. *A Chaucer Handbook*. 2nd ed. New York, 1947.

Frye, Northrop. *Anatomy of Criticism: Four Essays*. Princeton, 1957.

—. «The Argument of Comedy.» *English Institute Essays, 1948*. Ed. D. A. Robertson, Jr. New York, 1949. Pp. 58-73.

—. *A Natural Perspective: The Development of Shakespearean Comedy and Romance*. New York, 1965.

Gárbaty, Thomas Jay. «Chaucer in Spain, 1366: Soldier of Fortune or Agent of the Crown.» *ELN*, 5 (1967), 81-87.

—. «*Pamphilus, De Amore*: An Introduction and Translation.» *ChauR*, 2 (1967-68), 108-34.

—. «The *Pamphilus* Tradition in Ruiz and Chaucer.» *PQ*, 46 (1967), 457-70.

Garrido Pallardó, Fernando. *Los problemas de Calisto y Melibea y el conflicto de su autor*. Figueras, 1957.

Gaylord, Alan T. «Chaucer's Tender Trap: The *Troilus* and the 'Yonge, Freshe Folkes'.» *English Miscellany*, 15 (1964), 25-45.

—. «Friendship in Chaucer's *Troilus*.» *ChauR*, 3 (1969), 239-64.

—. «*Gentilesse* in Chaucer's *Troilus*.» *SP*, 61 (1964), 19-34.

Gerould, Gordon Hall. *Chaucerian Essays*. Princeton, 1952.

Getty, Agnes K. «Chaucer's Changing Conception of the Humble Lover.» *PMLA*, 44 (1929), 202-16.

Gill, Sister Anne Barbara. *Paradoxical Patterns in Chaucer's «Troilus», An Explanation of the Palinode*. Washington, 1960.

Gilman, Stephen. *The Art of La Celestina*. Madison, Wis., 1956.

—. «The Fall of Fortune: From Allegory to Fiction.» *FilR*, 4 (1957), 337-54.

—. «Fortune and Space in *La Celestina*.» *RF*, 66 (1955), 342-60.

—. «Rebirth of a Classic: *Celestina*.» In *Varieties of Literary Experience: Eighteen Essays in World Literature*. Ed. Stanley Burnshaw. New York, 1962. Pp. 283-305.

—. «A Rejoinder to Leo Spitzer.» *HR*, 25 (1957), 112-21.

—. Review of Carmelo Samonà, *Aspetti del retoricismo nella 'Celestina'*». *NRFH*, 10 (1956), 73-80.

—. «El tiempo y el género literario en *La Celestina*.» *RFH*, 7 (1945), 147-59.

Goldin, Frederick, *The Mirror of Narcissus in the Courtly Love Lyric*. Ithaca, N. Y., 1967.

Gordon, Ida L. *The Double Sorrow of Troilus*. Oxford, 1970.

—. «The Narrative Function of Irony in Chaucer's *Troilus and Criseyde.*» *Medieval Miscellany Presented to Eugène Vinaver.* Ed. F. Whitehead, A. H. Diverres, and F. E. Sutcliffe. New York, 1965. Pp. 146-56.

Gordon, R. K., ed. *The Story of Troilus.* New York, 1964.

Graydon, Joseph S. «Defense of Criseyde.» *PMLA,* 44 (1929), 141-77.

Green, Otis H. «Additional Note on the *Celestina* and the Inquisition.» *HR,* 16 (1948), 70-71.

—. «The Artistic Originality of *La Celestina.*» *HR,* 33 (1965), 15-31.

—. «*The Celestina* and the Inquisition.» *HR,* 15 (1947), 211-16.

—. *Courtly Love in Quevedo.* UColSSLL, 3. Boulder, Colorado, 1952.

—. «Courtly Love in the Spanish *Cancioneros.*» *PMLA,* 64 (1949), 247-301.

—. «Did the 'World' 'Create' Pleberio?» *RF,* 77 (1965), 108-10.

—. «Fernando de Rojas, *converso* and *hidalgo.*» *HR,* 15 (1947), 384-87.

—. «La furia de Melibea.» *Clavileño,* 4, xx (marzo-abril, 1953), 1-3.

—. «Imaginative Authority in Spanish Literature.» *PMLA,* 84 (1969), 209-16.

—. «Lo de tu abuela con el ximio *(Celestina,* Auto I).» *HR,* 24 (1956), 1-12.

—. «On Rojas' Description of Melibea.» *HR,* 14 (1946), 254-56.

—. *Spain and the Western Tradition: The Castilian Mind in Literature from El Cid to Calderon.* i. Madison, Wis., 1963.

Griffin, Robert. «*Aucassin et Nicolette* and the Albigensian Crusade.» *MLQ,* 26 (1965), 243-56.

Grimm, Charles. «Chrétien de Troyes's Attitude Towards Woman.» *RR,* 16 (1925), 236-43.

Guillaume de Lorris and Jean de Meun. *Le Roman de la Rose.* Ed. Ernest Langlois. 5 vols. SATF edition. Paris, 1914-44.

Gunn, Alan M. F. *The Mirror of Love: A Reinterpretation of the Romance of the Rose.* Lubbock, Texas, 1952.

Guyer, Foster Erwin. *Romance in the Making: Chrétien de Troyes and the Earliest French Romances.* New York, 1954.

Harden, Robert. «*Aucassin et Nicolette* as Parody.» *SP,* 63 (1966), 1-9.

Hart, Thomas R., Jr. *La alegoría en el Libro de buen amor.* Madrid, 1959.

Heidtmann, Peter. «Sex and Salvation in *Troilus and Criseyde.*» *ChauR,* 2 (1967-68), 246-53.

Herrick, Marvin T. *Tragicomedy: Its Origin and Development in Italy, France, and England.* ISLL, 39. Urbana, Illinois, 1955.

Highet, Gilbert. *The Anatomy of Satire.* Princeton, 1962.

Hill, Raymond Thompson and Thomas Goddard Bergin. *Anthology of the Provençal Troubadours.* YRS, 17. New Haven, 1941.

Holmes, Urban Tigner, Jr., and Sister M. Amelia Klenke. *Chrétien, Troyes, and the Grail.* Chapel Hill, 1959.

Howard, Donald R. «Literature and Sexuality: Book III of Chaucer's *Troilus.*» *MR,* 8 (1967), 442-56.

Howard, Edwin J. *Geoffrey Chaucer.* New York, 1964.

Huet, Gédéon. «Sur l'origine de *Floire et Blanchefleur.*» *Romania,* 28 (1899), 348-59.

Huizinga, J. *The Waning of the Middle Ages.* Trans. F. Hopman. London, 1924; reprinted Garden City, New York, 1954.

Huppé, Bernard F. and D. W. Robertson, Jr. *Fruyt and Chaf: Studies in Chaucer's Allegories.* Princeton, 1963.

Hussey, Maurice, A. C. Spearing, and James Winny. *An Introduction to Chaucer.* Cambridge, England, 1965.

Jackson W. T. H. «The *De Amore* of Andreas Capellanus and the Practice of Love at Court.» *RR,* 49 (1958), 243-51.

—. «Faith Unfaithful—The German Reaction to Courtly Love.» In *The Meaning of Courtly Love.* Ed. Newman. Pp. 55-76.

Jeanroy, Alfred. *La poésie lyrique des troubadours.* 2 vols. Toulouse, 1934.

—. *Les origines de la poésie lyrique en France au moyen âge.* París, 1925.

Jefferson, Bernard L. *Chaucer and the Consolation of Philosophy of Boethius.* Princeton, 1917; reprinted New York, 1968.

Jodogne, Omer. «La Parodie et la pastiche dans *Aucassin et Nicolette.*» *CAIEF,* 12 (1959), 53-65.

Jones, R. O. «Isabel la Católica y el amor cortés.» *RL*, 21 (1962), 55-64.
Jordan, Robert M. *Chaucer and the Shape of Creation: The Aesthetic Possibilities of Inorganic Structure*. Cambridge, Mass., 1967.
—. «The Narrator in Chaucer's *Troilus*.» *ELH*, 25 (1958), 237-57.
Kaske, R. E. «The *Aube* in Chaucer's *Troilus*.» In *Chaucer Criticism*, II. Ed. Schoeck and Taylor. Pp. 167-79.
Katzenellenbogen, Adolf. *Allegories of the Virtues and Vices in Medieval Art*. Trans. Alan J. P. Crick, New York, 1964.
Kean, P. M. «Chaucer's Dealings with a Stanza of *Il Filostrato* and the Epilogue of *Troilus and Criseyde*.» *MAe*, 33 (1964), 36-46.
Kelly, Amy. «Eleanor of Aquitaine and Her Courts of Love.» *Speculum*, 12 (1937), 3-19.
—. *Eleanor of Aquitaine and the Four Kings*. Cambridge, Mass., 1950.
Kelly, Douglas. «Courtly Love in Perspective: The Hierarchy of Love in Andreas Capellanus.» *Traditio*, 24 (1968), 119-48.
Kirby, Thomas A. *Chaucer's Troilus: A Study in Courtly Love*. Baton Rouge, 1940; reprinted Gloucester, Mass., 1958.
Kitchin, George. *A Survey of Burlesque and Parody in English*. London, 1931.
Kittredge, George Lyman. *Chaucer and His Poetry*. Cambridge, Mass., 1915.
—. *The Date of Chaucer's Troilus and Other Chaucer Matters*. Published for the Chaucer Society. London, 1909 for 1905.
Krappe, A. H. «Two Ancient Parallels to *Aucassin et Nicolette*.» *PQ*, 4 (1925), 180-81.
Kratins, Ojars. «Love and Marriage in Three Versions of 'The Knight of the lion'.» *CL*, 16 (1964), 29-39.
Langlois, Ernest. *Les Manuscrits du Roman de la Rose*. Lille, 1910.
—. *Origines et sources du Roman de la Rose*. París, 1891.
Lauter, Paul, ed. *Theories of Comedy*. New York, 1964.
Lavaud, René and René Nelli, eds. *Les Troubadours: Jaufre, Flamenca, Barlaam et Josaphat*. 2 vols. Paris, 1960.
Lazar, Moshé. *Amour courtois et «fin'amors» dans la littérature du XIIe siècle*. Paris, 1964.
—. «Lancelot et la 'mulier mediatrix': La Quête de soi à travers la femme.» *ECr*, 9 (1969), 243-56.
Lea, Henry C. *Chapters from the Religious History of Spain Connected with the Inquisition*, Philadelphia, 1890.
Le Gentil, Pierre. *La Poésie lyrique espagnole et portugaise à la fin du moyen âge*. i. Rennes, 1949.
Legouis, Emile. *Geoffrey Chaucer*. Trans. L. Lailavoix. London, 1913; reprinted New York, 1961.
Lehmann, Paul. *Die Parodie im Mittelalter*. First published 1922; 2nd ed. Stuttgart, 1963.
Levy, Raphael. «L'Emploi du mot *desport* dans *Aucassin et Nicolette*.» *MLN*, 64 (1949). 164-66.
Lewis, C. S. *The Allegory of Love: A Study in Medieval Tradition*. Oxford, 1936; reprinted New York, 1958.
—. «What Chaucer Really Did to *Il Filostrato*.» *Essays and Studies by Members of the English Association*. 17. Collected by W. H. Hadow. Oxford, 1932, Pp. 56-75.
Lida de Malkiel, María Rosa. «El ambiente concreto en *La Celestina*.» In *Estudios dedicados a James Homer Herriott*. [Madison, Wis.], 1966. Pp. 145-65.
—. «La hipérbole sagrada en la poesía castellana del siglo xv.» *RFH*, 8 (1946), 121-30.
—. *La originalidad artística de la Celestina*. Buenos Aires, 1962.
—. *Two Spanish Masterpieces: The Book of Good Love and The Celestina*. ISLL, 49, Urbana, Ill., 1961.
Loomis, Roger Sherman, ed. *Arthurian Literature in the Middle Ages: A Collaborative History*. Oxford, 1959.
—. *Arthurian Tradition and Chrétien de Troyes*. New York, 1949.
—. *A Mirror of Chaucer's World*. Princeton, 1965.
—. *The Development of Arthurian Literature*. London, 1963.
Lot-Borodine, Myrrha. *De l'amour profane à l'amour sacré*. Paris, 1961.
—. *La femme et l'amour au XIIe siècle d'après les poèmes de Chrétien de Troyes*. Paris, 1909; reprinted Genève, 1967.
—. *Le Roman idyllique au moyen âge*. Paris, 1913.

Lowes, John Livingston. *The Art of Geoffrey Chaucer*. London, 1931.
—. «Chaucer and Dante.» *MP*, 14 (1916-17), 705-35.
—. «Chaucer and Dante's *Convivio*.» *MP*, 13 (1915-16), 19-33.
—. *Geoffrey Chaucer and the Development of His Genius*. New York, 1934.
—. «The Loveres Maladye of Hereos.» *MP*, 11 (1913-14), 491-546.
Luquiens, Frederick Bliss. «The *Roman de la Rose* and Medieval Castilian Literature.» *RF*, 20 (1907), 284-320.
McCall, John P. «Chaucer's May 3.» *MLN*, 76 (1961), 201-05.
—. «Five-Book Structure in Chaucer's *Troilus*.» *MLQ*, 23 (1962), 297-308.
Macdonald, Dwight, ed. *Parodies: An Anthology from Chaucer to Beerbohm—and After*. New York, 1960.
Macdonald, Inez. «Some Observations on the *Celestina*.» *HR*, 22 (1954), 264-81.
McKean, Sister M. Faith. «Torelore and Courtoisie.» *RomN*, 3, ii (Spring, 1962), 64-68.
McPheeters, D. W. «The Corrector Alonso de Proaza and the *Celestina*.» *HR*, 24 (1956), 13-25.
—. «The Element of Fatality in the *Tragicomedia de Calisto y Melibea*.» *Symposium*, 8 (1954), 331-35.
—. «The Present Status of *Celestina* Studies.» *Symposium*, 12 (1958), 196-205.
Mahoney, John F. «Chaucerian Tragedy and the Christian Tradition.» *AnM*, 3 (1962), 81-99.
—. «The Evidence for Andreas Capellanus in Re-examination.» *SP*, 55 (1958), 1-6.
Malone, Kemp. *Chapters on Chaucer*. Baltimore, 1951.
Manly, John Matthews. *Chaucer and the Rhetoricians*. In *Proceedings of the British Academy*, 12, London, 1926.
Maravall, José Antonio. *El mundo social de La Celestina*. Madrid, 1964.
Marie de France. *Les Lais*. Ed. Jeanne Lods. Paris, 1959.
Markland, Murray F. «Pilgrims Errant: The Doubleness of Troilus and Criseyde.» *Research Studies of State College of Washington*, 33 (June, 1965), 64-78.
Mathew, Gervase. «Marriage and *Amour Courtois* in Late Fourteenth-Century England.» In *Essays Presented to Charles Williams*. London, 1947, Pp. 128-35.
Meech, Sanford B. *Design in Chaucer's Troilus*. Syracuse, 1959.
—. «Figurative Contrasts in Chaucer's *Troilus and Criseyde*.» *English Institute Essays: 1950*. Ed. Alan S. Downer. New York, 1951. Pp. 57-88.
Menéndez y Pelayo, Marcelino. *Orígenes de la novela*. iii, Madrid, 1910.
Micha, Alexandre. «En relisant *Aucassin et Nicolette*.» *MA*, 65 (1959), 279-92.
Misrahi, Jean. «Symbolism and Allegory in Arthurian Romance.» *RP*, 17 (1963-4), 555-69.
Mizener, A. «Character and Action in the Case of Criseyde.» *PMLA*, 54 (1939), 65-81. Reprinted in *Chaucer: Modern Essays in Criticism*. Ed. Edward Wagenknecht. New York, 1959. Pp. 348-65.
Moller, Herbert. «The Meaning of Courtly Love.» *JAF*, 73 (1960), 39-52.
Monsonégo, Simone. *Etude stylo-statistique du vocabulaire des vers et de la prose dans la Chantefable Aucassin et Nicolette*. Bibliothèque Française et Romane. Strasbourg, Série A, Manuels et Etudes Linguistiques, 10. Paris, 1966.
Moore, John A. «Ambivalence of Will in *La Celestina*.» *Hispania*, 47 (1964), 251-55.
Moore, John C. «Love in Twelfth-Century France: A Failure in Synthesis.» *Traditio*, 24 (1968), 429-43.
Morby, Edwin. «*The Celestina* as a Morality Play.» *RP*, 16 (1963), 323-31.
Mott, Lewis Freeman. *The System of Courtly Love Studied as an Introduction to the Vita Nuova of Dante*. New York, 1924.
Muscatine, Charles. *Chaucer and the French Tradition: A Study in Style and Meaning*. Berkeley and Los Angeles, 1957; reprinted 1964.
—. «The Feigned Illness in Chaucer's *Troilus and Criseyde*.» *MLN*, 63 (1948), 372-77.
Nagarajan, S. «The Conclusion to Chaucer's *Troilus and Criseyde*.» *Essays in Criticism*, 12 (1962), 1-8.
Nelli, R. *L'Erotique des troubadours*. Bibliothèque méridionale, 2e série, 38. Toulouse, 1963.
Newman, F. X., ed. *The Meaning of Courtly Love*. Papers of the first annual conference of the Center for Medieval and Early Renaissance Studies, State University of New York at Binghamton. Albany, 1968.

Nichols, Stephen G., Jr. «Ethical Criticism and Medieval Literature: *Le Roman de Tristan.*» In *Medieval Secular Literature: Four Essays.* Ed. William Matthews. Berkeley and Los Angeles, 1965. Pp. 68-89.

— and John A. Galm, eds. *The Songs of Bernart de Ventadorn.* Chapel Hill, 1962.

Orozco Díaz, Emilio. «El huerto de Melibea.» *Arbor.* 19 (May/August, 1951), 47-60.

—. «*La Celestina*, hipótesis para una interpretación.» *Insula*, 12, cxxiv (marzo, 1957), 1-10.

Ovid. *Heroides, Amours, Art of Love, Remedy of Love and Minor Works.* Trans. Henry T. Riley. London, 1896.

—. *The Loves, The Art of Beauty, The Remedies for Love, and The Art of Love.* Trans. Rolfe Humphries. Bloomington, Ind., 1957.

Owen, Charles A., Jr. «The Crucial Passages in Five of the *Canterbury Tales:* A Study in Irony and Symbol.» *JEGP*, 52 (1953), 294-311.

—. «The Significance of a Day in *Troilus and Criseyde.*» *MS*, 22 (1960), 366-70.

—. «The Significance of Chaucer's Revisions of *Troilus and Criseyde.*» *MP*, 55 (1957-58), 1-5; reprinted *Chaucer Criticism*, II. Ed. Schoeck and Taylor. Pp. 160-66.

Palmer, Margaret E. «An Interpretation of *La Celestina.*» A dissertation at the University of Washington, 1955.

Panofsky, Erwin. *Studies in Iconology: Humanistic Themes in the Art of the Renaissance.* Oxford, 1939; reprinted New York, 1962.

Paré, Gérard Marie. *Le Roman de la Rose et la scolastique courtoise.* Ottawa, 1941.

—. *Les idées et les lettres au XIIIe siècle, Le Roman de la Rose.* Montreal, 1947.

Paris, Gaston. *La Littérature française au moyen âge.* 5th ed. Paris, 1913.

—. «Lancelot du Lac II: Le Conte de la charrette.» *Romania*, 12 (1883), 459-534.

—. *Poèmes et légendes du moyen âge.* Paris, 1900.

—. Review of *Aucassin et Nicolette.* Trans. A. Bida, and *Aucassin und Nicolette.* Ed. Hermann Suchier. *Romania*, 8 (1879), 284-393.

Pasquale, Pasquale di, Jr. «'Sikernesse'and Fortune in *Troilus and Criseyde.*» *PQ*, 49 (1970), 152-63.

Patch, Howard R. «Chaucer and Mediaeval Romance.» *Essays in Memory of Barrett Wendell.* Cambridge, Mass., 1926. Pp. 95-108.

—. *The Goddess Fortuna in Medieval Literature.* Cambridge, Mass., 1927; reprinted London, 1967.

—. *On Rereading Chaucer.* Cambridge, Mass., 1939.

—. «Troilus on Determinism.» *Speculum*, 6 (1931), 225-43. Reprinted *Chaucer Criticism*, II. Ed. Schoeck and Taylor. Pp. 71-85.

—. «Troilus on Predestination.» *JEGP*, 17 (1918), 399-423. Reprinted in *Chaucer: Modern Essays in Criticism.* Ed. Wagenknecht. Pp. 366-84.

Pauphilet, Albert. *Jeux et sapience du moyen âge.* Paris, 1961.

—. *Le Legs du moyen âge: études de littérature médiévale.* Melun, 1950.

Payne, Robert O. *The Key of Remembrance: A Study of Chaucer's Poetics.* New Haven, 1963.

Penney, Clara Louisa. *The Book Called Celestina in the Library of the Hispanic Society of America.* New York, 1954.

Post, Chandler R. *Mediaeval Spanish Allegory, HSCL,* 4. Cambridge, Mass., 1915.

Poulet, Georges. *Études sur le temps humain.* EUPLL, 1. Edinburgh, 1949.

Preminger, Alex, ed. Frank J. Warnke and D. B. Hardison, Jr., assoc. eds. *Encyclopedia of Poetry and Poetics.* Princeton, 1965.

Prestage, Edgar, ed. *Chivalry: A Series of Studies to Illustrate its Historical Significance and Civilizing Influence,* by members of King's College. New York, 1928.

Preston, Raymond. *Chaucer.* London, 1952.

Price, Thomas R. «*Troilus and Criseyde*, A Study in Chaucer's Method of Narrative Construction.» *PMLA*, 2 (1896), 307-22.

Reinhard, John R. «The Literary Background of the Chantefable.» *Speculum*, 1 (1926), 157-69.

Reiss, Edmund. «Troilus and the Failure of Understanding.» *MLQ*, 29 (1968), 131-44.

Renart, Jean. *Le Lai de l'ombre.* Ed. Joseph Bédier. Paris. 1913.

Riquer, Martín de. «Fernando de Rojas y el primer acto de *La Celestina.*» *RFE*, 41 (1957), 373-95.

JUNE HALL MARTIN

Robbie, May Grant. «Three-faced Pandarus.» *CEJ*, 3 (1967), 47-54.
Robertson, D. W., Jr. «Chaucerian Tragedy.» *ELH*, 19 (1952), 1-37. Reprinted *Chaucer Criticism*, II. Ed. Schoeck and Taylor. Pp. 86-121.
—. «Chrétien's *Cligés* and the Ovidian Spirit.» *CL*, 7 (1955), 32-42.
—. «The Concept of Courtly Love as an Impediment to the Understanding of Medieval Texts.» In *The Meaning of Courtly Love*. Ed. Newman. Pp. 1-18.
—. «The Doctrine of Charity in Medieval Literary Gardens: A Topical Approach Through Symbolism and Allegory.» *Speculum*, 26 (1951), 24-49.
—. *A Preface to Chaucer: Studies in Medieval Perspectives*. Princeton, 1962.
—. «The Subject of the *De Amore* of Andreas Capellanus.» *MP*, 50 (1952-53), 145-61.
Robinson, F. N., ed. *The Works of Geoffrey Chaucer*. 2nd ed. Boston, 1957.
Rogger, Kaspar. «Etude déscriptive de la chantefable 'Aucassin et Nicolette'.» *ZRP*, 67 (1951), 409-57, and 70 (1954), 1-58.
Rojas, Fernando de. *La Celestina*. Ed. Julio Cejador y Frauca. 2 vols. Madrid, 1913; reprinted 1958.
—. *The Celestina*. Trans. Lesley Byrd Simpson. Berkeley, 1955.
—. *The Celestina*. Trans. Mack Hendricks Singleton. Madison, Wis., 1958.
—. *Tragicomedia de Calixto y Melibea*. Ed. M. Criado de Val y G. D. Trotter. Madrid, 1958.
Root, Robert Kilburn. *The Book of Troilus and Criseyde by Geoffrey Chaucer*. Princeton, 1945.
—. *The Poetry of Chaucer: A Guide to its Study and Appreciation*. New York, 1906.
Roques, Mario. «Deux notules sur des passages contestés du manuscrit d'*Aucassin et Nicolette*.» *Romania*, 75 (1954), 520-24.
—. «Pour Aucassin et Nicolette.» *Romania*, 76 (1955), 98.
—. «Corrections.» *Romania*, 76 (1955), 99-102.
Rousset, Paul. «Recherches sur l'émotivité à l'époque romane.» *CCM*, 2 (1959), 53-67.
Ruggerio, M. J. *The Evolution of the Go-Between in Spanish Literature Through the Sixteenth Century*. UCPMP, 78. Berkeley and Los Angeles, 1966.
Russell, Nicholas. «Characters and Crowds in Chaucer's *Troilus*.» *NQ*, 211 (1966), 50-52.
Russell, P. E. «La magia como tema integral de *La Tragicomedia de Calisto y Melibea*.» *Studia Philologica: Homenaje ofrecido a Dámaso Alonso*, 3, Madrid, 1963. Pp. 337-54.
—. «The Art of Fernando de Rojas.» *BHS*, 34 (1957), 160-67.
—. Review of José Antonio Maravall, *El mundo social de 'La Celestina.'* *BHS*, 43 (1966), 125-28.
Salter, Elizabeth. «Troilus and Criseyde: A Reconsideration.» *Patterns of Love and Courtesy: Essays in Memory of C. S. Lewis*. Ed. John Lawlor. London, 1966. Pp. 86-106.
Samonà, Carmelo. *Aspetti del retoricismo nella «Celestina.»* Facoltà di Magistero dell' Università di Roma, Studi di letteratura spagnola, Quaderno 2. Roma, 1953.
Sams, Henry W. «The Dual Time-Scheme in Chaucer's *Troilus*.» *MLN*, 56 (1941), 94-100. Reprinted *Chaucer Criticism*, II. Ed. Schoeck and Taylor. Pp. 180-85.
Sansone, G. E. *Idillio e ironia in Aucassin e Nicolette*. Bari, 1950.
Sargent, Barbara Nelson. «*The Lai de l'ombre* and the *De Amore*.» *RomN*, 7 (1965-66), 73-79.
—. «Parody in *Aucassin et Nicolette*: Some Further Considerations.» *FR*, 43 (1969-70), 597-605.
Scaglione, Aldo D. *Nature and Love in the Late Middle Ages*. Berkeley and Los Angeles, 1963.
Schless, Howard. «Chaucer and Dante.» *Critical Approaches to Medieval Literature: Selected English Institute Papers, 1958-1959*. Ed. Dorothy Bethurum. New York, 1960. Pp. 134-54.
Schlösser, Felix. *Andreas Capellanus: Seine Minnelehre und das christliche Weltbild des 12. Jahrhunderts*. Bonn, 1960.
Schoeck, Richard J. «Andreas Capellanus and St. Bernard of Clairvaux: The Twelve Rules of Love and the Twelve Steps of Humility.» *MLN*, 66 (1951), 295-300.

154

—, and Jerome Taylor, eds. *Troilus and Criseyde and the Minor Poems. Chaucer Criticism*, v. II. Notre Dame, 1961.

Serrano Poncela, Segundo. «El secreto de Melibea.» *CA*, 17 (1958), 488-510.

Severin, Dorothy Sherman. *Memory in «La Celestina»*. London, 1970.

Shanley, J. L. «The *Troilus* and Christian Love.» *ELH*, 6 (1939), 271-81. Reprinted in *Chaucer: Modern Essays in Criticism*. Ed. Wagenknecht.

Shedd, Gordon M. «*Flamenca:* A Medieval Satire on Courtly Love.» *ChauR*, 2 (1967-68), 43-65.

Shelly, Percy Van Dyke. *The Living Chaucer*. Philadelphia, 1940; reissued New York, 1968.

Shepherd, G. T. «Troilus and Criseyde.» In *Chaucer and Chaucerians: Critical Studies in Middle English Literature*. Ed. D. S. Brewer. University, Ala., 1966. Pp. 65-87.

Silverstein, Theodore. «Andreas, Plato, and the Arabs: Remarks on Some Recent Accounts of Courtly Love.» *MP*, 47 (1949-50), 117-26.

—. «Guenevere, or the Uses of Courtly Love.» In *The Meaning of Courtly Love*. Ed. Newman. Pp. 77-90.

Singleton, Charles S. «Dante: Within Courtly Love and Beyond.» In *The Meaning of Courtly Love*. Ed. Newman. Pp. 43-54.

Smith, Barbara. «Toward an Interpretation of *Aucassin et Nicolette*.» *Rendez-vous*, 3, i (1964), 43-59.

Spearing, A. C. *Criticism and Medieval Poetry*. New York, 1964.

Speirs, John. *Chaucer the Maker*. London, 1951.

Spitzer, Leo. *L'amour lointain de Jaufré Rudel et le sens de la poésie des troubadours*. UNCSRLL, 5. Chapel Hill, 1944.

—. «*Aucassin et Nicolette*, Line 2 Again.» *MP*, 48 (1950-51), 154-56.

—. *Classical and Christian Ideas of World Harmony*. Baltimore, 1963.

—. «A New Book on the Art of *The Celestina*.» *HR*, 25 (1957), 1-25.

—. «Le Vers 2 d'*Aucassin et Nicolette* et le sens de la chantefable.» *MP*, 45 (1947-48), 8-14.

«Star-Crossed Lovers.» *TLS*. (June 19, 1959), p. 368.

Stearns, Marshall W. «A Note on Chaucer's Attitude towards Love.» *Speculum*, 17 (1942), 570-74.

Stevenson, David Lloyd. *The Love Game Comedy*. New York, 1966.

Stone, Chistopher. *Parody*. London, [1914].

Stroud, Theodore A. «Boethius' Influence on Chaucer's *Troilus*.» *MP*, 49 (1951-52), 1-9. Reprinted *Chaucer Criticism*, II. Ed. Schoeck and Taylor. Pp. 122-35.

Susskind, Norman. «Love and Laughter in the *Romans Courtois*.» *FR*, 37 (1963-64), 651-57.

Sutherland, D. R. «The Language of the Troubadours and the Problem of Origins.» *FS*, 10 (1956), 199-215.

—. «The Love Meditation in Courtly Literature.» *Studies in Medieval French: Presented to Alfred Ewert*. Oxford, 1961. Pp. 165-93.

Sypher, Wylie, ed. *Comedy*. Garden City, New York, 1956.

Tatlock, J. S. P. «The Epilog of Chaucer's *Troilus*.» *MP*, 18 (1920-21), 625-59.

—. *The Mind and Art of Chaucer*. Syracuse, 1950.

—. «The People in Chaucer's *Troilus*.» *PMLA*, 56 (1941), 85-104.

Terry, Patricia, trans. *Lays of Courtly Love*. Garden City, New York, 1963.

Thomas. *Le Roman de Tristan*. Ed. Joseph Bédier. Paris, 1902-05.

Thomas Aquinas, Saint. *The Summa Theologica*. Trans. by fathers of the English Dominican Province. Encyclopedia Britannica, 2 vols. Great Books of the Western World, vv. 19-20. 1955.

Thomas, Mary Edith. *Medieval Skepticism and Chaucer*. New York, 1950.

Tourillon, Denise. *L'amour courtois: amour adultère*. Collection des amis de la Langue d'oc. Paris, 1965.

Trotter, G. D. «Sobre 'La furia de Melibea', de Otis H. Green.» *Clavileño*, 5. xxv (enero-febrero, 1954), 55-56.

— and Keith Whinnom, eds. *La comedia Thebaida*. London, 1969.

Urwin, Kenneth. «The Setting of *Aucassin et Nicolette*.» *MLR*, 31 (1936), 403-05.

Utley, Francis Lee. «Scene-Division in Chaucer's *Troilus and Criseyde*.» *In Studies in Medieval Literature, In Honor of Professor Albert Croll Baugh*. Ed. MacEdward Leach. Philadelphia, 1961. Pp. 109-38.

Valency, Maurice. *In Praise of Love*. New York, 1961.

Valle-Lersundi, Fernando del. «Documentos referentes a Fernando de Rojas.» *RFE*, 12 (1925), 385-96.

—. «Testamento de Fernando de Rojas, autor de 'La Celestina'.» *RFE*, 16 (1929), 366-88.

Van Marle, Raimond. *Iconographie de l'art profane au moyen âge et à la renaissance*, I. La Haye, 1931-32.

Villon, François. *Oeuvres*. Ed. Auguste Longnon. 4e ed., revue par Lucien Foulet. Paris, 1964.

Wagenknecht, Edward, ed. *Chaucer: Modern Essays in Criticism*. New York, 1959.

—. *The Personality of Chaucer*. Norman, Okla., 1968.

Wardropper, Bruce W. «Pleberio's Lament for Melibea and the Medieval Elegiac Tradition.» *MLN*, 79 (1964), 140-52.

Webber, Edwin J. «The *Celestina* as an *Arte de Amores*.» *MP*, 55 (1958), 145-53.

—. «Tragedy and Comedy in the *Celestina*.» *Hispania*, 35 (1952), 318-20.

Weigand, Hermann J. *Three Chapters on Courtly Love in Arthurian France and Germany: Lancelot—Andreas Capellanus—Wolfram Von Eschenbach's Parzival*. UNCSGLL, 17. Chapel Hill, 1956; reprinted New York, 1966.

Weiner, Jack. «Adam and Eve Imagery in *La Celestina*.» *PLL*, 5 (1969), 389-96.

Wells, Carolyn. *A Parody Anthology*. New York, 1904.

Wenzel, Siegfried. «Chaucer's Troilus of Book IV.» *PMLA*, 79 (1964), 542-47.

Weston, Jessie L. *From Ritual to Romance*. Garden City, New York, 1957.

Whinnom, Keith. *Spanish Literary Historiography: Three Forms of Distortion*. Exeter, 1967.

White, T. H., ed. and trans. *The Bestiary: A Book of Beasts*. A translation from a Latin bestiary of the twelfth century. New York, 1954; reprinted New York, 1960.

Whitehead, F. «Yvain's Wooing.» *Medieval Miscellany Presented to Eugène Vinaver*. Eds. F. Whitehead, A. H. Diverres, and F. E. Sutcliffe. New York, 1965. Pp. 321-36.

Wilhelm, James L. *Seven Troubadours: The Creators of Modern Verse*. University Park, Pa., 1970.

Williams, George. *A New View of Chaucer*. Durham, N. C., 1965.

Wimsatt, James. *Chaucer and the French Love Poets: The Literary Background of the Book of the Duchess*. UNCSCL, 43. Chapel Hill, 1968.

Wind, Bartina. «Ce jeu subtil, l'amour courtois.» In *Mélanges offerts à Rita Lejeune*, ii. Gembloux, 1969. Pp. 1257-61.

Winkler, E. «Or dient et content et fabloient.» *ZFSL*, 64 (1941), 184-202.

Woods, William S. «The Plot Structure in Four Romances of Chrétien de Troyes.» *SP*, 50 (1953), 1-15.

—. «The *Aube* in *Aucassin et Nicolette*.» *Mediaeval Studies in Honor of Urban Tigner Holmes, Jr*. UNCSRLL, 56. Chapel Hill, 1965. Pp. 209-15.

Worcester, David. *The Art of Satire*. Cambridge, Mass., 1940.

Young, Karl. «Chaucer's Renunciation of Love in *Troilus*.» *MLN*, 40 (1925), 270-76.

—. «Chaucer's *Troilus and Criseyde* as Romance.» *PMLA*, 53 (1938), 38-63.

—. *The Origin and Development of the Story of Troilus and Criseyde*. Chaucer Society, Second Series, 40. London, 1908 for 1904.

Zárate, Armando. «La poesía y el ojo en *La Celestina*.» *CA*, 164 (1969), 119-36.

Zatzikhoven, Ulrich von. *Lanzelet*. Ed. K. A. Hahn. Frankfurt, 1845; reprinted Berlin, 1965.

—. *Lanzelet*. Trans. Kenneth G. T. Webster; revised and introd. Robert Sherman Loomis. New York, 1951.

Zenker, Rudolf. *Die Lieder Peires von Auvergne*. Erlangen, 1900.

COLECCION TAMESIS

SERIE A - MONOGRAFIAS

SERIE D - REPRODUCCIONES EN FACSIMIL

CAYETANO ALBERTO DE LA BARRERA Y LEIRADO: *Catálogo bibliográfico y biográfico del teatro antiguo español, desde sus orígenes hasta mediados del siglo XVIII (Madrid, 1860)*, pp. xi + 727.

CRITICAL GUIDES TO SPANISH TEXTS

(Publicadas en colaboración con Grant and Cutler Limited)

J. E. VAREY: *Pérez Galdós: Doña Perfecta.*
JENNIFER LOWER: *Cervantes: Two novelas ejemplares.*
VERITY SMITH: *Valle-Inclán: Tirano Banderas.*